W9-BTI-740

Bridging Differences

Second Edition

INTERPERSONAL COMMTEXTS

Series Editors: Mark L. Knapp & John A. Daly,
both at the University of Texas

Designed for college and university undergraduates, the **Interpersonal Commtexts** series will also interest a much larger general audience. Ideal as basic or supplementary texts, these volumes are suited for courses in the development and practice of interpersonal skills; verbal and nonverbal behavior (the basis of interpersonal transactions); functions of communication in face-to-face interaction; the development of interpersonal behavior at various points in the lifespan; and intergroup and intercultural aspects of interpersonal communication. Readable and comprehensive, the **Interpersonal Commtexts** describe contexts within which interpersonal communication takes place and provide ways to study and understand the interpersonal communication process.

For information address:

SAGE Publications, Inc.
2455 Teller Road
Thousand Oaks, California 91320

SAGE Publications Ltd.
6 Bonhill Street
London EC2A 4PU
United Kingdom

SAGE Publications India Pvt. Ltd.
M-32 Market
Greater Kailash I
New Delhi 110 048 India

Printed in the United States of America

Library of Congress Cataloging-in-Publication Data

Gudykunst, William B.
    Bridging differences : effective intergroup communication /
William B. Gudykunst.— 2nd ed.
        p. cm. —(Interpersonal commtexts ; 3)
    Includes bibliographical references and index.
    ISBN 0-8039-5646-0 — ISBN 0-8039-5647-9 (pbk.)
    1. Intercultural communication. I. Title. II. Series.
HM258.G838 1994
303.48'2—dc20   93-43669

94 95 96 97 98 10 9 8 7 6 5 4 3 2 1

Sage Production Editor: Astrid Virding

Contents

Preface

I originally became involved in studying intercultural communication in the United States Navy when I served as an Intercultural
Relations Specialist in Japan. We designed and conducted training to help naval personnel and their families adjust to living in
Japan. While conducting intercultural training in Japan, I thought
intercultural communication (i.e., communication between people
from different cultures) was different from intracultural communication (i.e., communication with members of our own culture).

After getting out of the Navy, I went to Minnesota to work on
my Ph.D. with Bill Howell. While completing my Ph.D., I continued
to see intercultural communication as different from intracultural
communication and retained my interest in training and applications. After accepting a position as an assistant professor, however, I focused on conducting research and developing theory. In

trying to develop a way to explain communication between people from different cultures, I came to the conclusion that the processes operating when we communicate interculturally are the same as when we communicate intraculturally. To illustrate, our stereotypes always affect our communication. Stereotypes, however, lead to ineffective communication more frequently when the person with whom we are communicating comes from another culture than when the person comes from our own culture. One reason for this is that our stereotypes of our culture tend to be more accurate and favorable than our stereotypes of other cultures. Inaccurate and unfavorable stereotypes of other cultures and ethnic groups cause us to misinterpret messages we receive from members of those cultures and ethnic groups.

Given that the underlying process of communication is the same in intercultural and intracultural encounters, we need a way to refer to this common underlying process. Young Yun Kim and I used "communicating with strangers" to refer to this common process in our intercultural communication text, *Communicating With Strangers* (Gudykunst & Kim, 1984, 1992). I have drawn on that framework and the work of Harry Triandis, Henri Tajfel, Howie Giles, Chuck Berger, Ellen Langer, Walter Stephan, and Cookie Stephan, among others, to develop anxiety/uncertainty management (AUM) theory (Gudykunst, 1988, 1993) to explain interpersonal and intergroup communication (intercultural communication is a type of intergroup communication). I apply this theory to improving communication effectiveness in this book. My emphasis is on improving communication effectiveness between people from groups that differ in, for example, culture, ethnicity, gender, disability, age, or social class. The ideas presented, however, can be applied to communication with people within groups as well.

There are numerous people who have contributed, either directly or indirectly, to my thinking about communication and to this book. Exposure to Kurt Lewin's writing early in my graduate career convinced me that theories must have practical application. Bill Howell and George Shapiro reinforced this notion at Minnesota. Tsukasa Nishida, Gao Ge, Mitch Hammer, and Karen Schmidt have worked with me on many of the studies on which the theory is based, and Mitch co-authored the special version of the theory applied to intercultural adaptation (Gudykunst & Hammer, 1988a). Sandy Sudweeks, Paula Trubisky, Joyce Baker, David Doyle, Mark Cole, and I initially applied the theory to designing an intercultural training program. Participants in the Applications of Intercultural Communication course I taught at California State University, Fullerton, tested many of the ideas presented in intergroup training programs they designed and implemented.

Stella Ting-Toomey served as a sounding board for the theory and its application; she read a complete draft of the first edition and suggested the title. Stella also read a complete draft of the second edition while she was trying to complete her own intercultural book. Harry Triandis, Rich Wiseman, Jon Bruschke, and the Series Co-Editors, Mark Knapp and John Daly, also provided valuable feedback on a draft of the first edition of the book. Michael Bond has provided valuable feedback on my work over the years that I have incorporated in this book. The book would not have been written without the gentle prodding and support of Ann West, my editor at Sage for the first edition. Sophy Craze facilitated the production of the second edition at Sage. The time to write the first edition of the book was made possible by a Senior Faculty Research Grant from California State University, Fullerton.

William B. Gudykunst
Laguna Beach, CA

Greetings! I am pleased
to see that we are different.
May we together become greater
than the sum of both of us.

Vulcan Greeting
(*Star Trek*)

See at a distance an undesirable person;
See close at hand a desirable person;
Come closer to the undesirable person;
Move away from the desirable person.
Coming close and moving apart,
how interesting life is!

Gensho Ogura

Communicating With Strangers

Elie Wiesel, a recipient of the Nobel Peace Prize, believes that hate
directed toward members of different cultural and racial groups,
as well as toward members of different political and ideological
groups, is the major source of problems between people in the
twentieth century.[1] Hate is being expressed toward, and conflict
is occurring between, people of different groups everywhere we
look. To illustrate, nationality conflicts are taking place in the
former Soviet Union (e.g., between the Azerbaijanis and the Arme-
nians); ethnic conflict is occurring among the Serbians, Croatians,
and Muslims in the former Yugoslavia; conflict between neo-Nazis
and immigrants in Germany is leading to violence; conflict between Protestants and Catholics in Northern Ireland is still taking place; and conflict between Arabs and Jews in Israel has not
stopped, to name only a few of the intergroup conflicts occurring

in the world today.[2] There also is racial harassment on university campuses in the United States; hate crimes are being committed against members of various groups (e.g., members of different ethnic groups, homosexuals) at an increasing rate in cities throughout the United States; and there is conflict between pro-choice and right-to-life groups at abortion clinics in the United States. The animosity among the various groups is aggravated by the hate programs appearing on public access cable television in the United States (e.g., "Race and Reason"; see Zoglin, 1993).

Although the specific causes of the conflicts occurring throughout the world differ depending upon the situation, all incidents share one thing in common, polarized communication. *Polarized communication* occurs when the communicators have "the inability to believe or seriously consider one's view as wrong and the other's opinion as truth. Communication within human community becomes typified by the rhetoric of 'we' are right and 'they' are misguided or wrong" (Arnett, 1986, pp. 15-16). Polarized communication exists when groups or individuals look out for their own interests and have little or no concern for others' interests. Deborah Tannen (1993) believes that

> the devastating group hatreds that result in so much suffering in our own country and around the world are related in origin to the small intolerances in our everyday conversations—our readiness to attribute good intentions to ourselves and bad intentions to others; to believe there is one right way and ours is it; and to extrapolate from frustration with an individual in order to generalize to a group. (p. B5)

We express these small intolerances in our everyday conversations largely without being aware of doing so.

When we are not concerned for others' interests we are *morally exclusive.* "Moral exclusion occurs when individuals or groups are perceived as *outside the boundary in which moral values, rules, and considerations of fairness apply.* Those who are morally excluded are perceived as nonentities, expendable, or undeserving; consequently, harming them appears acceptable, appropriate or just" (Optow, 1990, p. 1). Lack of concern for others and moral exclusion are a function, at least in part, of the spiritual deprivation (i.e., the feeling of emptiness associated with separation from our fellow humans) that Mother Teresa sees as the major problem facing the world today (Jampolsky, 1989). Tannen (1993) points out that our "inability to feel committed to others we see like us is matched by an equally strong tendency to diminish the humanity of those we see as different" (p. B5).

One reason for our spiritual deprivation is the difficulties with which we must cope in our life. As Scott Peck (1978) says, "life is difficult" (p. 15). Most of us expect our life to be easy, but it is not. The difficult conditions in our life threaten our self-concepts (i.e., our views of ourselves; Staub, 1989). Also, whenever we perceive threats to achieving our goals, we perceive our self-concepts to be threatened (Lazarus, 1991). When our self-concepts are threatened, we try to improve the way we see ourselves. One way we accomplish this is by positively comparing ourselves to others or putting others down (Tajfel, 1978). When we feel superior to others or see others as inferior to us, we feel good about ourselves. Another way we deal with threats to our self-concepts is by becoming hostile or aggressive toward others, particularly those who are different from us in important ways (e.g., members of different cultures or ethnic groups, people with different gender orientations).

We also feel spiritual deprivation and unconnected when we do not know how to communicate with others. This is especially true for interactions between members of other cultures or ethnic groups in the United States, but it also is true for interactions between people with disabilities and people without disabilities, interaction between younger and older people, and interaction between members of different social classes. Because we have little contact with members of other groups (T. Rose, 1981), we do not have much practice in communicating with them. Many of us believe that our inability to communicate with members of other groups is due to one person not being competent in the other's language or dialect. Linguistic knowledge alone, however, is not enough to ensure that our communication with people from other groups will progress smoothly or be effective. Confucius said that "human beings are drawn close to one another by their common nature, but habits and customs keep them apart." Misunderstandings in intergroup encounters often stem from not knowing the norms and rules guiding the communication of people from different groups. If we understand others' languages or dialects, but not their communication rules, we can make fluent fools of ourselves.

Language and culture are not the only factors that can contribute to misunderstandings in intergroup encounters. Our attitudes (e.g., prejudice, ageism, sexism) and stereotypes create expectations that often lead us to misinterpret messages we receive from people who are different *and* lead people who are different to misinterpret the messages they receive from us. Spike Lee (1990), director of the film *Do the Right Thing*, for example, points out that expressing "racism is fashionable today." When people express their unconscious racist attitudes toward others, misunderstanding is inevitable and conflict is probable.

Our expectations regarding how people from other groups will behave are based on how we categorize them (e.g., he is Japanese; she is Mexican American; they are disabled). Our use of social categories, however, is not limited to our communication with people from different groups. We categorize others when we communicate with people from our own culture or ethnic group, but the categories are different (e.g., that person is a woman; he is a waiter; she or he is a "friend of a friend"). Until we get to know others, our interactions with them must be based on our expectations regarding how people in the category in which we place them will behave. Our initial interactions with people from our own groups and with people from other groups, therefore, are relatively similar. There are, of course, some phenomena that occur more frequently when we communicate with people from other groups than when we communicate with people from our own groups (e.g., we experience more anxiety when people come from different ethnic groups than when they are from our ethnic group). To be able to talk about the similarities in the underlying communication process, I refer to people who are not members of our own groups and who are different (on the basis of culture, ethnicity, gender, age, disability, social class, or other group memberships) as *strangers*[3] (based on Simmel's, 1908/1950, concept of "stranger").[4]

Donald Levine (1979) summarizes the importance of Simmel's concept of the stranger in understanding communication between members of different groups. He points out that

> it is the dialectic between closeness and remoteness that makes the position of strangers socially problematic in all times and places. When those who would be close, in any sense of the term, are actually close, and those who would be distant are distant, everyone is "in his [or her] place." When those who would be distant are close, however, the inevitable result is a degree of tension and anxiety which necessitates some special kind of response. . . . Group members derive security from relating in familiar ways to fellow group members and from maintaining distance from nonmembers through established insulating mechanisms. In situations where an outsider comes into the social space normally occupied by group members only, one can presume an initial response of anxiety and at least latent antagonism. (pp. 29-30)

To manage our antagonistic response, we must understand the factors that influence our communication with strangers.

Throughout this book, I draw attention to those factors that are given more weight when we communicate with strangers than with people from our own groups. Our stereotypes, for example, affect our communication with people from our own groups and our communication with strangers. Stereotypes are, however, less problematic in our communication with people from our own groups because our stereotypes of our own groups usually are more favorable and accurate than our stereotypes of strangers' groups. In order to improve our effectiveness in communicating with strangers, we must understand how unfavorable or inaccurate stereotypes affect the way we communicate.

Improving our communication with strangers requires that we become aware of how we communicate. William Howell (1982) argues that awareness and competence can be thought of as a stage process:[5] (a) unconscious incompetence where we misinterpret others' behavior, but are not aware of it; (b) conscious incompetence where we are aware that we misinterpret others' behavior, but we do not do anything about it; (c) conscious competence where we think about our communication behavior and consciously modify it to improve our effectiveness (I refer below to this stage as "mindfulness"); and (d) unconscious competence where we have practiced the skills for effective communication to the extent that we no longer have to think about them to use them. Throughout the book, I point out areas where we are unconsciously incompetent in communicating with strangers and provide suggestions on how we can become consciously competent. Moving to the level of unconscious competence requires practicing the skills discussed in the book.

I draw on a theory of interpersonal and intergroup communication I have been developing over the last several years (the most recent version is Gudykunst, 1993).[6] Kurt Lewin often is quoted as saying "there is nothing so practical as a good theory." I agree and go a step further: Training and practical advice must be theoretically based. Although this book is based on a communication theory, I do not present the theory in detail. Rather, I focus on practical applications of the theory. I translate the theory so that you can use it to improve your abilities to communicate effectively and manage conflict with strangers.

Each of us has a responsibility as a human being to communicate as effectively as we can with each other. To communicate effectively, we must transmit our messages in a way that strangers can understand what we mean, and we need to interpret strangers' messages in the way they meant them to be interpreted. If strangers do not try to communicate effectively with us, it does *not* relieve us of our responsibility. We also have a responsibility to react when we see others put down members of other groups. If we say nothing when we hear someone make a racist or sexist remark, for example, we are equally culpable (see the discussion of prejudice and the discussion of ethics in Chapter 3).

I do *not* mean to suggest that we try to communicate intimately or try to establish a personal relationship with all strangers we meet. This is impossible. We can, however, communicate as effectively as possible with strangers whatever our relationship (e.g., acquaintance, neighbor, co-worker, superior, subordinate) with them is. I also am not advocating that we hit our head against a brick wall. No matter how hard we try, it may be impossible to communicate effectively or establish a cooperative relationship with some people. In cases like this, we each have to make an individual decision when it is time to stop trying. Hugh Prather (1986) points out that we do not have to learn to deal with everyone and sometimes it is best to learn how to walk around people with whom we cannot get along. The important thing, in my opinion, is that we do our best to communicate effectively with the strangers we meet, before we decide to stop trying.

To understand how to improve our communication with strangers, we have to recognize our normal tendencies when we communicate with them. To help you assess your communication with strangers, I present questionnaires designed to assess your tendencies regarding the major constructs I discuss.[7] Completing the questionnaires is not critical to cognitively understanding the material presented, but it will assist you in improving your effectiveness in communicating with strangers. Therefore I urge you to complete the questionnaires presented and think about your typical behavior when communicating with strangers as you read the book. When completing the questionnaires, please keep in mind that they will only help you improve your communication if you answer them honestly.

Having summarized my approach and the purpose of the book, I will now turn to an overview of the process of communication. In the next section, I examine the role of symbols, messages, and meanings in communication. Following this, I isolate the aspects of communication (managing anxiety and uncertainty) that are central to the theory I use. I conclude by looking at some of the factors that have more of an influence on our behavior when we communicate with strangers than when we communicate with people from our own groups.

❏ An Overview of the Communication Process

We all communicate and consider ourselves to be experts.[8] We think we know what the problems of communication are and know how to solve them. Unfortunately, many of the things we take for granted about communication lead to ineffective communication, especially when we communicate with strangers. My purpose in this section is to provide an overview of the communication process.

Language often is equated with speech and communication.[9] There are, however, important differences. *Language* is a system of rules regarding how the sounds of the language are made, how sentences are formed, what meaning is assigned to words or combinations of words, and how the language is used. Language is a *medium* of communication. When the rules of language are translated into a *channel* of communication (e.g., the spoken word) using symbols, messages are created.

Symbols are things we use to represent something else. Virtually anything can be a symbol—words, nonverbal displays, flags, and so forth. Referents for symbols can include objects, ideas, or behaviors. The word "flag," for example, is used to represent a piece of cloth with stars and stripes that is attached to a staff and serves as the "national banner" in the United States. As the recent disagreements over the meaning of flag burning indicate, the symbol means different things to different people. For some, it is sacred and should not be burned or devalued under any circumstances. For others, it is not held in such high esteem and burning the flag is an expression of free speech. The point is that there is no natural connection between a specific symbol and its referent. The relationship between a symbol and its referent is arbitrary and varies from culture to culture. It also varies within cultures, as the example of the flag indicates. Although there is no direct relationship between the symbol and its referent, there are direct connections between our thoughts and a symbol and our thoughts and a symbol's referent (Ogden & Richards, 1923). If we think of the referent, the symbol comes to mind; if we think of the symbol, the referent comes to mind.

We combine a set of symbols into messages that we transmit to others. *Transmitting messages* involves putting our thoughts, feelings, emotions, and/or attitudes in a form recognizable by others. The messages we transmit are interpreted by others. *Interpreting messages* is the process of perceiving and making sense of the messages and other stimuli from the environment we receive through our senses (seeing, hearing, feeling, touching, smelling, and tasting). How we transmit and interpret messages is influenced by our life experiences (e.g., our experiences with others, the emotions we have felt). These life experiences include our unique individual experiences as well as our shared ethnic and cultural experiences. The important point to keep in mind is that no two individuals have the same life experiences. No two people will interpret a message in the same way.

There are several possible channels of communication through which messages can be transmitted. We can transmit a message through the spoken word, use nonverbal cues, or write it. If one person cannot speak or hear, sign language may be used. Alternatively, messages can be transmitted through mathematics or through artistic forms of expression such as painting, photography, or music. Only when the channel is the spoken word does speech occur.

> *No two people will interpret a message in the same way.*

MESSAGES AND MEANINGS

The term *communication* refers to the exchange of messages and the creation of meaning (e.g., assigning significance to messages). Meanings cannot be transmitted from one person to another. Only messages can be transmitted. When we send a message we attach a certain meaning to that message and choose the symbols and channel of communication accordingly. We rely on more than the behavior that the other person displays (e.g., she or he may laugh) when we construct our messages. We also rely on our interpretation of that behavior (e.g., he or she assumes we are funny *or* she or he is laughing at us). The way we construct and interpret messages is a function of our perceptions of ourselves, the other people involved, their objective behavior, and the way they send their messages to us. The person who interprets our message, however, attaches his or her own meaning to the message. The

meaning attached to the message is a function of the actual message transmitted, the channel used, the environment in which
the message is transmitted, the person who receives it, the relationship between the two people, and the way the message is
transmitted.

We do not transmit and interpret messages independently of
one another. We engage in both processes simultaneously. When
we transmit a message we are affected by how we interpret messages we are receiving from the other person and we may even
modify our message based on the feedback we receive while we
are transmitting the message.

Paul Watzlawick, Janet Beavin, and Don Jackson (1967) distinguished between the content and relationship dimensions of a
message. The *content dimension* of a message is the information in
the message (e.g., what is said). The *relationship dimension* of a
message is inferred from how the message is transmitted (including the specific words used), and it deals with how the participants
are relating to each other. The way we communicate offers a definition of the relationship between us. The children's saying "sticks
and stones may break my bones, but words will never hurt me"
is not accurate. The words we chose and the way we say them to
others can and do hurt.

When we communicate we present ourselves as we want others to see us and respond to how others present themselves to us.
We modify how we see ourselves based on the feedback we receive
from others.[10] If others consistently tell us we are incompetent,
for example, we begin to see ourselves as incompetent. Through
communication we can facilitate others' personal growth or destroy them. George Gerbner (1978) refers to our ability to destroy
others by our communication as "symbolic annihilation."

SOURCES OF COMMUNICATION BEHAVIOR

Our communication behavior is based on one of three sources.[11]
We might behave in a particular way because it is habitual.
Alternatively, we might communicate in a particular way because we are trying to accomplish certain objectives. Finally, we
may react emotionally without much conscious thought.

Habits. We engage is much of our behavior out of habit. We are not always aware of making decisions about the routines we enact. When we are communicating habitually, we are following a *script*—"a coherent sequence of events expected by the individual involving him [or her] either as a participant or an observer" (Abelson, 1976, p. 33). When we first encounter a new situation, we consciously seek cues to guide our behavior. As we have repeated experiences with the same event, we have less need to consciously think about our behavior. "The more often we engage in the activity, the more likely it is that we rely on scripts for the completion of the activity and the less likely there will be any correspondence between our actions and those thoughts of ours that occur simultaneously" (Langer, 1978, p. 39).

When we are engaging in habitual or scripted behavior, we are not highly aware of what we are doing or saying. To borrow an analogy from flying a plane, we are on automatic pilot. In Ellen Langer's (1978) terminology, we are mindless. We do not, however, communicate totally on automatic pilot; we pay sufficient attention so that we can recall key words in the conversations we have (Kitayama & Burnstein, 1988). When we communicate on automatic pilot, we interpret incoming messages based on the symbolic systems we learned as children. A large part of this system is shared with other members of our culture, our ethnic group, our religion, and our family, to name only a few of our group memberships. A part of our symbolic system, however, is unique and based on specific life experiences. No two people share the same symbolic systems.

Much of our habitual or scripted behavior involves superficial interactions with other members of our culture or ethnic group in which we rely mainly on group-based information about others. The meanings we attach to specific messages and the meanings others attach to these messages are relatively similar. This is due, in part, to the fact that the scripts we enact provide us with shared interpretations of our behavior. Although there are differences in our meanings, the differences are not large enough to make our communication ineffective. Under these conditions, we do not need to consciously think about our communication to be relatively effective.

The greeting ritual is one example of a script. The ritual for greeting others reduces the vast amount of uncertainty and anxiety present in initial interactions with strangers to manageable portions and allows us to interact with others as though there was relatively little uncertainty or anxiety. The norms and rules for the ritual provide us with predictions about how others will respond in the situation. When someone deviates from the script or we enter a new situation, we cannot fall back on the rituals' implicit predictions. Under these circumstances, we have to actively reduce our uncertainty and anxiety before we can make accurate predictions and communicate effectively.

Intentions. The second basis for our communication behavior is the intentions we form.[12] *Intentions* are instructions we give ourselves about how to communicate (Triandis, 1977). When we think about what we want to do in a particular situation, we form intentions. Intention, therefore, is a cognitive construct—it is part of our thought processes. We may not be able to accomplish our intentions, however. My intention, for example, may be to be non-judgmental in my interactions with others, but in actuality I may be very judgmental. My ability to accomplish my intentions is a function, at least in part, of my motivation, knowledge, and skills (discussed in Chapter 6).

We often are not highly aware of what our intentions are. One person may not intend to send a message to another person, but the other person may perceive that a message has been sent and react based on his or her interpretation. This is particularly problematic when the people come from different cultures. Consider the example of a businessperson from the United States negotiating a contract in an Arab culture. During the course of a meeting, the businessperson from the United States crosses her or his legs and in the process points the sole of her or his shoe toward an Arab. The person from the United States, in all likelihood, will not attach any meaning to this. The Arab, in contrast, will probably interpret this behavior as an insult and react accordingly. Although the person from the United States did not intend to send a message, one was received. Showing the sole of the foot does not mean anything in the United States. In Arab cultures, however, showing the sole of the foot to another person is considered an insult. The misunderstanding can only be explained by looking at behavior that was not intended to be meaningful.

Emotions. The final factor on which our communication behavior may be based is our affect, feelings, or emotions. We often react to others on a strictly emotional basis. If we feel we were criticized, for example, we may become defensive and strike out at the other person without thinking.

Emotions are our affective responses to changing relationships between ourselves and our environment (Lazarus, 1991). If we perceive that we are being threatened, for example, we will feel anxiety. We cannot, however, understand the emotion anxiety without taking into consideration what led to the perception of threat and the person perceiving the threat. Whether or not someone perceives a threat depends on his or her appraisal of the situation. Richard Lazarus (1991) argues that our appraisals of "harm or benefit, actual or potential, real or imagined" (p. 92) influence the emotion that is generated in a particular situation.

Lazarus (1991) points out that our appraisals of situations do not remain static, but are in flux. One of the reasons that our appraisals are in flux is that we constantly receive new information from the environment that we must appraise. These appraisals can influence how we interpret the feelings we have. Some of the changes that occur in our appraisals are due to our ability to cope. *Coping* involves our cognitive and behavioral efforts to manage our appraisals (Lazarus, 1991). Lazarus suggests that there are two ways of coping with emotions. One way to cope is to remove the problem. This form of coping is not highly successful in communication with others because we usually cannot remove the problem. Another way to cope involves changing the way we attend to or interpret our emotional responses. This involves managing our emotional reactions cognitively.[13] I argue later in this chapter that this is necessary for effective communication to occur, especially when we communicate with strangers.

SELF-CONCEPT AND COMMUNICATION

Our self-concepts are our views of ourselves. Our views of ourselves are derived from how we view ourselves in particular situations and from our views of ourselves as members of various groups, our identity. We have three general types of identities: human, social, and personal (J. C. Turner, 1987). Our *human identity* involves those views of ourselves that we believe we share with all other humans. Carlos Fuentes (1992) points out that

> people and their cultures perish in isolation, but they are born or reborn in contact with other men and women, with men and women of another culture, another creed, another race. If we do not recognize our humanity in others, we shall not recognize it in ourselves. (back cover)

To understand our human identities, we have to look for those things we share in common with all other humans.

Our *social identities* involve our views of ourselves that we share with other members of our ingroups. Ingroups are groups that are important to us with which we identify. Our social identities may be based on the roles we play (e.g., student, professor, parent), demographic categories (e.g., nationality, ethnicity, gender, age, social class), membership in formal or informal organizations (e.g., political party, religion, organization, social clubs), avocations or vocations (e.g., scientist, artist, gardener), or stigmatized groups (disabled, homeless person, person with AIDS).

The degree to which we identify with these various groups varies from situation to situation. To illustrate, although I am a North American, I do not think about being a member of my culture much in everyday life. When I visit another country, however, my North American identity (my cultural identity) becomes important. I think about being a North American, and my cultural identity plays a large role in influencing my behavior.

Our *personal identities* involve those views of ourselves that differentiate us from other members of our ingroups—those characteristics that define us as unique individuals. What we generally think of as our personality characteristics are part of our personal identities.[14]

Our communication behavior can be based on our personal, social, or human identities. In a particular situation, we may choose (either consciously or unconsciously) to define ourselves communicatively mainly as unique persons or as members of groups. When our communication behavior is based mostly on our personal identities, interpersonal communication takes place. When we define ourselves mostly in terms of our social identities, in contrast, intergroup communication occurs. It is important to recognize, however, that our personal and social identities influence all of our communication behavior, even though one may predominate in a particular situation. When our social identities have a greater influence on our behavior than our personal identities, however, there is an increased chance of misunderstandings occurring because we are likely to interpret others' behavior based on our group memberships. To overcome the potential for misunderstandings that can occur when our social identities predominate, we must recognize that we share common human identities with strangers. At the same time, we must acknowledge our differences and try to understand them and how they influence our communication.[15] I discuss issues of effective communication in more detail later in this chapter.

COMMUNICATIVE PREDICTIONS

"When people communicate they make predictions about the effects, or outcomes, of their communication behaviors; that is, they choose among various communicative strategies on the basis of predictions about how the person receiving the message will respond" (Miller & Steinberg, 1975, p. 7). Sometimes we are very conscious of the predictions we make and sometimes we are not highly aware of them. When we meet someone we find attractive and whom we want to see again, for example, we may think of alternative ways to arrange a next meeting or date, and then select the strategy we think will work best. Under conditions like this, we are aware of the predictions we make.

Gerald Miller and Mark Steinberg (1975) contend that we use three different types of information in making predictions about others: cultural, social, and personal.[16] People in any culture generally behave in a regular way because of the norms, rules, and values of their culture. This regularity allows *cultural information* to be used in making predictions. Gerald Miller and Michael Sunnafrank (1982) point out that "knowledge about another person's culture—its language, beliefs, and prevailing ideology— often permits predictions of the person's probable response to messages. . . . Upon first encountering . . . [another person], cultural information provides the only grounds for communicative predictions" (p. 226). If we are introduced to a person from the United States,[17] we can make certain assumptions about the person understanding introduction rituals. We implicitly predict, for example, that if we stick out our right hand to shake hands, she or he will do the same.

When we travel to another culture or interact with people from another culture in our culture, we cannot base our predictions of their behavior on our cultural rules and norms. This inevitably leads to misunderstanding. If we want to communicate effectively, we must use our knowledge of the other culture to make predictions. If we have little or no knowledge of the other person's culture, we have no basis for making predictions. "This fact explains the uneasiness and perceived lack of control most people experience when thrust into an alien culture; they not only lack information about the individuals with whom they must communicate, they are bereft of information concerning shared cultural norms and values" (Miller & Sunnafrank, 1982, p. 227).

Social predictions are based on our memberships in or aspirations to become members of particular social groups or social roles. Miller and Sunnafrank argue that social information is the principal kind we use to predict behavior of people from our culture. Groups memberships based on ethnicity, gender, religion, social class, disabilities, gender orientation, and so forth are used to predict others' behavior. Roles such as professor, physician, clerk, supervisor, among others, also provide a basis for the social predictions we make.

Our cultural and social predictions are based on the category in which we place the other person (e.g., member of my culture, not member of my culture). *Social categorization* is the way we order our social environment (i.e., the people with whom we come in contact) by grouping people in a way that makes sense to us (Tajfel, 1978). We may, for example, divide people into women and men, white and nonwhite, black and nonblack, "Americans" and foreigners, to name only a few of the sets of categories we use. In categorizing others and ourselves, we become aware of being members of social groups. A *social group* can be thought of as two or more people who define themselves as sharing a common bond (J. C. Turner, 1982). Once we place someone in a social category, our stereotype of people in that category is activated. *Stereotypes* are the mental pictures we have of a group of people. Our stereotypes create expectations about how people from our own and other cultures or ethnic groups will behave. These notions may be accurate or inaccurate and other persons may fulfill our expectations or violate them.

When we base our predictions on cultural or social information, we are assuming that the people within the category (e.g., the culture or ethnic group) are similar. Although individuals within a category share similarities (e.g., there are similarities people born and raised in the United States share), individuals within each of the categories also differ. When we are able to discriminate how individuals are similar to and different from other members of the same category, we are using psychological data to make predictions. The use of *personal information* involves taking into consideration when we make our predictions the specific person with whom we are communicating and how she or he will respond to our messages.

Miller and Steinberg point out that we rely on cultural and social information in the vast majority of the interactions we have. There is nothing wrong with this. It is natural, and it is necessary to allow us to deal with the complexity of our social environment. Imagine going into a restaurant and having to get to know your waiter or waitress so that you can make personal predictions about his or her behavior before placing your order. This would complicate our lives and is not necessary. We can communicate effectively with a waitress or waiter without using personal information about the individual. Social information is all that is necessary to get your order correct. The same is true for most other role relationships that do not involve extended inter-action (e.g., with clerks, mechanics).

When we communicate frequently with someone in a specific role relationship, using personal data becomes important. Physicians who treat all patients alike (e.g., use only social data) will not be very effective. Successfully treating patients requires knowledge of them both as patients and as individuals (e.g., specific information about the other person and how he or she is similar to and different from other members of her or his groups). Communicating effectively with strangers also requires differentiating individuals from the groups of which they are members. Relying completely on cultural or social information when communicating with strangers over an extended period of time inevitably leads to misunderstandings. Effective communication requires that some personal information be used to predict strangers' behavior.

❏ Managing Uncertainty and Anxiety

Interacting with strangers is a novel situation for most people. "The immediate psychological result of being in a new situation is lack of security. Ignorance of the potentialities inherent in the situation, of the means to reach a goal, and of the probable outcomes of an intended action causes insecurity" (Herman & Schield, 1961, p. 165). Attempts to deal with the ambiguity of new situations involves a pattern of information seeking (uncertainty reduction) and tension (anxiety) reduction (Ball-Rokeach, 1973).[18]

UNCERTAINTY

Often when we meet people in our own culture the norms and rules guiding our behavior in the situation provide sufficient information for us to be able to predict and explain others' behavior. This, however, is not always the case. Charles Berger (1979) argues that we try to reduce uncertainty when the person we meet is someone we expect to encounter again in the future or who provides rewards to us or behaves in a "deviant" fashion.[19] Given that strangers, especially those from other cultures or ethnic groups, are likely to behave in a deviant fashion, it is reasonable to say we try to reduce uncertainty when we communicate with strangers more than we do when we communicate with people who are familiar. It is important to recognize that we may not be conscious of our attempts to reduce our uncertainty.

Uncertainty and Communication. Charles Berger and Richard Calabrese (1975) point out there are two types of uncertainty present in our interactions with strangers. First, there is *predictive uncertainty,* the uncertainty we have about predicting others' attitudes, feelings, beliefs, values, and behavior. We need to be able, for example, to predict which of several alternative behavior patterns strangers will choose to employ. An illustration is the situation when we meet a person we find attractive at a party. Assuming we want to see this person again after the party, we try to think about different ways we can approach this person in order to convince him or her to see us again. The different approaches we think about are the predictions of alternative behaviors that reduce our uncertainty.

The second type of uncertainty is *explanatory uncertainty,* the uncertainty we have about explanations of strangers' behavior. Whenever we try to figure out why strangers behave the way they do, we are engaging in explanatory uncertainty reduction. The problem we are addressing is one of reducing the number of possible explanations for the strangers' behavior. This is necessary if we are to understand their behavior and be able to increase our ability to predict their behavior in the future.

There is greater uncertainty in our initial interactions with people from other groups than with people from our groups. This does not, however, mean that we will be motivated to actively reduce uncertainty more when we communicate with people from other groups than when we communicate with people from our own groups. Although people from other groups may behave in a deviant fashion (e.g., they do not follow *our* norms or communication rules), we rarely see them as sources of rewards and we may not anticipate seeing them again in the future. When we do not actively try to reduce our uncertainty regarding others' behavior, we rely on our categorizations to reduce our uncertainty and guide our predictions. As indicated earlier, this often leads to misunderstandings.

Thresholds for Uncertainty. Some degree of uncertainty exists in all relationships. We can never totally predict or explain another person's behavior. We all have maximum and minimum thresholds for uncertainty.[20] If our uncertainty is above our *maximum threshold*, we do not have enough information to predict or explain others' behavior comfortably. When our uncertainty is below our maximum threshold, we have sufficient information to make *some* predictions and explanations. We may not be highly confident of our predictions and our predictions may not be highly accurate, but we have sufficient information to be able to interact with the other person with some degree of comfort. If our uncertainty is below our *minimum threshold*, we see the other person's behavior as highly predictable. When this occurs, there may not be sufficient novelty in the relationship for us to sustain interest in interacting with the other person. We may also think that we can predict others' behavior, but our predictions may be inaccurate. When we see others' behavior as highly predictable we may misinterpret their messages because we do not consider the possibility that our interpretations are wrong.

Generally, as we get to know others our uncertainty regarding their behavior tends to decrease. Uncertainty, however, does not always decrease as relationships change over time. It also can increase. When we find out that others are engaged in competing relationships, when we lose closeness in a relationship, as well as when we find out that others have deceived or betrayed us, our uncertainty may increase (Planalp, Rutherford, & Honeycutt, 1988). Depending on the nature of the event and how we handle the uncertainty, increases in uncertainty can have positive or negative consequences for our relationships with others.

Assessing Your Uncertainty. Before proceeding, I want you to think about your uncertainty in communicating with strangers, people you do not know from other cultures or ethnic groups, for the first time. Take a moment to complete the assessment in Table 1.1 now.

Table 1.1 Assessing Your Uncertainty

The purpose of this questionnaire is to help you assess the amount of uncertainty you generally experience when you communicate with others. (NOTE: You can determine the amount of uncertainty you experience communicating with a specific person by substituting the person's name for "others" in each of the statements.) Respond to each statement by indicating the degree to which the adjectives are applicable when you interact with strangers. If you "Never" have the experience, answer 1 in the space provided; if you "Almost Never" have the experience, answer 2; if you "Sometimes" have the experiences and sometimes do not, answer 3; if you "Almost Always" have the experience, answer 4; if you "Always" have the experience, answer 5.

_____ 1. I am not confident when I communicate with others.
_____ 2. I can interpret others' behavior when we communicate.
_____ 3. I am indecisive when I communicate with others.
_____ 4. I can explain others' behavior when we communicate.
_____ 5. I am not able to understand others when we communicate.
_____ 6. I know what to do when I communicate with others.
_____ 7. I am uncertain how to behave when I communicate with others.
_____ 8. I can comprehend others' behavior when we communicate.
_____ 9. I am not able to predict others' behavior when we communicate.
_____ 10. I can describe others' behavior when we communicate.

To find your scores, first reverse the responses for the even-numbered items (i.e., if you wrote 1, make it 5; if you wrote 2, make it 4; if you wrote 3, leave it as 3; if you wrote 4, make it 2; if you wrote 5, make it 1). Next, add the numbers next to each of the items. Scores range from 10 to 50. The higher your score, the more uncertainty you experience when interacting with others.

Most of us experience some degree of uncertainty in communicating with strangers. If our level of uncertainty is above our maximum threshold, we need to try to reduce it in order to feel comfortable interacting with strangers. I discuss strategies to reduce uncertainty in Chapter 6.

ANXIETY

Anxiety is the feeling of being uneasy, tense, worried, or apprehensive about what might happen. It is an affective (i.e., emotional) response, not a cognitive or behavioral response like uncertainty. Anxiety is one of the fundamental problems with which all humans must cope (e.g., Lazarus, 1991; May, 1977). Jonathan H.

Turner (1988) believes that the amount of diffuse anxiety we experience influences our motivation to communicate with others. If our diffuse anxiety is too high, we are not motivated to communicate.

Anxiety in Intergroup Communication. When we communicate with members of other groups we not only have a high level of uncertainty, we also have a high level of anxiety. The anxiety we experience when we communicate with members of other groups usually is based on negative expectations. Actual or anticipated interaction with a member of a different ethnic group leads to anxiety. Walter Stephan and Cookie Stephan (1985) argue that we fear four types of negative consequences when interacting with strangers.

First, we fear *negative consequences for our self-concepts.* In interacting with members of other groups, we worry "about feeling incompetent, confused, and not in control . . . anticipate discomfort, frustration, and irritation due to the awkwardness of intergroup interactions" (Stephan & Stephan, 1985, p. 159). We also may fear the loss of self-esteem, that our social identities will be threatened, and that we will feel guilty if we behave in ways that offend members of other groups.

Second, we may fear *negative behavioral consequences* will result from our communication with members of other groups. We may feel that members of other groups will exploit us, take advantage of us, or try to dominate us. We also may worry about performing poorly in the presence of members of other groups or worry that physical harm or verbal conflict will occur.

Third, we fear *negative evaluations by members of other groups.* We fear rejection, ridicule, disapproval, and being stereotyped negatively. These negative evaluations, in turn, can be seen as threats to our social identities. We perceive communication with people from our own groups as more agreeable and less abrasive than communication with members of other groups (Hoyle, Pinkley, & Insko, 1989).

Finally, we may fear *negative evaluations by members of our ingroups.* If we interact with members of other groups, members of our ingroups may disapprove. We may fear that "ingroup members will reject" us, "apply other sanctions," or identify us "with the outgroup" (Stephan & Stephan, 1985, p. 160).

Thresholds for Anxiety. I believe that we have maximum and minimum thresholds of anxiety. If our anxiety is above our *maximum threshold*, we are so uneasy that we do not want to communicate with others and we are incapable of gathering accurate information about others. If our anxiety is below our *minimum threshold*, there is not enough adrenalin running through our system to motivate us to communicate with others. For us to be motivated to communicate with others, our anxiety has to be below our maximum threshold and above our minimum threshold. The role of anxiety in interpersonal communication is similar to its role in our performance on tests. If we are too anxious, we do not perform well on tests. Similarly, if we are not at all anxious, we do not perform well. Mihaly Csikszentmihalyi (1990) believes that there is an optimal level of anxiety that facilitates our having "flow" experiences (e.g., optimal experiences).

Individuals' minimum and maximum thresholds will differ. One way that we can tell if our anxiety is above our maximum threshold is by paying attention to our gut reaction. If we feel *a few* butterflies in our stomach, our anxiety probably is not above our maximum threshold. A few butterflies probably indicate a normal amount of anxiety (i.e., an amount between our minimum and maximum thresholds). When we do not feel *any* butterflies or nervousness, our anxiety is probably below our minimum threshold. If, however, we have a stomachache, our heart is racing, we are short of breath, and the palms of our hands are sweating, our anxiety is probably above our maximum threshold. The physical indicators each of us can use will differ. By paying attention to our gut reactions, we can figure out when our anxiety is so high that we do not feel comfortable communicating and when it is so low that we do not care what happens. Once we know where these points are, we can cognitively manage our anxiety. Anxiety management is discussed in Chapter 6.

Generally, as we get to know others, the anxiety we experience in interacting with them tends to decrease. I do not mean to imply, however, that anxiety continually decreases. Although there is a general trend for our anxiety to decrease the more we get to know others, our anxiety can increase or decrease at any particular point

Table 1.2 Assessing Your Anxiety

The purpose of this questionnaire is to help you assess the amount of general anxiety you experience when you communicate with others. (NOTE: You can determine the amount of anxiety you experience communicating with a specific person by substituting the person's name for "others" in each of the statements.) Respond to each statement by indicating the degree to which the adjectives are applicable when you interact with strangers. If you "Never" have the experience, answer 1 in the space provided; if you "Almost Never" have the experience, answer 2; if you "Sometimes" have the experiences and sometimes do not, answer 3; if you "Almost Always" have the experience, answer 4; if you "Always" have the experience, answer 5.

_____ 1. I feel calm when I communicate with others.
_____ 2. I get frustrated when I communicate with others.
_____ 3. I do not get ruffled when I communicate with others.
_____ 4. I am insecure when I communicate with others.
_____ 5. I feel composed when I communicate with others.
_____ 6. I feel anxious when I communicate with others.
_____ 7. I do not get excited when I have to communicate with others.
_____ 8. I feel stress when I communicate with others.
_____ 9. I feel relaxed when I communicate with others.
_____ 10. I am worried when I communicate with others.

To find your scores, first reverse the responses for the odd-numbered items (i.e., if you wrote 1, make it 5; if you wrote 2, make it 4; if you wrote 3, leave it as 3; if you wrote 4, make it 2; if you wrote 5, make it 1). Next, add the numbers next to each of the items. Scores range from 10 to 50. The higher your score, the more anxiety you experience when interacting with others.

SOURCE: Adapted from Stephan and Stephan (1985).
NOTE: I draw a distinction between uncertainty and anxiety which Stephan and Stephan do not. This is necessary to be consistent with the theory on which the book is based.

in a relationship depending on what is going on in the relationship and how we interpret it.

Assessing Your Anxiety. Before proceeding, I want you to think about your anxiety when communicating with strangers for the first time. Take a minute to complete the assessment in Table 1.2 now.

Scores on this questionnaire range from 10 to 50. There are *no* specific scores that we can use to indicate minimum and maximum thresholds. As indicated earlier, these are different for each of us. I suggest, however, that very low scores (e.g., 10-15) indicate little motivation to communicate with strangers. Similarly, very high scores (e.g., 45-50) probably suggest that we would avoid communicating with strangers.

❏ Effective Communication

In the movie *Cool Hand Luke*, Paul Newman plays Luke, a man put in prison for destroying a parking meter. While in prison, Luke constantly gets into trouble with the prison staff. At one point, when Luke had not done something that the warden asked him to do, the warden says to Luke, "What we have here is a failure to communicate." On the surface, the warden's statement makes sense. It is, however, incomplete. The warden and Luke communicated, but they did not communicate effectively.

EFFECTIVE COMMUNICATION DEFINED

To say we communicate does not imply an outcome. Communication is a process involving the exchange of messages and the creation of meaning. As indicated earlier, no two people ever attach the same meaning to a message. Whether or not a specific instance of communication is effective or not depends on the degree to which the participants attach similar meanings to the messages exchanged. Stated differently, communication is effective to the extent that we are able to minimize misunderstandings. "To say that meaning in communication is never totally the same for all communicators is not to say that communication is impossible or even difficult —only that it is imperfect" (B. A. Fisher, 1978, p. 257).

> *Communication is effective to the extent that we are able to minimize misunderstandings.*

When we communicate, we attach meaning to (or interpret) messages we construct and transmit to others. We also attach meaning to (or interpret) messages we receive from others. We are not always aware of this process, but we do it nevertheless. For two people to communicate effectively requires that the two attach relatively similar meanings to the messages sent and received (e.g., they interpret the messages similarly). William Powers and David Lowry (1984) refer to this as basic communication fidelity—"the degree of congruence between the cognitions [or thoughts] of two or more individuals following a communication event" (p. 58).

Harry Triandis (1977) argues that effectiveness involves making isomorphic attributions (*isomorphic* implies being similar; *attributions* involve assigning a quality or characteristic to something). Everett Rogers and Lawrence Kincaid (1981) take a slightly different position. They suggest that mutual understanding is the goal of communication. Mutual understanding is the extent to which one person's estimate of the meaning another person attaches to a message actually matches the meaning the other person attaches to a message.[21] Mutual understanding does not mean there is agreement. It is possible for us to have mutual understanding and either agree or disagree with each other. We also could have mutual misunderstanding and either agree or disagree.

WHY MISINTERPRETATIONS OCCUR

Communication is effective to the extent that the person interpreting the message attaches a meaning to the message similar to what was intended by the person transmitting it. This, however, is not what happens most of the time. The vast majority of the time we interpret others' messages using our own frame of reference. Robin Lakoff (1990) illustrates the problems that emerge when we interpret others' behavior based on our own frame of reference:

> We see all behavior from our own internal perspective: what would that mean if *I* did it? And, of course, if I, as a member of my own group, did what that person did in the presence of other members of my group, it would be strange or bad. . . . We don't usually extrapolate, we don't say, "Yes, but in *his* [or *her*] frame of reference, what would it mean?" We assume the possibility of direct transfer of meaning, that a gesture or act in Culture A can be understood in

the same way by members of Culture B. Often this is true: there are universals of behavior, but as often that is a dangerous assumption; and by cavalierly ignoring the need for translation, we are making misunderstanding inevitable. (pp. 165-166)

When we are communicating with strangers and base our interpretations on our symbolic systems, ineffective communication often occurs.

The misunderstandings that occur when we communicate with strangers may be due to many different sources, including but not limited to: (a) the messages may be transmitted in a way that they cannot be understood by others (e.g., pronunciation or accents may hinder understanding), (b) the communication rules of the cultures from which the communicators come may differ and influence how messages are interpreted (e.g., one person is being indirect and the other person is interpreting the messages using direct rules for communication), (c) one of the communicators may not be able to adequately speak the other's language (e.g., one person is just learning the other's language and is not fluent), (d) one person may not understand how to accomplish a certain task or interpret a specific utterance within a social context (e.g., a person who does not speak English well may try to complain to an English speaker and actually apologize), (e) one person may make errors in attributions because of his or her group identity or intergroup expectations (e.g., a North American expects a Japanese to be indirect and does not recognize a direct answer to a question when it is given), and (f) the communicators may not be familiar with the topic being discussed.[22] The participants in intergroup encounters may or may not recognize that misunderstandings are occurring. When misunderstandings are recognized within a conversation, communicators have three options: (a) to stop the thread of conversation taking place by shifting topics, (b) to negotiate the misunderstanding, and (c) to ignore the misunderstanding and continue the conversation (Gass & Varonis, 1991).

To illustrate the misunderstandings that can occur, consider a European American teacher interacting with an African American student raised in the lower-class subculture. The teacher asks the student a question. In answering the question, the student does not look the teacher in the eyes. The teacher, in all likelihood, would interpret the student's behavior as disrespectful or assume that the student is hiding something. Establishing eye contact is expected in the European American middle-class subculture in the United States when you are telling the truth and being respectful. The student's intent in fact may have been to show respect to the teacher given that children in the lower-class African American subculture in the United States are taught not to make eye contact with people they respect. Situations like this lead to misunderstanding and ineffective communication.

To further illustrate the misunderstandings that can occur when we communicate with strangers, consider the following example presented by Harry Triandis (1975, pp. 42-43). The example is drawn from the files of his colleague George Vassiliou, a Greek psychiatrist, and it involves a segment of interaction between a supervisor from the United States and a subordinate from Greece. In the segment, the supervisor wants the employee to participate in decisions (a norm in the United States), whereas the subordinate expects to be told what to do (a norm in Greece):

Behavior	Attribution
American: How long will it take you to finish this report?	American: I asked him to participate.
	Greek: His behavior makes no sense. He is the boss. Why doesn't he tell me?
Greek: I do not know. How long should it take?	American: He refuses to take responsibility.
	Greek: I asked him for an order.
American: You are in the best position to analyze time requirements.	American: I press him to take responsibility for his own actions.
	Greek: What nonsense! I better give him an answer.
Greek: Ten days.	American: He lacks the ability to estimate time; this estimate is totally inadequate.
American: Take 15. It is agreed you will do it in 15 days?	American: I offer a contract.
	Greek: These are my orders. Fifteen days.

In fact the report needed 30 days of regular work. So the Greek worked day and night, but at the end of the 15th day, he still needed one more day's work.

American: Where is my report?	American: I am making sure he fulfills his contract.
	Greek: He is asking for the report.
Greek: It will be ready tomorrow.	(Both attribute that it is not ready.)
American: But we agreed that it would be ready today.	American: I must teach him to fulfill a contract.
	Greek: The stupid, incompetent boss! Not only did he give me wrong orders, but he does not appreciate that I did a 30-day job in 16 days.
The Greek hands in his resignation.	The American is surprised.
	Greek: I can't work for such a man.

As these two examples illustrate, our culture and ethnicity influence the attributions (i.e., explanations of the causes) we make about others' behavior. The unique aspects of our symbolic systems also can be problematic when we are communicating with people we know reasonably well. In fact, it appears that we have more misunderstandings with people we know well than with people we do not know well.[23] One reason for this is that we *assume* that people we know well have meanings that are similar to ours (i.e., our uncertainty is below our minimum threshold). Because the topics of conversations we hold with people we know (including co-workers) are often more important than those we hold with people we do not know well, small differences in meanings attached to messages may lead to misunderstandings.

RECOGNIZING OUR UNCONSCIOUS INTERPRETATIONS

It is important to recognize that the misunderstandings that we have with others are the result of our interpretations of their behavior, not their behavior per se.[24] I may say, for example, "You make me angry." This is not an accurate statement. Although it is true I would not have experienced anger if you had not behaved in a certain way, my anger is based on how I interpreted your behavior, not your actual behavior.

To decrease the chance of misinterpretations of others' messages based on our unconscious interpretations, we must be aware of our normal tendencies. Aaron Beck (1988) outlines five principles that are useful in understanding how misinterpretations occur:

1. We can never know the state of mind—the attitudes, thoughts, and feelings—of other people.
2. We depend on signals, which are frequently ambiguous, to inform us about the attitudes and wishes of other people.
3. We use our own coding system, which may be defective, to decipher these signals.
4. Depending on our own state of mind at a particular time, we may be biased in our method of interpreting other people's behavior, that is, how we decode.
5. The degree to which we believe that we are correct in divining another person's motives and attitudes is not related to the actual accuracy of our belief. (p. 18)

Understanding these principles can help us improve the quality of our communication with others. Using the principles, however, requires that we be mindful.

MINDFULNESS

We must become aware of our communication behavior in order to correct our tendency to misinterpret others' behavior and communicate more effectively. Social psychologists refer to this as becoming mindful of our behavior.[25] Ellen Langer (1989) isolates three qualities of *mindfulness*: "(1) creation of new categories; (2) openness to new information; and (3) awareness of more than one perspective" (p. 62). She points out that "categorizing is a fundamental and natural human activity. It is the way we come to know the world. Any attempt to eliminate bias by attempting to eliminate the perception of differences is doomed to failure" (p. 154).

Langer argues that what we need to do is learn to make more, not fewer, distinctions. To illustrate, Langer uses an example of people who are in the category "cripple." If we see all people in this category as the same, we start treating the category in which we place a person as his or her identity. If we draw additional distinctions within this category (e.g., create new categories), on the other hand, it stops us from treating the person as a category. If we see a person with a "lame leg," we do not necessarily treat her or him as a "cripple."

Openness to new information and awareness of more than one perspective are related to focusing on the process rather than the outcome. Langer argues that

> an outcome orientation in social situations can induce mindlessness. If we think we know how to handle a situation, we don't feel a need to pay attention. If we respond to the situation as very familiar (as a result, for example, of overlearning), we notice only minimal cues necessary to carry out the proper scenarios. If, on the other hand, the situation is strange, we might be so preoccupied with the thought of failure ("what if I make a fool of myself?") that we miss nuances of our own and others' behavior. In this sense, we are mindless with respect to the immediate situation, although we may be thinking quite actively about outcome related issues. (p. 34)

Langer believes that focusing on the process (e.g., how we do something) forces us to be mindful of our behavior and pay attention to the situations in which we find ourselves. It is only when we are mindful of the process of our communication that we can determine how our interpretations of messages differ from others' interpretations of those messages.

Sometimes we become mindful of our communication without any effort on our part because of the circumstances in which we find ourselves. We become mindful of our communication: "(1) in novel situations where, by definition, no appropriate script exists, (2) where external factors prevent completion of a script, (3) when scripted behavior becomes effortful because substantially more of the behavior is required than is usual, (4) when a discrepant outcome is experienced, or (5) where multiple scripts come into conflict" (Berger & Douglas, 1982, pp. 46-47).

We often are mindful of our behavior when we communicate with strangers because they act in a deviant or unexpected fashion or we lack a script to guide our communication with them. The problem is that we usually are mindful of the outcome, not the process. Because we tend to interpret others' behavior based on our own frame of reference, to communicate effectively with strangers we need to become mindful of the process of our communication, even when we are engaging in habitual behavior. I am not suggesting that we try to be mindful at all times. This would be impossible. Rather, I am suggesting that when we know there is a high potential for misunderstanding, we need to be mindful and consciously aware of the process of communication that is taking place.

❏ Notes

1. See Bill Moyer's PBS program "Beyond Hate" for a summary of Wiesel's position on hate.

2. The *Los Angeles Times* (June 8, 1993, p. H8) estimates that there are over 50 places in the world where ethnic conflict is occurring today. This estimate counts the United States as one spot where such tensions exist.

3. This idea originally was used in *Communicating With Strangers* (Gudykunst & Kim, 1984, 1992). This book has much more "applied" than the earlier text. My focus here is on presenting material that can be used to improve communication effectiveness. I take a "culture general" approach; that is, I present general strategies for reducing uncertainty and anxiety that can be applied when you communicate with people from a variety of cultural and ethnic groups.

4. Stranger is a figure-ground phenomenon. Who is the stranger depends on the context. To simplify application of the material presented here I use the perspective of a person being approached by a stranger. In presenting the material, I arbitrarily use either the perspective of the "sender" or "receiver." I believe that these processes occur simultaneously, but separating the processes simplifies the presentation.

5. Howell (1982) suggests a fifth stage, "conscious supercompetence," which is not included here. I have described his stages in the language I use throughout the book.

6. I have modified and extended the theory since this published version was completed. A complete elaboration will appear in Gudykunst (in press). Where I draw on extensions in this book, I will outline the theoretical rationale in notes.

7. Most of the questionnaires presented are adapted from reliable and valid measures used in research. Some I developed for the purpose of the book. Although

I have not assessed the psychometric properties of the questionnaires, I believe they are all reasonable measures of the concepts under discussion.

8. Some of the ideas for this introduction were drawn from B. A. Fisher (1978).

9. My view of the nature of communication draws upon many different sources (e.g., Barnlund, 1962; Berger & Bradac, 1982; Berlo, 1960; Miller & Steinberg, 1975). It is influenced most by Miller and Steinberg (1975). I disagree with them in one important area, however. They argue that communication is an intentional activity. I will argue that communication can occur unintentionally. Here and throughout the book I will attempt to keep references to a minimum. The general sources for this section are specified above. When I use a specific scholar's position, I will cite the source in the text.

10. See J. Stewart (1990) for a detailed discussion of the transactional model of communication.

11. The sources of behavior discussed below are based originally on the work of Harry Triandis (1977, 1980, 1984). The specific discussion here is drawn from my extension of his work (Gudykunst, 1987; Gudykunst & Ting-Toomey, 1988).

12. Some scholars (e.g., Miller & Steinberg, 1975) argue that we must have intentions to call our messages communication. Obviously, I think this is only one of the sources of our communication behavior.

13. I will draw on models of cognitive therapy throughout the book, especially Beck (1988).

14. Deaux (1993) argues that the distinction between social and personal identity is somewhat arbitrary. "Personal identity is defined, at least in part, by group memberships, and social categories are infused with personal meaning" (p. 5). Trafimow, Triandis, and Goto (1991), however, demonstrated that personal and social aspects of the self are stored in different "baskets" in memory.

15. See Boulding (1988) for a discussion of "species identity."

16. Miller and Steinberg's (1975) actual terms are cultural, sociological, and psychological.

17. Although it is awkward usage, I will talk about people from the United States rather than "Americans." The reason for this is that use of the term Americans to refer to people from the United States often is considered offensive by people from Mexico and Latin and South America, who are also "Americans." Where possible, I will use North Americans, but this term is also problematic.

18. These two functions are drawn from my theory of interpersonal and intergroup communication (Gudykunst, 1988, 1993). I extended the work of Charles Berger and his associates (e.g., Berger & Bradac, 1982; Berger & Calabrese, 1975) on uncertainty reduction and W. G. Stephan and C. W. Stephan (1985) on anxiety reduction.

19. Kellermann (1986) has presented research questioning the anticipated interaction assumption. Kellermann and Reynolds (1990) provide data supporting the deviance and incentive (reward) value assumptions.

20. Kellermann and Reynolds (1990) found that tolerance for uncertainty influences our communication. This finding indirectly supports the argument made here.

21. Rogers and Kincaid (1981) actually use the term *cognitions* instead of *attaching mean- ing*. I have used attaching meaning to be consistent with the position I outline below. McLeod and Chaffee (1973) refer to mutual understanding as "accuracy" in their coorientational model.

22. Some of the sources presented are drawn from Banks, Gao, and Baker (1991).

23. Beck (1988) cites research on marital communication (e.g., Noller, 1980) to support this claim.

24. See Chapter 7 in Beck (1988) for an extended discussion of this process.

25. See Langer (1989). Langer's work provides the conceptual foundation for most of this section.

2

Understanding Group Differences

In this chapter, I examine the various sources of group differences that influence the way we communicate. Because the focus of the book is on national cultures and ethnic subcultures, I examine these sources of diversity in the most detail. There are, however, several other sources of diversity that affect our communication everyday. I therefore also discuss gender, disability, age, and social class as social categorizations that affect our communication.

❏ Culture

Culture can be seen as including everything that is human made (e.g., Herskovits, 1955) or as a system of shared meanings (e.g., Geertz, 1973), to name only two possible conceptualizations. Culture also has been equated with communication. Edward T. Hall (1959), for example, believes that "culture is communication and communication is culture" (p. 169).

DEFINING CULTURE

There are many definitions of culture, but it is necessary to select one to guide our analysis. I find Roger Keesing's (1974) definition useful:

> Culture, conceived as a system of competence shared in its broad design and deeper principles, and varying between individuals in its specificities, is then not all of what an individual knows and thinks and feels about his [or her] world. It is his [or her] theory of what his [or her] fellows know, believe, and mean, his [or her] theory of the code being followed, the game being played, in the society into which he [or she] was born. . . . It is this theory to which a native actor [or actress] refers in interpreting the unfamiliar or the ambiguous, in interacting with strangers (or supernaturals), and in other settings peripheral to the familiarity of mundane everyday life space; and with which he [or she] creates the stage on which the games of life are played. . . . But note that the actor's [or actress's] "theory" of his [or her] culture, like his [or her] theory of his [or her] language may be in large measure unconscious. Actors [or actresses] follow rules of which they are not consciously aware, and assume a world to be "out there" that they have in fact created with culturally shaped and shaded patterns of mind. We can recognize that not every individual shares precisely the same theory of the cultural code, that not every individual knows all the sectors of the culture . . . no one native actor [or actress] knows all the culture, and each has a variant version of the code. Culture in this view is ordered not simply as a collection of symbols fitted together by the analyst but as a system of knowledge, shaped and constrained by the way the human brain acquires, organizes, and processes information and creates "internal models of reality." (p. 89)

Keesing emphasizes that culture is our theory of the "game being played" in our society. He suggests that we generally are not highly aware of the rules of the game being played, but we behave as though there was general agreement on the rules. To illustrate, if we met a stranger from Mars and the Martian asked us to explain the rules of our culture, we probably would not be able to describe many of the rules because we are not highly aware of them. Keesing

Culture is our theory of the "game being played" in our society.

argues that we use our theory of the game being played to interpret unfamiliar things we come across. We also use the theory in interacting with the other people we encounter in our society. Keesing also points out that members of a culture do *not* all share exactly the same view of the culture. No one individual knows all aspects of the culture, and each person has a unique view of the culture. The theories that members of a culture share, however, overlap sufficiently so that they can coordinate their behavior in everyday life.

NORMS AND RULES

We learn to be members of our culture from our parents, from teachers in schools, from our religious institutions, from our peers, and from the mass media. Originally, we learn about our culture from our parents. Our parents begin to teach us the norms and communication rules that guide behavior in our culture. *Norms* are guidelines of how we should behave or should not behave that have a basis in morality. *Rules,* in contrast, are guidelines for the ways we are expected to communicate. Rules are not based in morality (Olsen, 1978). Our parents do *not* explicitly tell us the norms and rules of our culture. They do not, for example, tell us that when we meet someone for the first time we should stick out our right hand and shake three times. Rather, they teach us the norms and rules by modeling how to behave and correcting us when we violate a norm or rule.

As we grow older and begin to interact with other children, these children reinforce the norms and rules we learned from our parents. We also learn additional norms and rules of our culture. We learn how to be cooperative and how to compete with others from our peers. When we attend religious services or school we learn other norms and rules of our culture. Another way we learn about our culture is through the mass media, especially television. Television teaches us many of the day-to-day norms of our culture and provides us with a view of reality. Television has become the medium through which most of us learn what others' expectations are for our behavior. It appears that the more television we watch, the more our views of reality overlap with others (Gerbner, Gross, Morgan, & Signorielli, 1980).

CULTURES AND SUBCULTURES

As indicated earlier, Keesing's (1974) definition emphasizes that our culture provides us with a system of knowledge that allows us to know how to communicate with others and how to interpret their behavior. The term *culture* usually is reserved for the systems of knowledge used by relatively large numbers of people. The boundaries between cultures *usually* coincide with political, or national, boundaries between countries. To illustrate, we can speak of the culture of the United States, the Mexican culture, the Japanese culture, and so forth. In some countries, however, there is more than one culture.[1] Consider Canada as an example; there is the Anglophone (i.e., English-speaking) culture derived from Great Britain and there is the Francophone culture derived from France.

I do *not* mean to imply that cultures are homogeneous (i.e., that the members are alike). All cultures are heterogeneous to some degree. The heterogeneity is due, at least in part, to the existence of subcultures within the larger culture. *Subcultures* are groups within a culture whose members share many of the values of the culture, but also have some values that differ from the larger culture. We can talk about ethnic subcultures, subculture of the disabled, elderly subculture, social class subcultures, a student subculture, a business subculture, a medical subculture (people who work in medicine), a homosexual subculture, and so forth. The subcultures of which we are members influence the norms and rules we use to guide our behavior. The norms and rules we use to guide our communication overlap to some extent in every culture. If they did not overlap, people would not be able to coordinate their actions. The more individuals' implicit theories overlap, the more homogeneous the culture. Although the United States is not highly homogeneous, there clearly is sufficient homogeneity for most people to know how to behave and coordinate their communication in most situations.

Before proceeding, one other issue needs to be mentioned. Throughout this book, I focus on how our culture influences our communication. The relationship between culture and communication, nevertheless, is reciprocal. Our culture influences our communication *and* our communication influences our culture. The influence of our communication on our culture, however, does not take place over short periods of time. If people in a culture begin to communicate differently, over time, this will change the culture. Further, most of the time we automatically follow the rules and norms of our culture when we communicate because this does not require effort. Not following the rules and norms of our culture, in contrast, requires effort.

❑ How Cultures Differ

To understand similarities and differences in communication across cultures, it is necessary to have a way of talking about how cultures differ. It does not make any sense to say that "Fumio communicates indirectly because she is a Japanese" or that "Kimberly communicates directly because she is from the United States." This does not tell us why there are differences between the way people communicate in the United States and Japan. There has to be some aspect of the cultures in Japan and the United States that are different and this difference, in turn, explains why Japanese communicate indirectly and people from the United States communicate directly. In other words, there are dimensions on which cultures can be different or similar that can be used to explain communication across cultures. I refer to these as dimensions of cultural variability.

There are several different conceptualizations of how cultures differ. It is impossible to discuss them all in a short book like this. I emphasize the two that I have found most useful in understanding similarities and differences in communication across cultures: individualism-collectivism and low- and high-context communication.[2] I also discuss more briefly three other dimensions of cultural variability that influence our communication: uncertainty avoidance, power distance, and masculinity.

INDIVIDUALISM-COLLECTIVISM

Individualism-collectivism is the major dimension of cultural variability used to explain cross-cultural differences in behavior.[3] Emphasis is placed on individuals' goals in individualistic cultures, whereas group goals have precedence over individuals' goals in collectivistic cultures. Members of individualistic cultures, for example, promote self-realization:

> Chief among the virtues claimed by individualist philosophers is self-realization. Each person is viewed as having a unique set of talents and potentials. The translation of these potentials into actuality is considered the highest purpose to which one can devote one's life. The striving for self-realization is accompanied by a subjective sense of rightness and personal well-being. (Waterman, 1984, pp. 4-5)

Collectivistic cultures, in contrast, require that individuals fit into the group. This is illustrated by the culture in Kenya:

> In Kenyan tribes nobody is an isolated individual. Rather, his [or her] uniqueness is a secondary fact. . . . First, and foremost, he [or she] is several people's contemporary. His [or her] life is founded on these facts economically, socially and physically. In this system group activities are dominant, responsibility is shared and accountability is collective. . . . Because of the emphasis on collectivity, harmony and cooperation among the group tend to be emphasized more than individual function and responsibility. (Saleh & Gufwoli, 1982, p. 327)

In individualistic cultures, "people are supposed to look after themselves and their immediate family only," whereas in collectivistic cultures, "people belong to ingroups or collectivities which are supposed to look after them in exchange for loyalty" (Hofstede & Bond, 1984, p. 419). The "I" identity has precedence in individualistic cultures over the "we" identity, which takes precedence in collectivistic cultures. The emphasis in individualistic societies is on individuals' initiative and achievement, whereas emphasis is placed on belonging to groups in collectivistic societies. People in individualistic cultures tend to be universalistic and apply the same value standards to all. People in collectivistic cultures, in contrast, tend to be particularistic and therefore apply different value standards for members of their ingroups and outgroups.

Importance of Ingroups. Harry Triandis (1988) argues that the relative importance of ingroups is one of the major factors that differentiate individualistic and collectivistic cultures. *Ingroups,* according to Triandis, are groups that are important to their members. Individualistic cultures have many specific ingroups (e.g., family, religion, social clubs, profession, to name only a few) that might influence behavior in any particular social situation. Because there are many ingroups, any individual ingroup exerts relatively little influence on behavior. In collectivistic cultures there are few general ingroups (e.g., work group, university, family, to name the major ingroups that influence behavior in collectivistic cultures) that have a strong influence on behavior across situations.

Although the ingroup may be the same in individualistic and collectivistic cultures, the sphere of its influence is different. The sphere of influence in an individualistic culture is very specific (i.e., the ingroup affects behavior in very specific circumstances), whereas the sphere of influence in a collectivistic culture is very general (i.e., the ingroup affects behavior in many different aspects of a person's life).

Collectivistic cultures emphasize goals, needs, and views of the ingroup over those of the individual; the social norms of the ingroup, rather than individual pleasure; shared ingroup beliefs, rather than unique individual beliefs; and a value on cooperation with ingroup members, rather than maximizing individual outcomes. Ingroups have different rank-orders of importance in collectivistic cultures; some, for example, put family ahead of all other ingroups, whereas others put business enterprises ahead of other ingroups (Triandis, 1988). To illustrate, the company often is considered the primary ingroup in Japan (Nakane, 1970), whereas the family is the primary ingroup in many other collectivistic cultures (e.g., Latin America).

Independent and Interdependent Self-Construals. The way people in individualistic and collectivistic cultures view themselves (i.e., their self-concepts) tends to differ. Hazel Markus and Shinobu Kitayama (1991) call the different self-conceptions *independent construal of self* and *interdependent construal of self.* Independent self-construals tend to predominate in individualistic cultures and interdependent self-construals tend to predominate in collectivistic cultures.

When an independent construal of the self predominates we view ourselves as unique individuals with clear boundaries that separate us from others. Markus and Kitayama view the sense of individuality that accompanies an independent construal of self as involving a sense of

> oneself as an agent, as a producer of one's actions. One is conscious of being in control over the surrounding situation, and of the need to express one's own thoughts, feelings, and actions to others. . . . . Such acts as standing out are often intrinsically rewarding because they elicit pleasant, ego-focused emotions (e.g., pride) and also reduce unpleasant ones (e.g., frustration). Furthermore, the acts of standing out, themselves, form an important basis for self-esteem. (p. 246)

Based on the independent construal of self, we see ourselves as unique individuals and do not have to take others into consideration in deciding how to behave.

When an interdependent construal of self predominates, we view ourselves as part of a social relationship. We view our self not totally separate from others, but interlinked with others. Markus and Kitayama (1991) point out that the sense of self-conception that accompanies an interdependent construal of self focuses on an

> attentiveness and responsiveness to others that one either explicitly or implicitly assumes will be reciprocated by these others, as well as the willful management of one's other-focused feelings and desires so as to maintain and further the reciprocal interpersonal relationship. One is conscious of where one belongs with respect to others and assumes a receptive stance toward these others, continually adjusting and accommodating to these others in many aspects of behavior. . . . Such acts of fitting in and accommodating are often

intrinsically rewarding because they give rise to pleasant, other-focused emotions (e.g., feeling of connection) while diminishing unpleasant ones (e.g., shame) . . . because of the self-restraint required in doing so forms an important basis of self-esteem. (p. 246)

Based on the interdependent construal of the self, we take others involved in our self-conception into consideration in deciding how we should behave.

Personal identities in individualistic and collectivistic cultures appear to be based on independent self-construals. Social identities in collectivistic cultures tend to be based on an interdependent self-construal. Social identities in individualistic cultures, however, do not have to be based an interdependent self-construal. The social identity based on occupation in an individualistic culture, for example, would be based on an independent self-construal, because people do not see themselves as interlinked with others in their occupation. The social identity as a member of a family (parent, son/daughter), however, might be based on an interdependent self-construal in an individualistic culture.

We all use *both* independent and interdependent self-construals when we think about ourselves. One of the two self-construals, however, tends to predominate in the way we think about ourselves. Stated differently, we use one of the two self construals more than the other when we think about ourselves. In the United States, for example, we may think of ourselves in interdependent terms with respect to our family, but most of us tend to use an independent self-construal to guide our behavior in the remainder of our lives.

Individualism and collectivism both exist in every culture, but one tends to predominate. Cultures in which individualism tends to predominate include, but are not limited to: Australia, Great Britain, Belgium, Canada, Denmark, France, Germany, Ireland, Italy, New Zealand, Sweden, and the United States. Cultures in which collectivism tends to predominate include, but are not limited to: Argentina, Brazil, China, Costa Rica, Egypt, Ethiopia, Greece, Guatemala, India, Japan, Kenya, Korea, Mexico, Nigeria, Panama, Saudi Arabia, and Venezuela. Generally, most Arab, African, Asian, and Latin cultures are collectivistic.

LOW- AND HIGH-CONTEXT COMMUNICATION

Individualism-collectivism provides a powerful explanatory framework for understanding cultural similarities and differences in interpersonal communication. Whereas individualism-collectivism defines broad differences between cultures, Edward T. Hall's (1976) low- and high-context scheme focuses upon cultural differences in communication processes.

Hall (1976) differentiates cultures on the basis of the communication that predominates in the culture. A *high-context message* is one in which "most of the information is either in the physical context or internalized in the person, while very little is in the coded, explicit, transmitted part of the message" (Hall, 1976, p. 79). A *low-context message*, in contrast, is one in which "the mass of information is vested in the explicit code" (p. 70). Although no culture exists at either end of the continuum, the culture of the United States is placed toward the lower end, slightly above the German, Scandinavian, and Swiss cultures. Most Asian cultures, such as the Japanese, Chinese, and Korean, in contrast, fall toward the high-context end of the continuum.

The level of context influences all other aspects of communication:

> High-context cultures make greater distinction between insiders and outsiders than low-context cultures do. People raised in high-context systems expect more of others than do the participants in low-context systems. When talking about something that they have on their minds, a high-context individual will expect his [or her] interlocutor to know what's bothering him [or her], so that he [or she] doesn't have to be specific. The result is that he [or she] will talk around and around the point, in effect putting all the pieces in place except the crucial one. Placing it properly—this keystone—is the role of his [or her] interlocutor. (Hall, 1976, p. 98)

It appears that low- and high-context communication are the predominant forms of communication in individualistic and collectivistic cultures, respectively.

As suggested earlier, members of low-context, individualistic cultures tend to communicate in a direct fashion, whereas members of high-context, collectivistic cultures tend to communicate in an indirect fashion. Donald Levine (1985) describes communication in the Amhara culture in Ethiopia (a collectivistic culture):

> The Amhara's basic manner of communicating is indirect, often secretive. Amharic conversation abounds with general, evasive remarks, like *Min yeshallal?* ("What is better?") when the speaker has failed to indicate what issue he [or she] is referring to, or *Setagn!* ("Give me!") when the speaker fails to specify what it is he [or she] wants. When the speaker then is quizzed about the issue at hand or the object he [or she] desires, his [or her] reply still may not reveal what is really on his [or her] mind; and if it does, his [or her] interlocutor will likely as not interpret that response as a disguise. (p. 25)

Levine goes on to describe communication in the United States (an individualistic culture) in this way:

> The [U.S.] American way of life, by contrast, affords little room for the cultivation of ambiguity. The dominant [North] American temper calls for clear and direct communication. It expresses itself in such common injunctions as "Say what you mean," "Don't beat around the bush," and "Get to the point." (p. 28)

UNCERTAINTY AVOIDANCE

In comparison to members of cultures low in uncertainty avoidance, members of cultures high in uncertainty avoidance have a lower tolerance "for uncertainty and ambiguity, which expresses itself in higher levels of anxiety and energy release, greater need for formal rules and absolute truth, and less tolerance for people or groups with deviant ideas or behavior" (Hofstede, 1979, p. 395). There is a strong desire for consensus in high uncertainty avoidance cultures, therefore, deviant behavior is not acceptable. People in high uncertainty avoidance cultures tend to display emotions more than people in low uncertainty avoidance cultures. People in low uncertainty avoidance cultures have lower stress levels and weaker superegos and accept dissent and taking risks more than people in high uncertainty avoidance cultures.

Geert Hofstede (1991) points out that uncertainty avoidance should not be equated with risk avoidance. People in uncertainty avoiding cultures shun ambiguous situations. People in such cultures look for a structure in their organizations, institutions, and relationships which makes events clearly interpretable and predictable. Paradoxically, they are often prepared to engage in risky behavior to reduce ambiguities, like starting a fight with a potential opponent rather than sitting back and waiting. (p. 116)

Hofstede summarizes the view of people in high uncertainty avoidance cultures as "what is different, is dangerous," (p. 119) and the credo of people in low uncertainty avoidance cultures as "what is different, is curious" (p. 119).

Uncertainty avoidance is useful in understanding differences in how strangers are treated. People in high uncertainty avoidance cultures try to avoid ambiguity and therefore develop rules and rituals for virtually every possible situation in which they might find themselves, including interacting with strangers. Interaction with strangers in cultures high in uncertainty avoidance may be highly ritualistic or very polite. If people from high uncertainty avoidance cultures interact with strangers in a situation where there are not clear rules, they may ignore the strangers—treat them as though they do not exist.

Different degrees of uncertainty avoidance exist in every culture, but one tends to predominate. Cultures that tend to be high in uncertainty avoidance include, but are not limited to: Egypt, Argentina, Belgium, Chile, France, Greece, Guatemala, Japan, Korea, Mexico, Peru, Portugal, and Spain. Cultures that tend to be low in uncertainty avoidance include, but are not limited to: Canada, Denmark, Great Britain, Hong Kong, India, Jamaica, Sweden, and the United States.

POWER DISTANCE

Power distance is "the extent to which the less powerful members of institutions and organizations accept that power is distributed unequally" (Hofstede & Bond, 1984, p. 419). Individuals from high power distance cultures accept power as part of society. As such, superiors consider their subordinates to be different from themselves and vice versa. People in high power distance cultures see power as a basic fact of life in society and stress coercive or referent power, whereas people in low power distance cultures believe power should be used only when it is legitimate and prefer expert or legitimate power. Hofstede (1991) points out that

> in small power distance countries there is limited dependence of subordinates on bosses, and a preference for consultation, that is, *interdependence* between boss and subordinate. The emotional distance between them is relatively small: subordinates will quite readily approach and contradict their bosses. In large power distance countries there is considerable dependence of subordinates on bosses. Subordinates respond by either *preferring* such dependence (in the form of autocratic or paternalistic boss), or rejecting it entirely, which in psychology is known as *counterdependence:* that is dependence, but with a negative sign. (p. 27)

The power distance dimension clearly focuses on the relationships between people of different statuses (e.g., superiors and subordinates in organizations).

Power distance is useful in understanding strangers' behavior in role relationships, particularly those involving different degrees of power or authority. People from high power distance cultures, for example, do not question their superiors' orders. They expect to be told what to do. People in low power distance cultures, in contrast, do not necessarily accept superiors' orders at face value, they want to know why they should follow them. When people from the two different systems interact, misunderstanding is likely unless one or both understand the other person's system.

Low and high power distance tendencies exist in all cultures, but one generally predominates. Cultures in which high power distance tends to predominate include, but are not limited to: Egypt, Ethiopia, Ghana, Guatemala, India, Malaysia, Nigeria, Panama, Saudi Arabia, and Venezuela. Cultures in which low power distance tends to predominate include, but are not limited to: Austria, Canada, Denmark, Germany, Ireland, Israel, New Zealand, Sweden, and the United States.

MASCULINITY-FEMININITY

People in highly masculine cultures value things, power, and assertiveness, whereas people in cultures low on masculinity or high on femininity value quality of life and nurturance (Hofstede, 1980). Members of highly masculine cultures emphasize differentiated sex roles, performance, ambition, and independence. Members of cultures low on masculinity, in contrast, value fluid sex roles, quality of life, service, and interdependence.

Masculinity-femininity is useful in understanding cultural differences and similarities in opposite-sex and same-sex relationships. People from highly masculine cultures, for example, tend to have little contact with members of the opposite sex when they are growing up. They tend to see same-sex relationships as more intimate than opposite-sex relationships. For people from a feminine culture to communicate effectively with strangers from a masculine culture, especially if they are male and female, they must understand the others' orientation toward sex roles.

As with the other dimensions of cultural variability, both masculinity and femininity tendencies exist in all cultures. One tendency, however, generally predominates. Cultures in which masculinity tends to predominate include, but are limited to: Austria, Italy, Jamaica, Japan, Mexico, Switzerland, and Venezuela. Cultures in which femininity tends to predominate include, but are not limited to: Chile, Costa Rica, Denmark, Finland, the Netherlands, Norway, and Sweden. The United States falls in the middle on this dimension.

❑ Cultural Identity

Before examining ethnicity and other forms of diversity that influence the way we communicate, we need to briefly look at our cultural identity. Our *cultural identity* is our social identity that focuses on our membership in our culture. This identity has a tremendous influence on our communication in everyday life, but we generally are not highly aware of its influence. We become aware of the influence of our cultural identity on our communication when we find ourselves in another culture or in a situation in our culture where we are interacting with members of other cultures.

There are two issues that need to be addressed with respect to our cultural identity. First, how strongly do we identify with our culture? Second, what is the content of our cultural identity?

STRENGTH OF CULTURAL IDENTITY

The strength of our cultural identity involves the degree to which our culture influences how we define ourselves.[4] As noted earlier, we tend to see our culture as more important in how we define ourselves when we are in another culture than when we are in our own culture. The degree to which we identify with our culture influences the degree to which we expect others to follow the rules and norms of our culture.

Table 2.1 contains a questionnaire designed to assess the strength of your cultural identity. Take a few minutes to complete it now.

Scores on the cultural identity questionnaire range from 10 to 50. The higher your score, the stronger you identify with your culture. As I indicated above, we are more aware of our cultural identity when we find ourselves in another culture than when we are in our own culture. If your score is low, it may not mean that you do not identify strongly with your culture, but only that you are not aware of how important your culture is to you. If you visit another culture and complete this questionnaire after you have been there for a day or two, you will probably see that your score is higher than when you completed it just now.

INDIVIDUALISTIC AND COLLECTIVISTIC ORIENTATIONS

The second aspect of our cultural identity is the content of our cultural identity. Each of the dimensions of cultural variability discussed in this chapter contributes to the content of our cultural identities. The one that influences our communication with strangers the most, however, appears to be individualism-collectivism. I therefore focus on this dimension here.

Table 2.1 Assessing the Strength of Your Cultural Identity

The purpose of this questionnaire is to help you think about the degree to which you identify with being a member of your national culture. Respond to each statement by indicating the degree to which the statement is true regarding the way you typically think about yourself. When you think about yourself is the statement "Always False" (answer 1), "Mostly False" (answer 2), "Sometimes True and Sometimes False" (answer 3), "Mostly True" (answer 4), or "Always True" (answer 5)?

_____ 1. Being a member of my culture is important to me.
_____ 2. Thinking about myself as a member of my culture is not central to how I define myself.
_____ 3. I have a positive view of my culture.
_____ 4. I rarely think about being a member of my culture.
_____ 5. Being a member of my culture plays a large role in my life.
_____ 6. It does not bother me if others do not recognize me as a member of my culture.
_____ 7. I enjoy being a member of my culture.
_____ 8. I rarely choose to express my culture in the way I communicate.
_____ 9. I like the things that make me a member of my culture and different from people in other cultures.
_____ 10. If I were born again, I would want to be born as a member of a different culture.

To find your score, first reverse the responses for the even-numbered items (i.e., if you wrote 1, make it 5; if you wrote 2, make it 4; if you wrote 3, leave it as 3; if you wrote 4, make it 2; if you wrote 5, make it 1). Next, add the numbers next to each of the statements. Scores range from 10 to 50. The higher your score, the more you identify with the group.

SOURCE: Adapted in part from Hofman (1985).

Individualistic and collectivistic tendencies exist in all cultures, but one generally predominates. Everyone, however, has individualistic and collectivistic thoughts. It is possible, therefore, for there to be collectively oriented persons in an individualistic culture and individualistically oriented persons in collectivistic cultures. Harry Triandis and his associates (Triandis, Leung, Villareal, & Clack, 1985) argue that individuals' collectivistic tendencies involve three factors: subordinating individual goals to group goals, viewing the ingroup as an extension of the self, and having a strong ingroup identity.

Shalom Schwartz (1990) argues that individualistic and collectivistic values do not necessarily conflict. With respect to individualistic values, he points out that "hedonism (enjoyment), achievement, self-direction, social power, and stimulation values all serve self interests of the individual, but not necessarily at the expense of any collectivity. . . . These same values might be promoted by leaders or members of collectivities as goals for their ingroup" (p. 143). With respect to collectivistic tendencies, he indicates that

> prosocial, restrictive conformity, security, and tradition values all focus on promoting the interests of others. It is other people, constituting a collective, who benefit from the actor's [or actress's] concern for them, self-restraint, care for their security, and respect for shared traditions. But this does not necessarily occur at the expense of the actor [or actress]. (p. 143)

Cultures and individuals thus can have both individualistic and collectivistic tendencies.[5]

The questionnaire in Table 2.2 is designed to help you assess the degree to which you are individualistic and/or collectivistic. Take a few minutes to complete the questionnaire now.

Scores on the questionnaire range from 10 to 50 for both individualistic and collectivistic tendencies. The higher your scores, the more your individualistic and collectivistic tendencies. Although you probably have a tendency toward one orientation more than the other, you can have high or low scores on both. The important thing to keep in mind is that your tendencies affect your communication with people who have different tendencies.

When we communicate with people from other cultures, we start from the assumption that all members of the other culture are similar to each other. People from individualistic cultures, for example, assume that people in collectivistic cultures act collectively. This provides valuable information on how to communicate with people from collectivistic cultures. To illustrate, it allows us to predict that people in collectivistic cultures emphasize their social identities over their personal identity when they communicate.[6] To communicate effectively with specific members of collectivistic cultures, however, we must also recognize

Table 2.2 Assessing Your Individualistic and Collectivistic Tendencies

The purpose of this questionnaire is to help you assess your individualistic and collectivistic tendencies. Respond by indicating the degree to which the values reflected in each phrase are important to you: "Opposed to My Values" (answer 1), "Not Important to Me" (answer 2), "Somewhat Important to Me" (answer 3), "Important to Me" (answer 4), or "Very Important to Me" (answer 5).

_____ 1. Obtaining pleasure or sensuous gratification
_____ 2. Preserving the welfare of others
_____ 3. Being successful by demonstrating my individual competency
_____ 4. Restraining my behavior if it is going to harm others
_____ 5. Being independent in thought and action
_____ 6. Having safety and stability for members of my ingroups
_____ 7. Obtaining status and prestige
_____ 8. Having harmony in my relations with others
_____ 9. Having an exciting and challenging life
_____ 10. Accepting cultural and religious traditions
_____ 11. Being recognized for my individual work
_____ 12. Avoiding the violation of social norms
_____ 13. Leading a comfortable life
_____ 14. Living in a stable society
_____ 15. Being logical in my approach to work
_____ 16. Being polite to others
_____ 17. Being ambitious
_____ 18. Being self-controlled
_____ 19. Being able to choose what I do
_____ 20. Enhancing the welfare of others

To find your individualism score, add your responses to the odd-numbered items. To find your collectivism score, add your responses to the even-numbered items. Both scores will range from 10 to 50. The higher your scores, the more individualistic or collectivistic you are.

SOURCE: Adapted from Rokeach (1972) and Schwartz (1990).

that not all people in collectivistic cultures emphasize their collectivistic tendencies; some are highly individualistic. In other words, we must be ready to look for individual differences.

❏ Ethnicity and Ethnic Identity

There are many different ways to define ethnicity. We can, for example, impose ethnic labels on others. When we impose labels on others, however, we may not impose the label the other person would use to describe him- or herself (Barth, 1969). George DeVos (1975) suggests that ethnicity involves the use of some aspect of a group's cultural background to separate it from others. Howard Giles and Patricia Johnson (1981), in contrast, see an ethnic group as "those individuals who identify themselves as belonging to the same ethnic category" (p. 202).

In actuality, we can impose an ethnic label on others *and* they identify with an ethnic group. When we categorize ourselves as members of a group, we also categorize others as not members of our group and therefore members of another group (J. C. Turner, 1987). Categorization of ethnicity may be based on cultural, social, psychological, or biological characteristics (Gordon, 1964).

There have been changes in recent years in the way people in the United States view ethnicity.[7] In the past, an assimilationist view of ethnicity predominated and was not questioned. *Assimilation* refers to the process of giving up one culture and taking on the characteristics of another. Robert Park (1950), for example, argues that the "cycle of contact, competition, accommodation, and eventual assimilation [among ethnic groups] is apparently progressive and unreversible" (p. 13).[8] The assimilationist view often leads to the use of "race" as a metaphor, where "Americanness" is defined as "white" (Morrison, 1992, p. 42). Explaining the culture of the United States using this metaphor will not work, however, when whites become a numerical minority sometime in the next century. The changes in the ethnic composition of the United States is changing what it means to be an "American." "The deeper significance of America's becoming a majority nonwhite society is what it means to the national psyche, to individuals' sense of themselves and their nation—their idea of what it is to be an American" (Henry, 1990, p. 30).

Pluralism is now viewed as an alternative to assimilation. In *pluralism*, ethnicity is viewed as "an internal attitude which predisposes, but does not make compulsory, the display of ethnic identification in interaction. When it facilitates self-interest, ethnic identity will be made self-evident; it is left latent when it would hinder" (Hraba & Hoiberg, 1983, p. 385). When members of a group decide to exert their ethnicity depends upon the particular circumstances in which they find themselves (Glazer & Moynihan, 1975). In the pluralistic view, maintaining ethnic identity is valued or accepted.

ETHNIC IDENTITY IN THE UNITED STATES

Although the degree to which we assert our social identities varies from situation to situation, the general degree to which we identify with particular groups appears to remain relatively stable over time. Eugeen Roosens (1989), for example, points out that asserting an ethnic identity helps us define who we are. Specifically, he suggests that our ethnicity offers

> communality in language, a series of customs and symbols, a style, rituals, and appearance, and so forth, which can penetrate life in many ways. These trappings of ethnicity are particularly attractive when one is continually confronted by others who live differently. . . . If I see and experience myself as a member of an ethnic category or group, and others—fellow members and outsiders—recognize me as such, "ways of being" become possible for me that set me apart from the outsiders. These ways of being contribute to the *content* of my self-perceptions. In this sense, I *become* my ethnic allegiance; I experience any attack on the symbols, emblems, or values (cultural elements) that define my ethnicity as an attack on myself. (pp. 17-18)

Stanley Lieberson (1985) argues that there has been a transformation regarding how ethnic identity is manifested for people of European descent in the United States. He concludes that ethnic distinctions based on ancestry from specific European countries are fading and people recognize being white, but do not have a "clearcut identification with and/or knowledge of a specific European origin" (p. 159).[9] As evidence for this change, Richard Alba (1990) points to the tremendous intermarriage among people from different European countries—three of every four marriages involve marrying someone from a different country of origin. Individuals in marriages in which the couple trace their origins to different European countries, however, do not perceive their partner to be from a different ethnic group. I refer to whites from Europe as *European Americans* throughout this book.

Although I talk about people from Europe as a group not recognizing a specific country of origin, I also recognize that there are places in the United States where European Americans clearly differentiate their country of origin (e.g., Boston, New York, Chicago). There are differences in patterns of communication among European Americans with different countries of origin, but the differences are relatively small when European Americans are compared to members of other ethnic groups.

Alba points out that European Americans can choose whether to express their ethnic identity and that European Americans vary in the degree of importance they attach to it. He concludes that Herbert Gans's (1979) notion of symbolic ethnicity accurately describes the manifestation of ethnicity among European Americans today. *Symbolic ethnicity* refers to

> *European Americans can choose whether to express their ethnic identity.*

"the desire to retain a sense of being ethnic, but without any deep commitment to the ethnic social ties and behavior" (Alba, 1990, p. 306). Mary Waters (1990) concurs with Alba's conclusion:

> The reality is that white ethnics have a lot more choice and room for maneuver than they themselves think they do. The situation is very different for members of racial minorities, whose lives are strongly influenced by their race or national origin regardless of how much they choose not to identify themselves in ethnic or racial terms. (p. 157)

European Americans, however, do not necessarily recognize the differences between their experience of ethnicity and the way non-European Americans experience it.[10] The voluntary aspect of European Americans asserting their ethnicity and the enjoyment they receive from it (e.g., it is asserted at ethnic celebrations) make it difficult for European Americans to understand the way ethnicity affects non-European Americans (Waters, 1990).

The influence of ethnic identity for non-European Americans is illustrated by the way Philip Gotanda (1991), a Japanese American playwright, describes his experiences. Gotanda was raised in the United States, but lived in Japan. His time in Japan helped him understand his ethnicity:

> After I'd been living in Japan for about a year, I had an extraordinary experience. . . . I was walking down the streets and I looked over to my left and I saw a bank of televisions all lined up, and they were filled with a Japanese newscaster. I looked up at the billboard and there was a Japanese face, I looked at the magazines on display and they were filled with Asian faces; I looked ahead and I saw a sea of people coming toward me, all about my same height, with black hair, with skin that looked exactly like mine. . . . What I experienced for the first time was this extraordinary thing called anonymity—the sense of being able to be part of a group, of everything around me reinforcing what I was. I didn't have to second guess my obviousness, to be constantly aware that I was different. . . . In that instant in Tokyo something lifted from me, and I was able to move freely. . . . Of course, the longer I was in Japan the more I became aware of the fact that I wasn't strictly Japanese either, that I would never be Japanese Japanese—that I was Japanese-American. (pp. 9-10)

Gotanda's experience clearly illustrates that ethnicity is not symbolic for non-European Americans in the United States. It is something they must address every day of their life.

LANGUAGE AND ETHNIC IDENTITY

The language we speak is a major way we mark boundaries between our ethnic group and others.[11] This is true in informal conversations with strangers, acquaintances, and friends, as well as in formal communication situations (e.g., when we talk to our supervisor at work).

Richard Rodriguez (1982) illustrates the importance of language in describing the effect of hearing his father speak English to a European American gas station attendant when he was growing up:

> I cannot forget the sounds my father made as he spoke. At one point his words slid together to form one word—sounds as confused as the threads of blue and green oil in the puddle next to my shoes. His voice rushed through what he had left to say. And, toward the end, reached falsetto notes, appealing to his listeners' understanding.

I looked away to the lights of passing automobiles. I tried not to hear anymore. (p. 15)

In contrast to the alienation he felt when he heard his father speaking English, Rodriguez felt comfort when members of his family spoke to him in Spanish:

> A family member would say something to me and I would feel specially recognized. My parents would say something to me and I would feel embraced by the sounds of their words. Those words said: I am speaking with ease in Spanish. I am addressing you in words I never use with los gringos. I recognize you as someone special, close, like no one outside. You belong with us. In the family. (p. 15)

Another way language affects our identity is through the labels we use to define ourselves. Michael Hecht and Sidney Ribeau (1991) argue that in the middle of the 1980s African Americans in the United States used different labels to refer to themselves. Some individuals, for example, used the label *Black* because it is acceptable and based on consensus (in the larger culture). Blacks reported being willing to talk, being verbally aggressive, and using slang. Blacks also described themselves as patriotic, accepting of the status quo, and attempting to assimilate into the larger culture. Individuals who used the label *Black Americans*, in contrast, gained their identity from being both black and American. Like Blacks, Black Americans attempted to assimilate into the larger culture. Black Americans' communication style, however, was characterized by the use of dialect and code switching. *Afro-Americans* also derived their identity from being black and American, but they did not want to assimilate into the larger culture, only succeed in it. Afro-Americans reported that their communication style was distinguished by the use of ethnic forms of nonverbal communication and the use of black dialect.

In the 1990s, it appears that the vast majority of blacks prefer to use the label *African American* when they refer to themselves. Two individuals provide the reasons for the use of this term:

> I grew up in a time when "black" was the accepted term. It was used on application forms and among family and friends. I changed

to African American because it seemed more accurate and more enduring to our culture.

[In the past] I didn't prefer "black," it was just used. However, when I began to realize that the term "black" was just making us be seen in terms of skin color (and not including our ethnic heritage), I embraced the term African American. After all, a "white, American, Irish person" is Irish American. We've done just as much for the country, and we have a heritage from *our* mother land, so why not express it! (Larkey, Hecht, & Martin, 1993, p. 312)

Note that there is *not* a hyphen in the label African American. In fact, most non-European Americans no longer use a hyphen for their ethnicity (e.g., Japanese American, Mexican American). Although it may seem like a minor point, omitting or including a hyphen may be interpreted as providing self-concept support (omitting) or denying a self-concept (including it). (The issue of self-concept support is discussed in more detail in Chapter 7.) We therefore need to pay attention to the labels others use to refer to themselves.

Concern over the use of ethnic labels is not limited to African Americans. Many people born in Mexico, Puerto Rico, and Cuba find the panethnic term (i.e., a term used for all of these cultures combined) *Hispanic* archaic and offensive (e.g., see Gonzalez, 1992). Participants in a recent Latino Political Survey report that they prefer the term *Latino* over *Hispanic* (summarized in Gonzalez, 1992).[12] Even the pronunciation of the term can be a statement of identity (the preferred pronunciation is lah-TEEN-oh). Sandra Cisneros (the author of *Woman Hollering Creek*) points out that "to say Latino is to say you came to my culture in a manner of respect" (quoted by Gonzalez). Cisneros believes that people who prefer the term Hispanic want to fit into the mainstream culture (that is, give up their original culture), whereas people who use Latino want to maintain their ethnicity.

Before proceeding, I want to point out that all panethnic terms (e.g., Latino, Asian Americans) are misleading as they imply homogeneity across the groups included under the term. People who were born in, or whose ancestors come from, Mexico, Cuba, and Puerto Rico, for example, share some similarities based on a common language, but there are many cultural differences among the three groups that cannot be ignored. Respondents in the Latino Political Survey clearly indicate that they prefer labels based on their country of origin (e.g., Mexican American, Cuban American), rather than panethnic terms like Latino (Gonzalez, 1992). Similarly, first-generation Asian Americans may share a collectivistic upbringing, but there are many differences among Chinese Americans, Japanese Americans, Korean Americans, and Vietnamese Americans, to name only a few of the Asian groups often lumped together.

The labels individuals use regarding their ethnic group membership can tell us a lot about them. People who trace their heritage to Mexico, for example, might use several different terms to refer to themselves. To illustrate, people who label themselves as Chicanos or Chicanas define themselves differently than people who use the label Mexican American. The people who define themselves as a Chicanos or Chicanas probably have political goals (e.g., promoting La Raza and community solidarity), whereas people who define themselves as Mexican Americans do not. To communicate effectively with members of either group, it would be important to know that they prefer one label or another. This is important, as indicated earlier, because effective communication requires that we support others' self-concepts, including their preferred ethnic identity. Personal and social identities are both important in how we view ourselves, how we view others, and how others view us. Amy Gutmann (1992) points out that

> full public recognition as equal citizens may require two forms of respect: (1) respect for the unique identities of each individual, regardless of gender, race, or ethnicity [personal identity], and (2) respect for those activities, practices, and ways of viewing the world that are particularly valued by or associated with members of disadvantaged groups, including women, Asian-American, African-Americans, Native Americans, and a multitude of other groups in the United States [social identities]. (p. 8)

We need to respect the identities others claim for themselves if we want to develop a relationship with them.

STRENGTH OF ETHNIC IDENTITY

We all identify to some degree with our ethnic group. The more strongly we identify with our ethnic group, the more our ethnicity influences our behavior. Strongly identifying with our ethnic group, however, does *not* necessarily mean that we put members of other groups down or are biased toward our ethnic group. The degree to which we are biased toward our ethnic group is a function of our collective self-esteem. *Collective self-esteem* is the extent to which we evaluate our group memberships positively (Crocker & Luhtanen, 1990). If we strongly identify with our ethnic group and only derive collective self-esteem from our ethnicity we will be biased toward our ethnic group and we may have problems in interacting with members of other ethnic groups. If we strongly identify with our ethnic group and we derive collective self-esteem from group memberships other than our ethnicity (e.g., religion, occupation), we will not necessarily be biased toward our ethnic group.

To understand the influence of ethnicity on behavior we have to take into consideration our cultural identity too. If we identify strongly with our ethnic group and do *not* identify strongly with our culture, our ethnicity will have a strong influence on our behavior in most, if not all, situations. If we identify strongly with our ethnic group *and* we identify strongly with our culture, we can choose how to behave in different situations. Our behavior, for example, may be based mostly on our cultural identity at work and on our ethnic identity at home or when we are with close friends from our ethnic group. Throughout the book, when I discuss ethnic differences in communication behavior there should always be a caveat: ethnic differences in communication may only occur between individuals who strongly identify with their ethnic group.

Table 2.3 contains a questionnaire designed to assist you in assessing the strength of your ethnic identity. Take a few minutes to complete the questionnaire now.

The scores on the questionnaire range from 10 to 50. The higher your score, the more you identify with your ethnic group. Keep your score in mind. In later chapters, I will discuss how the

Table 2.3 Assessing the Strength of Your Ethnic Identity

The purpose of this questionnaire is to help you think about the degree to which you identify with being a member of your ethnic group. Respond to each statement by indicating the degree to which the statement is true regarding the way you typically think about yourself. When you think about yourself is the statement "Always False" (answer 1), "Mostly False" (answer 2), "Sometimes True and Sometimes False" (answer 3), "Mostly True" (answer 4), or "Always True" (answer 5)?

_____ 1. If I were born again, I would want to be born as a member of a different ethnic group.
_____ 2. Being a member of my ethnic group is important to me.
_____ 3. I rarely think about being a member of my ethnic group.
_____ 4. Being a member of my ethnic group plays a large role in my life.
_____ 5. Thinking about myself as a member of my ethnic group is not central to how I define myself.
_____ 6. I like the things that make me a member of my ethnic group and different from people in other ethnic groups.
_____ 7. I rarely choose to express my ethnicity in the way I communicate.
_____ 8. I have a positive view of my ethnic group.
_____ 9. I do not enjoy being a member of my ethnic group.
_____ 10. If others do not recognize me as a member of my ethnic group it upsets me.

To find your score, first reverse the responses for the odd-numbered items (i.e., if you wrote 1, make it 5; if you wrote 2, make it 4; if you wrote 3, leave it as 3; if you wrote 4, make it 2; if you wrote 5, make it 1). Next, add the numbers next to each of the statements. Scores range from 10 to 50. The higher your score, the more you identify with the group.

SOURCE: Adapted in part from Hofman (1985).

strength of your identification with your ethnic group can influence your communication with members of other groups. The questionnaire only assesses the strength of your identification with your ethnic group. It does not assess what it means to be a member of this group.

❏ Identities Based on Gender, Disability, Age, and Social Class

Our cultural and ethnic identities are only two of the social identities that influence the way we communicate. We have many other social identities that can be sources of misinterpretations and ineffective communication; for example, gender, disability, age, social class, gender orientation, occupation, religion, and so forth. Religion can be used as a basis for determining ethnicity if the religion provides a distinct subculture. Jews are the main religious group that meet this criteria in the United States and this group is the target of negative intergroup attitudes (i.e., anti-Semitism).[13] In this section, I discuss four major social identities that affect our behavior. I begin with the most obvious and discuss the four in decreasing order of our awareness of how they influence our behavior.

GENDER

One of the major social identities affecting our communication is our gender and the way we define our gender role. There are differences in how women define themselves depending on whether internal or external criteria for group memberships are used. There are no agreed-upon external criteria for womanhood and when women compare their internal definitions with external criteria there is always an inconsistency. This inconsistency often leads to a feeling of marginality and an unsatisfactory social identity for women in comparison to men (Breakwell, 1979).

Women attach different meaning to the category woman. There are traditional women, for example, who identify strongly with their group, see their roles as preferable to men's roles, and accept the existing gender roles (Condor, 1986). Women subcategorize themselves differently:

> I've got a lot of things in common with other women. Interests and such like. Of course, by "other women," I mean wives and mothers like me. Women with family commitments, not career girls.
>
> When I talk about "women," I am taking it for granted that you understand that I am talking about women with careers outside the home. (Condor, 1986)

Women thus may identify with each other based on gender group membership or in terms of personal characteristics (Gurin & Townsend, 1986).

There are differences in the way men and women relate to the world that affect their social identities. Henri Tajfel's (1978) social identity theory focuses on social identity as a cognitive process of differentiation and comparison. Women's social identity is based on more communal processes than differentiation processes (e.g., Williams, 1984).[14] Further, "women are more inclined [than men] to value relationships with other people from groups other than their own" (Skevington, 1989, p. 56). This may suggest that men and women engage in intergroup behavior differently.[15]

There also are important differences in the ways men and women communicate. Aaron Beck (1988), for example, points out that women tend to see questions as a way of keeping a conversation going. Men, in contrast, see questions as requests for information. Women tend to make connections between what their partner said and what they have to say. Men, on the other hand, do not use conversational bridges as much and may appear to ignore what their partner just said in a conversation. Men tend to view aggressiveness as a way of communicating, whereas women tend to interpret aggressiveness as an attack. Women may discuss problems and only be looking for reassurances. Men, on the other hand, interpret the discussion of a problem as a request for a solution.[16] These differences in communication patterns suggest that there are subcultural

> differences between men and women . . . in their conceptions of friendly conversation, their rules for engaging in it, and, probably most important, their rules for interpreting it. We argue that [North] American men and women come from different sociolinguistic subcultures, having learned to do different things with words in a conversation, so that when they attempt to carry a conversation with one another, even if both parties are attempting to treat one another as equals, cultural miscommunication results. (Maltz & Borker, 1982, p. 200)

Male-female communication therefore can be considered a form of intergroup communication.

DISABILITY

Another social identity that affects our communication is whether or not one of the people is disabled. We categorize others based on their physical appearance and evaluate novel appearances negatively (McArthur, 1982). When nondisabled people communicate with people who are visibly disabled in some way, they tend to experience uncertainty and anxiety, and avoid interaction when possible (e.g., there is a bias toward the ingroup).[17] Nondisabled people communicating with a person in a wheelchair, for example, predict more negative outcomes and are less aware of the person in the wheel chair than when communicating with other nondisabled individuals (Grove & Werkman, 1991). Similar observations can be made about interactions with other people who we view as stigmatized (e.g., blind, deaf, AIDS victims, mentally ill; see Goffman, 1963). The bias toward the ingroup is a two-way street. To illustrate, there is a sign in the American Sign Language with the right index finger circling forward in front of the forehead that indicates a deaf person who thinks like a hearing person. This sign is *not* meant as a compliment and its use demonstrates a bias toward the deaf ingroup (Barringer, 1993).

Lerita Coleman and Bella DePaulo (1991) point out that the visability of others' conditions influences whether we see them as disabled:

> External markers of a disability, such as the use of sign language by the deaf, canes and guide dogs by the blind, and wheelchairs by amputees and paraplegics, render those special conditions even more salient. However, even conditions almost completely invisible can be perceived as disabling and can engender miscommunications if they are known to others. . . . For example, women who have recently had mastectomies may find themselves to be the object of unusual regard in their initial interactions with others immediately following the surgery. (p. 64)

They also suggest that conditions that are not physically disabling (e.g., facial scars) may be psychologically disabling.

Coleman and DePaulo argue that both nondisabled and disabled individuals contribute to miscommunications when they interact. The nondisabled, for example, have negative stereotypes of the disabled. Disabled people are seen as "dependent, socially introverted, emotionally unstable, or depressed, hypersensitive, and easily offended, especially with regard to their disability" (p. 69). Nondisabled people may expect that disabled people will view them as prejudiced against the disabled. When nondisabled people interact with the disabled, they may experience anxiety, fear, and surprise. These reactions often are displayed nonverbally (e.g., in the voice or on the face), even though the nondisabled may try to control their reactions. If nondisabled individuals become aware of a disabled person's disability after they begin communicating, it often changes the way they communicate. To illustrate, a blind person tells what happened when a taxi driver became aware of the disability:

> I could tell that at first the taxi driver didn't know that I was blind because for a while he was quite a conversationalist. Then he asked me what these sticks were for (a collapsible cane). I told him it was a cane, and then he got so different. . . . He didn't talk about the same things as he did at first. (Davis, 1977, p. 85)

Changes in communication like this clearly have an effect on the disabled person.

Disabled people also contribute negative expectations to their interactions with nondisabled individuals. Coleman and DePaulo point out that the disabled may be "bitter and resentful about their disability" (p. 75). Disabled people also may expect to be perceived negatively by nondisabled individuals; "for example, blind people think that sighted persons perceive them as slightly retarded and hard of hearing" (p. 75). It is important to recognize that disabled persons' disabilities may affect their communication with nondisabled people. To illustrate, blind people cannot make eye contact and hearing-impaired people who read lips cannot pick up nuances of communication in tone of voice.

There are idioms in English such as "the blind leading the blind" and "that's a lame excuse" to which disabled individuals react negatively (Pogrebin, 1987). Also, the labels that nondisabled use to refer to disabled can cause problems in communication. To illustrate, "A man who wears leg braces says the issue is accuracy. I'm not handicapped, people's attitudes about me handicap me" (Pogrebin, 1987, p. 218). "Differently abled" and "physically challenged" also do not appear to be accepted widely by disabled individuals either. Letty Cotton Pogrebin (1987) quotes Harilyn Rousso, a psychotherapist with cerebral palsy as saying:

> Friends who care most sometimes think they're doing you a favor by using euphemisms or saying "I never think of you as disabled." The reason they don't want to acknowledge my disability is that they think it is so negative. Meanwhile, I'm trying to recognize it as a valued part of me. I'm more complex than my disability and I don't want my friends to be obsessed by it. But it's clearly there, like my eye color, and I want my friends to appreciate and accept me with it. (p. 219)

Some disabled prefer the label "cripple" or "gimp" because these terms are not euphemisms and recognize the realities facing the disabled. As with members of different ethnic groups, it is important that we know what the individuals with whom we are communicating want to be called.

AGE

Members of other groups do not have to be visibly disabled for us to experience uncertainty and anxiety and want to avoid communicating with them; for example, young people often avoid communicating with old people. We categorize others based on age when we guess their age based on their physical appearance, when they tell us their age, when they make references to age categories (e.g., indicating they are retired), and when others talk about experiences in the past, to name only a few of the cues we use for categorizing others based on age. Age-based identities can take place at the beginning of our interactions with others or emerge out of our communication with them (N. Coupland, Nussbaum, & J. Coupland, 1991).

Arnold Rose (1965) argues that several factors have contributed to the development of age-based identities in the United States: (a) the growing number of old people, (b) the development of retirement communities that segregate old people, (c) the increase in retirement that decreases interaction between young and old on the job, (d) the amount of money available to older people, and (e) the emergence of groups and organizations exclusively for old people. Older people demonstrate all of the signs of group identification. There is a desire to associate with fellow-agers, especially in formal associations, and to exclude younger adults from these associations. There are expressions of group pride. . . . There are manifestations of a feeling of resentment at "the way older people are being mistreated," and indications of their taking social action to remove the sources of their resentment. (Rose, 1965, p. 14)

Intergeneration interaction is clearly a form of intergroup communication.

Young people view elderly people as less desirable interaction partners than other young people or middle-aged people (Tamir, 1984). When young people are communicating with the elderly they use several different strategies to adapt their behavior (N. Coupland, J. Coupland, Giles, & Henwood, 1988). First, young people adapt their behavior by over-accommodating to the elderly because they assume the elderly are handicapped (e.g., hard of hearing). Second, young people communicate with the elderly in ways that reflect the attitude that the elderly are dependent on the young. This allows young people to control the elderly. Third, young people may speak differently from the elderly to establish their identity as young people (e.g., using slang the elderly do not understand). Fourth, young people may over-accommodate to the elderly to nurture them (e.g., young people might use baby talk when talking to the elderly). Fifth, young people may not adapt their behavior to the elderly. The elderly, in turn, may perceive this as lack of interest in them.

The elderly also use strategies in adapting their behavior to the young (N. Coupland et al., 1988). First, the elderly may not accommodate their behavior to the young. One reason for this is that they may have little contact with young people and not know how to adapt their behavior. Second, the elderly may use self-protecting strategies because they anticipate negative interactions with young people. Third, the elderly may anticipate that they will not perform well when they communicate with young people. Fourth, the elderly may engage in self-stereotyping (e.g., they may have negative stereotypes of being old). Fifth, the elderly may speak differently from the way young people do because they want to establish their social identity.

Self-concept support is necessary for effective intergenerational communication. One of the major concerns of older people is maintaining healthy self-concepts. Older people's self-concepts are threatened by the process of aging and attitudes toward old people (Tamir, 1984). "Lack of self-affirmation by others can lead to a vicious circle of decreasing self-worth and continued negative and self-effacing encounters" (Tamir, 1984, p. 36). Older people will find interactions with younger people who support the older people's self-concept more satisfying than interactions with younger people who do not support their self-concepts.

SOCIAL CLASS

We all identify with a social class whether we are aware of it or not. Social class

> is much more than a convenient pigeonhole or merely arbitrary divisional unit—like minutes, ounces, I.Q. points or inches—along a linear continuum. It is a distinct reality which embraces the fact that people live, eat, play, mate, dress, work, and think at contrasting and dissimilar levels. These levels—social classes—are the blended product of shared and analogous occupational orientations, educational backgrounds, economic wherewithal, and life experiences. Persons occupying a given level need not be conscious of their class identity. But because of their approximately uniform backgrounds and experiences and because they grew up perceiving or "looking at things" in similar ways, they will share comparable values, attitudes, and life-styles. (Hodges, 1964, p. 13)

The social class to which we belong may be the class with which we identify if we are satisfied with our position in society. Alternatively, if we are seeking upward mobility, our class identity may be based on the social class to which we aspire.

Sociologists tend to divide the social classes in the United States into upper class, upper middle class, middle class, lower middle class, and lower class. No matter how we divide up the class structure, we sort ourselves and others into social classes when we interact. The criteria we use for sorting ourselves and others are usually based on income, occupation, education, beliefs and attitudes, style of life, or kind of family (Jackman & Jackman, 1983).

Paul Fussell (1983) points out that we also can tell people's social class by their hometown, their houses, their yards, the decorations in their houses, as well as the clothes they wear and the cars they drive.

Our class identity influences the way we communicate. We can tell others' class background from the way they speak. Persons using the standard dialect (e.g., the dialect used by newscasters on national broadcasts) are attributed higher social status than those using a nonstandard dialect (see Chapter 5 for more on dialect). Fussell, for example, points out that the use of double negatives (e.g., "I can't get no satisfaction") and erroneous grammatical number (e.g., "He don't," "I wants it") clearly distinguish lower-class speakers from middle-class speakers. Word pronunciation and vocabulary distinguish between middle-class and upper-middle- and upper- class speakers.

Basil Bernstein (1973) argues that lower- and middle-class speakers learn to emphasize different communication codes and that these codes reinforce class identity.[18] Middle-class speakers are taught to speak using an *elaborate code* with (a) verbal explicitness (e.g., direct messages), (b) verbal elaboration, (c) a focus on verbal aspects of messages, (d) no reliance on shared meanings between communicators, (e) not taking others' intentions for granted, (f) orientation toward individual persons, and (g) planning messages. Lower-class speakers, in contrast, are socialized to *restricted codes*, which involve (a) using metaphors and indirectness, (b) not being verbally elaborate, (c) stressing nonverbal aspects of communication, (d) relying on shared identities and meanings between communicators, (e) taking others' intentions for granted, (f) being oriented toward the group, and (g) not engaging in much planning. Class differences in the use of these codes is one of frequency. Middle-class speakers use elaborated codes more than restricted codes, but they do use restricted codes. Similarly, lower-class speakers use restricted codes more than elaborate codes, but they can use elaborate codes.

Our class identity and our status in particular communication situations (e.g., are we superiors or subordinates, teachers or students, physicians or patients) influence our communication. Class identification tends to be stronger in lower classes than in middle or upper classes (M. Jackman & R. Jackman, 1983). Our communication in particular situations in turn influences how we define particular situations and the social identities we choose to emphasize in the particular situation. In thinking about how our class identity influences our communication it is important to keep in mind that our class identity interacts with other identities, particularly ethnicity. It can be argued, for example, that there is little difference between the way middle-class European Americans and African Americans communicate. There are, however, significant differences between the ways middle-class European Americans and lower-class African Americans communicate (see Gudykunst & Lim, 1985).

To conclude, no matter what the criteria for strangers' group memberships, we do not have scripts to follow when communicating with them. The only basis we have for communicating with strangers is their group memberships and our stereotypes about the group. Strangers' communication may be based on any one (or more) of their social identities. To communicate effectively, we need to understand which social identities are influencing strangers' behavior and how they define themselves with respect to these identities.

Our stereotypes tend to provide us with negative expectations and we therefore try to avoid (either consciously or unconsciously) communicating with people who are different. In the next chapter, I discuss the role of expectations in communication. Specifically, I examine positive versus negative expectations and how they influence our predictions of others' behavior and our interpretations of the messages we receive from them. I also look at specific factors on which our expectations are based, including others' group memberships, our stereotypes, intergroup attitudes (e.g., prejudice, ethnocentrism, and sexism), and our perceptions of similarity.

❏ Notes

1. There are other ways of talking about culture. Joel Garreau (1981), for example, isolates nine nations of North America (e.g., Mexamerica, Dixie, Quebec, The Islands, New England, The Foundry, The Breadbasket, Ecotopia, The Empty Quarter). He argues that each of the nine nations shares a common culture.

2. For a complete discussion of the various dimensions that could be used see Gudykunst and Ting-Toomey (1988).

3. See Hofstede (1980), Kluckhohn and Strodtbeck (1961), and Triandis (1988) for extended discussions of this dimension of cultural variability. It should be noted that this dimension is not only isolated by theorists in "western" cultures, but also is isolated by theorists from "eastern" cultures (see Chinese Culture Connection, 1987, for an example).

4. See Fitzgerald (1993) for a discussion of the interrelated meanings of culture, communication, and identity.

5. Greeley (1989) argues that individualism-collectivism differences can be applied to religious denominations; Protestants are individualistic and Catholics are collectivistic.

6. Triandis, Brislin, and Hui (1988) provide concrete suggestions for individualists interacting with collectivists and collectivists interacting with individualists.

7. I do not mean to say that everyone's ideas of ethnicity have changed. The predominant view, however, has changed from assimilationist to pluralistic.

8. Park actually used the term *race* not *ethnic group*. I am avoiding the use of *race* throughout the book. There are several reasons for this. The major reason is that the term is emotionally loaded for many people, whereas ethnicity is not as emotionally loaded. Moreover, it is the shared cultural characteristics of a racial group (i.e., its ethnicity) that influences members' communication patterns.

9. See Omi and Winant (1986) for a discussion of how racial categories form and change over time.

10. There is no good term to use to refer to non-European Americans (e.g., African Americans, Japanese Americans). Some writers use "people of color," but this term has problems because European Americans are "of color" too. Although it is awkward, I have chosen *non-European Americans*.

11. Edwards (1985) makes the point that language is not necessary for an ethnic group to survive as a unique group.

12. The Latino Political Survey "Latino Voices" was conducted by Rodolfo de la Garza and Chris Garcia.

13. With respect to religion, anti-Semitism is on the rise in recent years. See Rubin (1990) for an excellent discussion of anti-Semitism. Tempest's (1990) article also provides a summary of recent examples of anti-Semitism.

14. This position is consistent with Gilligan's (1982) work on differences in moral development between men and women.

15. To the best of my knowledge there is no specific research supporting this contention. For a complete elaboration of the logic and suggestions for research, see Skevington (1989).

16. Beck (1988) also indicates there are differences in the intimacy of the topics men and women discuss. I have not included these differences because the research findings are mixed.

17. For a review of this research, see Dahnke (1983). See Shearer (1984) for disabled persons' views of their communication with nondisabled.

18. Bernstein's (1973) distinction is similar to Hall's (1976) low- and high-context messages discussed earlier in this chapter: low-context messages are similar to elaborate codes and high-context messages are similar to restricted codes. See Haslett (1990) for a summary of research supporting Bernstein's distinction.

3

Our Expectations of Strangers

In the previous chapters, I indicated that we have expectations about how others are going to communicate. Sometimes we are highly aware of our expectations and sometimes we are not. In this chapter, I discuss expectations in detail. I begin by examining the nature of expectations. I then look at specific sources of our expectations for others' behavior, focusing on those sources that contribute to misinterpretations and misunderstandings when we communicate with strangers. Because our expectations tell us how we should behave and how others should behave, I conclude this chapter with a discussion of ethical issues in communicating with strangers.

❑ The Nature of Expectations

Expectations involve our anticipations and predictions about how others will communicate with us. Our expectations are derived from social norms, communication rules, and others' personal characteristics of which we are aware. Expectations also emerge from our intergroup attitudes and the stereotypes we hold. Intergroup attitudes and stereotypes are given more weight when we are communicating with people who are different or unknown than when we communicate with people who are similar or known.

EXPECTATIONS ARE CULTURALLY BASED

"People who interact develop expectations about each other's behavior, not only in the sense that they are able to predict the regularities, but also in the sense that they develop preferences about how others *should* behave under certain circumstances" (J. Jackson, 1964, p. 225). Our culture and ethnicity provide guidelines for appropriate behavior and the expectations we use in judging competent communication. To illustrate, Judee Burgoon and Jerold Hale (1988) point out that in the European American middle-class subculture[1]

> one expects normal speakers to be reasonably fluent and coherent in their discourse, to refrain from erratic movements or emotional outbursts, and to adhere to politeness norms. Generally, normative behaviors are positively valued. If one keeps a polite distance and shows an appropriate level of interest in one's conversational partner, for instance, such behavior should be favorably received. (p. 61)

The problem is that norms for what is a polite distance and what constitutes an emotional outburst vary across cultures and subcultures within a culture.

An example may help clarify the problems that occur when people from different cultures communicate. In the European American middle-class subculture, people expect that friends will stand an acceptable distance away from us when talking (e.g., an arm's length away). Arabs, in contrast, expect friends to stand close enough so that they can smell each other's breath. To deny the smell of your breath to a friend is considered an insult in most Arab cultures. If a European American and an Arab are following their own cultural norms and are not aware that the other person's norm is different, they will inevitably misinterpret each other's behavior.

EVALUATING VIOLATIONS OF OUR EXPECTATIONS

If a stranger violates our expectations to a sufficient degree that we recognize the violation, we become aroused and have to assess the situation (Burgoon & Hale, 1988). The degree to which the other person provides us with rewards affects how we evaluate the violation and the person committing the act. As used here, *rewards* do not mean only money (although that might be a consideration if the other person is our boss or a client). Rather, rewards include the benefits we obtain from our interactions with the other person (e.g., status, affection). If the other person provides us with rewards, we choose the most positive of the possible interpretations of violations available to us; "for example, increased proximity during conversation may be taken as a sign of affiliation if committed by a high reward person but as a sign of aggressiveness if committed by a low reward person" (Burgoon & Hale, 1988, p. 63).

Positively evaluated violations of our expectations have positive consequences for our communication with violators (e.g., do not lead to misinterpretations, increase intimacy). Negatively evaluated violations, in contrast, lead to negative outcomes (e.g., misinterpretations, decreases in intimacy). There are, however, exceptions for negative violations. If the other person provides rewards and commits an extreme violation of our expectations, positive outcomes (e.g., higher credibility or interpersonal attraction) are possible (Burgoon & Hale, 1988).

Walter Stephan (1985) argues that we often believe our expectations have been fulfilled when we communicate with strangers, regardless of how the stranger behaves. Stephan suggests that we tend not to change our behavior when others disconfirm our expectations. He goes on to point out that the affective consequences of confirmation or disconfirmation depend to a great degree on whether the expectancy is positive or negative. Confirmation of positive expectancies and disconfirmation of negative expectancies would be expected to elicit favorable affective responses to the behavior, such as pride and happiness. Disconfirmation of positive expectancies and confirmation of negative expectancies may lead to negative affect, such as sadness or low self-esteem or resentment and hostility directed toward the self or the holder of the expectancy. (p. 637)

As Burgoon and Hale point out, however, whether the other person can provide rewards influences how we interpret the confirmation or disconfirmation of our expectations.

Before proceeding, it is important to recognize that strangers with whom we communicate usually are not viewed as potential sources of rewards. Rather, we tend to see the costs as outweighing the rewards when we communicate with strangers. There are exceptions, however. Mark Knapp points out that interacting with people who are different "is enjoyable when the interaction is brief, when the differences are few and on peripheral beliefs, and when the chance of rejection is small, that is, when the costs of pursuing dissimilar relations are negligible relative to the rewards" (cited in Crockett & Friedman, 1980, p. 91).

NEGATIVE INTERGROUP EXPECTATIONS

Our communication with strangers usually is based on negative expectations. Actual or anticipated interaction with a member of a different ethnic group, for example, leads to anxiety.[2] Walter Stephan and Cookie Stephan (1985) point out that "intergroup anxiety often has a basis in reality. People sometimes do make embarrassing mistakes, are taken advantage of, and are rejected by ingroup and outgroup members" (p. 160) when communicating with strangers. One of the emotional reactions we have to our expectations of strangers being disconfirmed is that we become frustrated. "Frustration involves feelings of intense discomfort stemming from the blockage of paths toward goals. . . . Frustration, in turn, often leads to aggressive behavior or people try to vent their negative feelings" (Brislin, Cushner, Cherrie, & Yong, 1986, p. 250).

Several factors are associated with the amount of intergroup anxiety we experience. Thinking about the behavior in which we need to engage when communicating with strangers, for example, can reduce our anxiety about interacting with them (Janis & Mann, 1977). Further, if we focus on finding out as much as we can and forming accurate impressions of strangers, the biases we have, based on our anxiety and negative expectations, will be reduced (Neuberg, 1989). Stephan and Stephan (1989) also suggest that the less intergroup contact we have experienced, the less ethnocentric we are and the more positive our stereotypes, the less intergroup anxiety we experience.

❏ Intergroup Attitudes

"An attitude is a learned predisposition to respond in an evaluative (from extremely favorable to extremely unfavorable) manner toward some attitude object" (Davidson & Thompson, 1980, p. 27). I focus on four specific attitudes that affect our communication with members of other groups: ethnocentrism, prejudice, sexism, and ageism.

ETHNOCENTRISM

William Graham Sumner (1940) defines *ethnocentrism* as "the view of things in which one's own group is the center of everything, and all others are scaled and rated with reference to it" (p. 13). Robert LeVine and Donald Campbell (1972) isolate two facets of ethnocentrism. One involves our orientation toward our ingroup. If we are highly ethnocentric, we see our ingroup as virtuous and superior, and we see our ingroup values as universal (i.e., applying to everyone). The second facet of ethnocentrism involves our orientation toward outgroups. If we are highly ethnocentric, we see outgroups as contemptible and inferior, we reject outgroups' values, we blame outgroups for ingroup troubles, and we try to maintain social distance from outgroups.

We can think about ethnocentrism as the tendency to interpret and evaluate others' behavior using our own standards. This tendency is natural and unavoidable. Everyone is ethnocentric to some degree. Although it is possible to have a low degree of ethnocentrism, it is impossible to be nonethnocentric. Ethnocentrism leads us to view our ways of doing things as the natural and right ways of doing things. The major consequence of this in an inter-

Everyone is ethnocentric to some degree.

group context is that we tend to view our ingroup way of doing things as superior to the outgroup's way of doing things. In other words, ethnocentrism is a bias toward the ingroup that causes us to evaluate different patterns of behavior negatively, rather than try to understand them.

The opposite of ethnocentrism is cultural relativism. *Cultural relativism* involves trying to understand others' behavior in the context of the culture or group of the person engaging in the behavior. We cannot understand others' behavior if we use our own cultural or ethnic frame of reference to interpret their behavior. Kurt Vonnegut, Jr., says

> I didn't learn until I was in college about all other cultures, and I should have learned that in first grade. A first grader should understand that his or her culture isn't a rational invention; that there are thousands of other cultures and they all work pretty well; that all cultures function on faith rather than truth; that there are lots of alternatives to our own society. Cultural relativity is defensible and attractive. It also is a source of hope. It means we don't have to continue this way if we do not like it.[3]

Some degree of cultural relativism is necessary to understand strangers' behavior. Cultural relativism, however, should not be extended to moral relativism (this issue is discussed in more detail in the section on ethics).

Ethnocentric Speech. The attitudes we hold influence the way we speak to other people. The speed with which we talk or the accent we use may be varied in order to generate different feelings of distance between us and members of other groups with whom we communicate (i.e., to make the distance seem smaller or greater). The concept of *communicative distance* can be used to explain this linguistic diversity:

> A communicative distance cannot be measured directly. It is not even visible. But we can be sure of its presence when we hear certain words or expressions. In other words, our awareness of a communicative distance in the midst of a conversation depends to a large extent on certain linguistic devices which serve, from the speaker's point of view, to set up the communicative distance, or from the hearer's point of view, to let the hearer know that it has already been set up by the speaker. (Peng, 1974, p. 33)

Janet Lukens (1978) expands this conceptualization of communicative distance to isolate what she calls *ethnocentric speech,* our speech patterns that are based on our ethnocentrism. Young Kim and I (Gudykunst & Kim, 1984) extend Lukens's analysis to include communicative distances based on cultural relativism.

To begin, it is important to recognize that there are different levels of ethnocentrism and cultural relativism. Five positions on a continuum can be isolated: very low cultural relativism/very high ethnocentrism, high ethnocentrism/low cultural relativism, moderate ethnocentrism/moderate cultural relativity, low ethnocentrism/high cultural relativism, and very high cultural relativism/very low ethnocentrism.[4]

The *distance of disparagement* involves very high levels of ethnocentrism and very low levels of cultural relativism. This distance reflects animosity of the ingroup toward the outgroup (Lukens, 1978). It arises when the two groups are in competition for the same resources. This level is characterized by the use of pejorative expressions about the outgroup and the use of ethnophaulisms (i.e., name calling). At this distance imitation and mockery of speech styles are characteristic.

The *distance of avoidance* is established to avoid or minimize contact with members of an outgroup (Lukens, 1978). One technique commonly used to accomplish this is an ingroup dialect. "The emphasizing of an ethnic dialect and other linguistic differences between the in-group and outsiders may be purposefully used by in-group members to make themselves appear esoteric to the out-group thus lessening the likelihood for interaction" (p. 45). At this distance members of the ingroup also may use terms of solidarity (e.g., "black pride"). Feelings of ingroup pride and solidarity are increased through the use of such terms. In establishing the distance of avoidance, jargon common to the ingroup is used extensively.

The *distance of indifference* is the speech form used to "reflect the view that one's own [group] is the center of everything" (Lukens, 1978, p. 42). This distance, therefore, reflects an insensitivity to other group's perspectives. One example of the speech used at this distance is "foreigner talk," the form of speech used when talking to people who are not native speakers of a language. It usually takes the form of loud and slow speech patterns, exaggerated pronunciation, and simplification (e.g., deletion of articles). "We tend to believe that, if we speak slowly enough or loudly enough, anyone can understand us. I have done this myself quite without realizing it, and others have tried to reach me in the same way in Japanese, Chinese, Thai, Punjabi, Navajo, Spanish, Tibetan, and Singhalese" (Downs, 1971, p. 19).

The *distance of sensitivity* reveals a sensitivity to group differences (Gudykunst & Kim, 1984). Our speech at this level reflects our desire to decrease the communicative distance between ourselves and others. When speaking at this level with a member of a different ethnic group, for example, we would use the term for the person's ethnic group that he or she prefers, even if it is different than the one we typically use. When men are speaking with women at this distance, for example, they will avoid using the term "lady" if it causes offense to the women with whom they are speaking.

The *distance of equality* reflects our desire to minimize the distance between ourselves and others (Gudykunst & Kim, 1984). This distance involves an attitude of equality, one where we demonstrate we are interpreting the language and behavior of others in terms of their group's standards. Speech at this distance avoids evaluations of the other group. The use of his or her instead of using he as a generic pronoun, for example, would reflect a distance of equality.

Table 3.1 Assessing Your Ethnocentrism

The purpose of this questionnaire is to assess your ethnocentrism. Respond to each statement by indicating the degree to which the statement is true regarding the way you typically think about yourself. When you think about yourself, is the statement "Always False" (answer 1), "Mostly False" (answer 2), "Sometimes True and Sometimes False" (answer 3), "Mostly True" (answer 4), or "Always True" (answer 5)? Answer honestly, not how you think you should.

_____   1. I do not apply my values when judging people who are different.
_____   2. I see people who are similar to me as virtuous.
_____   3. I cooperate with people who are different.
_____   4. I prefer to associate with people who are like me.
_____   5. I trust people who are different.
_____   6. I am obedient to authorities.
_____   7. I do not fear members of other groups.
_____   8. I try to maintain distance from members of other groups.
_____   9. I blame other groups for troubles I have.
_____ 10. I believe that my values are universal values.

To find your score, first reverse the responses for the odd-numbered items (i.e., if you wrote 1, make it 5; if you wrote 2, make it 4; if you wrote 3, leave it as 3; if you wrote 4, make it 2; if you wrote 5, make it 1). Next, add the numbers next to each of the statements. Scores range from 10 to 50. The higher the score, the more ethnocentric you are.

SOURCE: Based on Brewer's (1981) description of ethnocentrism.

Assessing Your Ethnocentrism. Table 3.1 contains a brief questionnaire designed to help you assess your level of ethnocentrism. Take a moment to complete the questionnaire. In responding to the statements, please keep in mind it will not help you to understand your communication behavior if you answer the questions as you think you should. For the questionnaire to be useful, the questions must be answered honestly.

Scores on the questionnaire range from 10 to 50. The higher your score, the more ethnocentric you are. I will not provide average scores because they would not be useful in helping you improve your communication. The thing to keep in mind is that the more ethnocentric you are, the more likely you are to misinterpret messages from strangers. You can manage the effect of your ethnocentrism on your communication when you are mindful.

PREJUDICE

Prejudice involves making a prejudgment based on member-ship in a social category. Prejudice can be positive or negative, but there is a tendency for most of us to think of it as negative. Consistent with this view, Gordon Allport (1954) defines *negative ethnic prejudice* as "an antipathy based on a faulty and unflexible generalization. It may be felt or expressed. It may be directed toward a group as a whole, or toward an individual because he [or she] is a member of that group" (p. 10).

Dimensions of Prejudice. We tend to think of prejudice in terms of a dichotomy; either I am prejudiced or I am not. It is more useful, however, to think of the strength of our prejudice as varying along a continuum from low to high. This suggests that we all are prejudiced to some degree. We also are all racist, sexist, ageist, and so forth to some degree. As with ethnocentrism, this is natural and unavoidable. It is the result of our being socialized as mem-bers of our ingroups. Even people with low levels of prejudice prefer to interact with people who are similar to themselves, because such interactions are more comfortable and less stressful than interactions with strangers.

We all are prejudiced to some degree.

We also can think of prejudice as varying along a second contin-uum ranging from very positive to very negative. We tend to be positively prejudiced toward our ingroup and negatively preju-diced toward outgroups. A recent survey, for example, suggests the trend for younger European Americans to have more positive attitudes toward African Americans may be on the decline. The Anti-Defamation League survey reports that 35% of European Americans over age 50 are highly prejudiced against African Americans, whereas 23% between 30 and 49, and 31% of those between 18 and 29 are highly prejudiced.[5]

Viewing prejudice as varying along a continuum from low to high may distort our intergroup attitudes. It appears that people in the United States today experience inner conflict regarding members of other ethnic groups. We have both favorable and unfavorable attitudes that are not necessarily related to each other. Both attitudes are important to us. With respect to African Americans, for example, the majority of European Americans are disposed "(a) to be in sympathy with [African Americans] as a group that is unfairly disadvantaged by past and present discrimination but also (b) to be critical of them for not doing enough to help themselves" (Hass, Katz, Rizzo, Bailey, & Moore, 1992, p. 787). When we are aware of our incompatible beliefs regarding other ethnic groups, we experience psychological discomfort and stress. Recognizing our incompatible beliefs may damage our self-image as a humane person (Hass et al., 1992). We therefore try to manage the way we present ourselves to others in the way we talk.

Prejudiced Talk. It generally is not acceptable to make overt prejudiced or racist comments in public.[6] It may be acceptable within some ingroups (e.g., Ku Klux Klan, Skinheads), but in public talk most people try to present themselves as nonprejudiced. If we are going to make a negative comment about people who are different, we preface our comment with a claim of not being prejudiced. To illustrate, one interviewee in Tuen van Dijk's (1984) study responded in this way:

[Interviewer]: Did you ever have any unpleasant experiences [with foreigners]?
[Interviewee]: I have nothing against foreigners. But their attitude, their aggression is scaring. We are no longer free here. You have to be careful. (p. 65)

Prejudiced talk clusters in four categories: (a) "they are different (in culture, mentality)," (b) "they do not adapt themselves," (c) "they are involved in negative acts (nuisance, crime)," and (d) "they threaten our (social, economic) interests" (van Dijk, 1984, p. 70).[7]

We display our prejudice and racism in our everyday actions and we are often not aware of doing it (Essed, 1991). To illustrate, a clerk in a store may follow an African American customer around the store, but not watch a European American. If the African American has not done anything suspicious, this is a clear case of racism. Prejudice and racism appear in the mass media frequently and we often do not recognize it because we are so used to hearing it. After Martin Luther King, Jr., was shot, for example, European American reporters asked African American leaders questions like "Who is going to hold your people together?" Some said things like "When our leader died [referring to John F. Kennedy], his widow held us together." Many people hear reporting like this but do not recognize the racism inherent in it.

The way we talk about and to people who are different is, in large part, a function of how we want to be seen by our ingroup, not the other person's group. Tuen van Dijk (1984) points out that

> people "adapt" their discourse to the rules and constraints of interaction and communication social settings. Especially when delicate topics, such as "foreigners," are concerned, social members will strategically try to realize both the aims of positive self-presentation and those of effective persuasion. Both aims, however, derive from the position of social members within their group. Positive self-presentation is not just a defense mechanism of individuals as persons, but also as respected, accepted, and integrated social members of ingroups. And the same holds for the persuasive nature of prejudiced talk; people do not merely lodge personal complaints or uneasiness about people of other groups, but intend to have their experiences, their evaluations, their opinions, their attitudes, and their actions shared by other members of the ingroup. (p. 154)

Everyone engages in prejudiced talk to some degree. It is inevitable when we communicate on automatic pilot. We can, however, reduce the degree to which we engage in prejudiced talk if we are mindful of our communication.

We can also influence the amount of prejudiced talk in which others engage. Flether Blanchard, Teri Lilly, and Leigh Ann Vaughn (1991) point out that when we express antiprejudice sentiments, others are less likely to make prejudiced comments in our presence.[8] Similarly, Ervin Staub (1989) claims that "bystanders can exert a powerful influence. They can define the meaning of events and move others toward empathy and indifference. They can promote values and norms of caring, or by passivity or participation in the system they can affirm the perpetrators" (p. 87). If we

Table 3.2 Assessing Your Prejudice

The purpose of this questionnaire is to assess your prejudice. Respond to each statement by indicating the degree to which the statement is true regarding the way you typically think about other groups. When you think about other groups, is the statement "Always False" (answer 1), "Mostly False" (answer 2), "Sometimes True and Sometimes False" (answer 3), "Mostly True" (answer 4), or "Always True" (answer 5)? Answer honestly, not how you think you should.

_____ 1. Affirmative action programs discriminate against whites.
_____ 2. Members of other groups have not received as much support as they deserve to make up for past discrimination.
_____ 3. Members of other groups have received more attention in the media than they deserve.
_____ 4. I understand why members of other groups are angry at my group.
_____ 5. Members of other groups should not push themselves where they are not wanted.
_____ 6. Members of other groups are cooperative.
_____ 7. Members of other groups are too demanding in their push for equal rights.
_____ 8. Discrimination against members of other groups is a problem today.
_____ 9. Members of other groups are receiving unfair privileges in society today.
_____ 10. I have positive feelings about members of other groups.

To find your score, first reverse the responses for the even-numbered items (i.e., if you wrote 1, make it 5; if you wrote 2, make it 4; if you wrote 3, leave it as 3; if you wrote 4, make it 2; if you wrote 5, make it 1). Next, add the numbers next to each statement. Scores range from 10 to 50. The higher your score, the greater your prejudice.

SOURCE: Adapted in part from McConahay (1986).

find that others are making prejudiced remarks in our presence, for example, we can say that this is *not* acceptable to us. By simply stating our opinion in this way, we decrease the likelihood that others will continue to make prejudiced remarks in our presence. If we do not speak out when others make prejudiced comments or behave in a discriminatory manner, we are responsible for the consequences of others' remarks or behavior.

Assessing Your Prejudice. Table 3.2 contains a questionnaire designed to assess your level of prejudice. Take a couple of minutes to complete it now. Answer the questions honestly.

Scores on the questionnaire range from 10 to 50. The higher your score on the questionnaire, the greater your level of prejudice. Everyone will be prejudiced to some degree. This is unavoidable. The important thing to keep in mind is that we can manage how our prejudices influence our communication by being mindful when we communicate with strangers.

SEXISM

Sexism occurs when we assign characteristics to others based on their sex (Nilsen, Bosdmajian, Gershuny, & Stanley, 1977). Although we can be sexist toward either males or females, sexism usually is viewed as prejudice against women. Sexism is manifested by viewing women as genetically inferior, supporting discriminatory practices against women, engaging in hostility toward women who do not fulfill traditional sex roles, not supporting the women's movement, using derogatory names to refer to women or negatively stereotyping women, and treating women as sexual objects (Benson & Vincent, 1980). Although both men and women are sexist, men tend to be more sexist than women. If we look at individual sex roles, however, it appears that masculine men and feminine women are more sexist than men and women who are androgenous or have an undifferentiated sex role (Faulkender, 1985).

Sexism in Language Usage. Sexism is manifested mainly through our language. There are three major forms of sexism in language: (a) the ignoring of women, (b) the way women are defined, and (c) the deprecation of women (Henley, Hamilton, & Thorne, 1985). The first way that language usage is sexist is in how *women are ignored.* Probably the main way that our language usage ignores women is through the use of masculine words to include both males and females (Schmidt, 1991). There are many words in the English language, for example, that include the word "man" that traditionally have been meant to include women. Examples of these words include, but are not limited to, chairman, mailman, spokesman, and mankind. Another way that women are ignored in language usage is through using "he" as a generic pronoun.

Many of us learned that when we write or talk pronouns for males can be used to refer to both males and females. This, however, is not how we actually process the information. When we use male pronouns, it elicits a vision of a male for the reader or listener (Schneider & Hacker, 1973).

Before proceeding, I want to comment on my use of pronouns in this book. I have tried whenever possible to use plural forms so that gender-specific personal pronouns do not have to be used. Where this is not possible, I alternate "he or she" and "she or he" and so forth. I also edit quotes from other authors to make them nonsexist. Although these changes make sentence structure more complicated than I would like in some places, they are necessary to avoid sexist language.

The second way that our language usage can be sexist is in *how women are defined.* One way women are ignored is in our tendency to address women by their first names in situations where we would not address a man by his first name (McConnell-Ginet, 1978). Also "women, much more than men, are addressed through terms of endearment such as honey, cutie, and sweetie, which function to devalue women by depriving them of their name while renaming them with trivial terms" (Schmidt, 1991, p. 30).

The third way that our language is sexist is in *deprecating women.* In English, for example, there are over 200 terms for calling a woman sexually promiscuous, but fewer than 25 for calling a man sexually promiscuous (Stanley, 1977). There are more masculine terms (more than 350) in the English language than feminine (fewer than 150), but there are more negative feminine terms than masculine (Nilsen, 1977).

Assessing Your Sexism. The questionnaire in Table 3.3 is designed to help you assess your sexism. Take a few minutes to complete it now.

Scores on the questionnaire range from 10 to 50. The higher your score on the questionnaire, the more sexist you are. If your score is higher than you would like it to be, you need to keep in mind that you can choose to behave in a nonsexist fashion and to use nonsexist language when you are mindful of your communication.

Table 3.3 Assessing Your Sexism

The purpose of this questionnaire is to assess your sexism. Respond to each statement by indicating the degree to which the statement is true regarding the way you typically think about men and women. When you think about women and men, is the statement "Always False" (answer 1), "Mostly False" (answer 2), "Sometimes True and Sometimes False" (answer 3), "Mostly True" (answer 4), or "Always True" (answer 5)? Answer honestly, not how you think you should.

_____ 1. Husbands should make decisions in the family.
_____ 2. Women and men are equal in all respects.
_____ 3. Men are more courageous than women.
_____ 4. Men and women can handle pressure equally well.
_____ 5. Women are more emotional than men.
_____ 6. Women can lead as effectively as men.
_____ 7. Men should be the dominant sex.
_____ 8. Women and men are equal in intelligence.
_____ 9. Women are influenced by others more than men.
_____ 10. Men and women should have the same rights.

To find your score, first reverse the responses for the even-numbered items (i.e., if you wrote 1, make it 5; if you wrote 2, make it 4; if you wrote 3, leave it as 3; if you wrote 4, make it 2; if you wrote 5, make it 1). Next, add the numbers next to each statement. Scores range from 10 to 50. The higher your score, the greater your sexism.

AGEISM

"Many, if not most, of the 'problems of aging' stem from or are exacerbated by prejudice and discrimination against the aged" (Palmore, 1982, p. 333). *Ageism* involves negative attitudes toward people who are older than we are (usually people we consider "old"). Teenagers, for example, may be prejudiced against people over 30, whereas a person who is middle aged may be prejudiced against people who are retired. Ageism is based on "a deep-seated uneasiness on the part of the young and middle-aged—a personal revulsion to and distaste for growing older" (Butler, 1969, p. 243). It also can emerge from competition between the groups (young and old) over scarce resources and jobs (Levin & Levin, 1980). Overall, attitudes toward aging tend to be negative (Palmore, 1982).

Ageism in Language Usage. Ageism is manifested in our language usage. Although the term "old" has connotations of experience, skill and wisdom, it also is used in derogatory terms for others (e.g., "old hag," "old fogy"; Covey, 1988). The English language includes a wide variety of terms with negative overtones for referring to old people (e.g., "battle-ax," "geezer"); and the attributes used to talk about the elderly (e.g., "cantankerous," "grumpy") often have negative connotations (Nuessel, 1984). More than one half of the jokes in English about aging reflect a negative view of old people, with a greater portion of jokes about women than men being negative. Terms such as aged and elderly are perceived to be negative, whereas terms such as senior citizen and retired person are evaluated more positively by people of all age groups (Barbato & Feezel, 1987).

Assessing Your Ageism. Table 3.4 contains a questionnaire designed to help you assess your ageism. Take a few minutes to complete it now.

Scores on the questionnaire in Table 3.4 range from 10 to 50. The higher your score, the greater your ageism. The higher your score, the greater the possibility of misunderstandings when you are communicating with someone older than you. If you have a high score, you can choose to stop your negative reaction to old people when you are mindful of your communication.

❏ Stereotypes

Stereotypes are the pictures we have in our heads for the various social categories we use. Like ethnocentrism and prejudice, stereotyping is a natural result of the communication process. We cannot not stereotype. Miles Hewstone and Rupert Brown (1986) isolate three essential aspects of stereotypes: (a) we categorize others based on easily identifiable characteristics; (b) we assume that certain attributes apply to most or all of the people in the category, and that people in the category are different than people in other categories with respect to these attributes; and (c) we assume that individual members of the category have the attributes associated with their groups.

Table 3.4 Assessing Your Ageism

The purpose of this questionnaire is to assess your ageism. Respond to each statement by indicating the degree to which the statement is true regarding the way you typically think about others' age. When you think about someone's age, is the statement "Always False" (answer 1), "Mostly False" (answer 2), "Sometimes True and Sometimes False" (answer 3), "Mostly True" (answer 4), or "Always True" (answer 5)? Answer honestly, not how you think you should.

_____ 1. I find it more difficult to communicate with an old person than with a young person.
_____ 2. I am not afraid of growing old.
_____ 3. I see old people as cantankerous.
_____ 4. I learn a lot when I communicate with elderly people.
_____ 5. I prefer to interact with people my own age.
_____ 6. I do not see all old people as alike.
_____ 7. I see old people as individuals, not as a group.
_____ 8. My communication with people older than me is as effective as my communication with people my own age.
_____ 9. I have to speak loudly and slowly for old people to understand me.
_____ 10. I look forward to growing old.

To find your score, first reverse the responses for the even-numbered items (i.e., if you wrote 1, make it 5; if you wrote 2, make it 4; if you wrote 3, leave it as 3; if you wrote 4, make it 2; if you wrote 5, make it 1). Next, add the numbers next to each statement. Scores range from 10 to 50. The higher your score, the greater your ageism.

Nature of Stereotypes. Henri Tajfel (1981) draws a distinction between stereotypes and social stereotypes:

> "stereotypes" are certain generalizations reached by individuals. They derive in large measure from, or are an instance of, the general cognitive process of categorizing. The main function of the process is to simplify or systematize, for purposes of cognitive and behavioral adaptation, the abundance and complexity of the information received from its environment by the human organism. . . . But such stereotypes can become _social_ only when they are shared by large numbers of people within social groups. (pp. 146-147)

Some of our stereotypes are unique and based on our individual experiences, but some are shared with other members of our ingroups. The stereotypes we share with others are our social stereotypes.

Social stereotypes often are used in the media and we learn many of our stereotypes from the media. Anyone who watches Saturday morning cartoons, for example, knows that villains are non-Europeans. With respect to ageing, the "dirty old man" is used frequently in the media and aging is depicted as involving evil, failures, and unhappiness in television dramas (Arnoff, 1974). Similarly, disabled people often are presented as bitter, self-pitying, and maladjusted, whereas nondisabled are portrayed as *not* having trouble accepting the disabled's identities (Longmore, 1987). Virtually all stereotypes of the old, disabled, and non-Europeans presented in the media are negative and inaccurate.

Stereotypes also are used in advertising. To illustrate, I recently was given an advertisement for a cleaning service that indicated that the company had "German thoroughness, Swedish spotlessness, Polish flexibility," and was "Discrete as a Swiss bank, Cheap as Russian promises." Although some of these are positive stereotypes, others are negative and will be offensive to members of those groups.

Our stereotypes are multidimensional images.[9] They vary in complexity (e.g., the number of traits included), specificity (e.g., how specific the traits are), favorability (e.g., the positive or negative valence of the traits), the degree of consensus there is on the traits (i.e., social versus individual stereotypes), and whether or not they are valid (i.e., the degree to which our stereotype of a group coincides with the stereotype members of that group have of themselves; Vassiliou, Triandis, Vassiliou, & McGuire, 1972).

The size of the group we are stereotyping influences the way we think about the group (Mullen, 1991). In general, the smaller the group, the more simple our stereotypes of the group. Group size also influences how we form our stereotypes. The smaller the group, the more likely we are to create stereotypes based on what we consider the average or typical member to be like. The larger the group, the more likely we are to base our stereotype on the example of group members with whom we have interacted.[10]

STEREOTYPES AND COMMUNICATION

Stereotypes provide the content of our social categories. We have social categories in which we place people and it is our stereotype that tells us what people in that category are like.[11] Stereotyping is the result of our tendency to overestimate the degree of association between group membership and psychological attributes. Although there may be some association between group membership and psychological characteristics of members, it is much smaller than we assume when we communicate on automatic pilot. Only 28% to 37% of the people in a culture, for example, have the traits attributed to them (Wallace, 1952). In some cases, there is more similarity between people in the same occupation across cultures than there is between people in different occupations within a culture (Inkeles, 1974).

Our stereotypes influence the way we process information. We remember more favorable information about our ingroups and more unfavorable information about outgroups (Hewstone & Giles, 1986). This, in turn, affects the way we interpret incoming messages from members of ingroups and outgroups. Our processing of information is "biased in the direction of maintaining the preexisting belief systems. . . . These processes, then, can produce the *cognitive confirmation* of one's stereotypic beliefs" (Hamilton, Sherman, & Ruvolo, 1992, p. 138).

Our stereotypes also create expectations regarding how members of other groups will behave. Stereotypes are activated automatically when we have contact with strangers (Devine, 1989). Unconsciously, we assume that our expectations are correct and behave as though they are. David Hamilton and his associates (1992) point out that

> stereotypes operate as a source of expectancies about what a group as a whole is like (e.g., Hispanics) as well as about what attributes individual group members are likely to posses (e.g., Juan Garcia). Their influence can be pervasive, affecting the perceiver's attention to, encoding of, inferences about, and judgments based on that information. And the resulting interpretations, inferences, and judgments typically are made so as to be consistent with preexisting beliefs that guided them. (p. 142)

We thus unconsciously try to confirm our expectations when we communicate with members of other groups.

Our stereotypes constrain others' patterns of communication and engender stereotype-confirming communication. Stated differently, stereotypes create self-fulfilling prophecies. We tend to see behavior that confirms our expectations, even when it is absent. We ignore disconfirming evidence when communicating on automatic pilot. Hamilton and his associates (1992) point out that

> perceivers can influence a person with whom they interact by constraining the person's behavior. However, perceivers typically do not recognize this influence or take it into consideration when interpreting the target's behavior. Although a target person's behavior may be affected by perceiver-induced constraints, it is often interpreted by the perceiver as a manifestation of the target's personality. (p. 149)

To illustrate, if we assume someone else is not competent and communicate with them based on this assumption they will appear incompetent (even if they are actually competent). We do not recognize our influence on the other person's behavior, and we judge the other person to be incompetent. We often do this when we communicate with disabled and older people.

Stereotypes, in and of themselves, do not lead to miscommunication or communication breakdown. If, however, inaccurate or negative stereotypes are held rigidly, they lead to inaccurate predictors of others' behavior and misunderstandings. In addition to inaccurate stereotypes, simple stereotypes of other groups can lead to misunderstandings. To increase our effectiveness in communicating with strangers, we need to increase the complexity of our stereotypes (e.g., include a large number of traits in the stereotype and differentiate subgroups within the group being stereotyped) and question our unconscious assumption that most, if not all, members of a group fit a single stereotype (Stephan & Rosenfield, 1982).

Patricia Devine (1989) argues that conscious control of our reactions when our stereotypes are activated is necessary to control our prejudice:

> Nonprejudiced responses are . . . a function of intentional controlled processes and require a conscious decision to behave in a nonprejudiced fashion. In addition, new responses must be learned and well practiced before they can serve as competitive responses to the automatically activated stereotype-congruent response. (p. 15)

This position is consistent with Langer's notion that mindfulness is necessary to reduce prejudice.

Individual members of a group may or may not fit a stereotype we have of that group. Stella Ting-Toomey (1989) isolates four possible options between the way individuals identify with a group and the way they behave: (a) individuals may see themselves as a typical group member and behave typically, (b) individuals may see themselves as a typical group member and behave atypically, (c) individuals may see themselves as atypical group members and behave atypically, and (d) individuals may see themselves as atypical group members and behave typically. It is actually more complicated than this, however, because our perceptions of the other person as a typical or atypical member of her or his group may not be the same as hers or his.

The accuracy of our predictions depends on whether the traits that we include in our stereotype of another group are similar to the ones in the other group's stereotype of its group (i.e., are our stereotypes valid). If the traits we apply to another group agree with the traits members of that group apply to themselves, our stereotype should lead to accurate interpretations of the behavior of members of the group who are typical. Valid stereotypes, however, will lead to misinterpretations of the behavior of atypical members of the group.

When we place someone in a category our stereotype of people in that category helps us predict his or her behavior if we perceive that person is typical of her or his group.[12] We are able to reduce our uncertainty because we *assume* that our stereotypes tell us how typical group members communicate (Krauss & Fussell, 1991). If the other person has informed us of his or her category membership, our predictions may be accurate. To illustrate, if we are communicating with a woman of Mexican descent and she tells us she is a Chicana, not a Mexican American, we can make some accurate predictions of her behavior if our stereotypes of people from Mexico differentiates Chicanos/Chicanas from Mexican Americans. If our stereotype does not include this differentiation, then our predictions will probably not be accurate. It is rare, however, for others to tell us their group memberships directly (Kellermann, 1993).

Rather than using others' self-categorizations (the group memberships they announce), we tend to base our categorizations on skin color, dress, accents, the car a person drives, and so forth (Clark & Marshall, 1981). The cues we use, however, are not always appropriate ways to categorize others (i.e., an inappropriate categorization occurs when we put someone in a category he or she would not place her- or himself). This is true for all social categories, including ethnicity. To illustrate, recall from Chapter 2 that we vary in the degree to which we identify with our ethnic groups and cultures. If we categorize others who do *not* identify strongly with their ethnic group and make predictions based on this categorization, our prediction will, in all likelihood, be inaccurate. Predictions based on ethnicity will probably only be accurate for group members who identify strongly with their ethnic group and do not identify strongly with their culture.

Another source of inaccuracy in our predictions based on our stereotypes is that the boundaries between many social groups are fuzzy (Clark & Marshall, 1981). What, for example, is the boundary between educated and uneducated people? Or between young and old? Even skin color may not be a good predictor of category membership. To illustrate, there are light-colored African Americans who look like European Americans. These individuals may be categorized as European American based only on skin color. They may, however, identify strongly with being an African American. Obviously, predictions about their behavior based on skin color will be inaccurate.

Even if others are typical members of the groups in which we categorize them, the inferences we make about them based on their group memberships may *not* be accurate. One reason for this is that our stereotypes are not valid (i.e., our stereotypes of the person's group is different from her or his stereotype of the group). Another reason our predictions may not be accurate is that the group membership we are using to categorize the other person may not be affecting his or her behavior in this situation. We are all members of many social groups that influence our behavior and provide us with different social identities. When communicating with strangers, we might categorize them based on one group membership (e.g., ethnicity) and assume that their social identities based on this category are influencing their behavior. The strangers, however, may be basing their behavior on a different social identity (e.g., social class, gender, role). To increase our accuracy in making predictions, we must try to understand which social identity is guiding a stranger's behavior in a particular situation.

STEREOTYPES AND COMMUNICATION BREAKDOWNS

Miles Hewstone and Howard Giles (1986) present a stereotype-based model of intergroup communication breakdown. They define *communication breakdown* as a feeling of dissatisfaction that detracts from the full potential of an encounter. For the breakdown to be intergroup in nature, the individuals must attribute their dissatisfaction as being due to membership in contrasting social groups.

Hewstone and Giles (1986) point out that the context in which we interact with strangers influences whether communication breakdowns occur. *Context* involves the historical and changing relationship between social groups. It includes the past efforts that members of different groups have made toward mutual social and linguistic accommodation. *Accommodation* refers to our tendency to adapt our behavior to others' behavior. We can move toward others (convergence) or move away from them (divergence). Using our own language when around people who do not speak it (divergence), for example, is one way we may exert a positive social identity (Giles, Bourhis, & Taylor, 1977). We tend to react favorably to outgroup members who linguistically move toward us (e.g., speak our language or dialect).[13] Our reaction, however, depends upon the intent we attribute to the speaker. If we perceive speakers' intent to be positive, we will evaluate their convergence positively. Hewstone and Giles suggest that as mutual convergence increases, there is less of a likelihood of communication breakdowns occurring. Also, as we perceive that the members of other groups are making evaluative comparisons with our group, there is an increased potential for communication breakdowns to occur.

Our perceptions of the situation and of the characteristics of the strangers with whom we are communicating (e.g., Are there more strangers than members of our own group present? Are the strangers typical of their group?) affects how important our social identities are in the encounter. Our stereotypes of outgroup members lead us to depersonalize them (i.e., think of them as members of a group and not as individuals). When this occurs, we place little emphasis on the individual characteristics of outgroup members, because the stereotypes associated with the groups are guiding our behavior. We use our stereotypes of outgroups to explain communication difficulties and thus confirm our negative feelings associated with the outgroup. Hewstone and Giles (1986) speculate that participants in intergroup breakdowns are likely to seek advice and consolation from members of the ingroup and ultimately attribute the cause of the breakdown to the outgroup members.

ASSESSING YOUR STEREOTYPES

To get an idea of what your stereotypes are, complete the questionnaire in Table 3.5. To complete this questionnaire you need to think of a specific group to which you belong (e.g., your culture or ethnic group) and another group (e.g., another culture or ethnic group). Take a few minutes to complete the questionnaire now.

The specific adjectives you checked constitute the content of your stereotype. The content of your stereotypes can vary in complexity (i.e., the number of traits). The content also can vary in the degree of consensus (i.e., do other members of your group assign the same traits to your group) and validity (i.e., do members of the other group assign the same traits to themselves as you assign to them).

❏ Changing Our Intergroup Expectations

Throughout this chapter I have discussed our expectations for strangers. Our expectations are not static; they can and do change,

Table 3.5 Assessing Your Stereotypes

The purpose of this questionnaire is to help you understand what your stereotypes of your own and other groups are. Several adjectives are listed below and there is space for you to add adjectives if the ones you want to use are not listed. Because stereotypes are specific to particular groups, you will have to think of specific groups. Think of one group of which you are a member (e.g., your cultural or ethnic group) and an outgroup (e.g., another culture or ethnic group). Put a check mark in the column "My Group" next to the adjectives that apply to your group. Put a check mark in the column marked "Other Group" next to the adjectives that apply to the outgroup you have selected. After you put your check marks, go back through the list and rate each adjective you checked in terms of how favorable a quality the adjective is: 1=very unfavorable, 2=moderately unfavorable, 3=neither favorable nor unfavorable, 4=moderately favorable, and 5=very favorable. Put these ratings in the column to the right of the adjectives.

My Group	Other Group		Favorableness
____	____	Intelligent	____
____	____	Materialistic	____
____	____	Ambitious	____
____	____	Industrious	____
____	____	Compassionate	____
____	____	Deceitful	____
____	____	Conservative	____
____	____	Practical	____
____	____	Shrewd	____
____	____	Arrogant	____
____	____	Aggressive	____
____	____	Warm	____
____	____	Sophisticated	____
____	____	Conceited	____
____	____	Neat	____
____	____	Alert	____
____	____	Friendly	____
____	____	Cooperative	____
____	____	Impulsive	____
____	____	Stubborn	____
____	____	Conventional	____
____	____	Progressive	____
____	____	Sly	____
____	____	Tradition loving	____
____	____	Pleasure loving	____

(continued)

Table 3.5 Continued

My Group	Other Group		Favorableness
____	____	Competitive	____
____	____	Honest	____
____	____	Modern	____
____	____	Emotional	____
____	____	Logical	____
____	____	Sincere	____
____	____	____	____
____	____	____	____

The adjectives you checked constitute the content of your stereotypes. To find out how favorable the stereotypes are add the numbers next to the adjectives you checked and divide by the number of adjectives you checked. Compute separate favorableness scores for the stereotype of your group and the other group. Scores range from 1 to 5. The higher the score, the more favorable your stereotype.

SOURCE: Adapted in part from Katz and Braly (1933).

consciously and unconsciously. Marilyn Brewer and Norman Miller (1988) argue that when we communicate with strangers there are three ways that our experiences with individual strangers can generalize to change our attitudes toward their groups:

1. *Change in attitudes toward the group as a whole.* This is the most direct form of generalization, where positive experiences with individual members of a broad social category lead to alterations in the affect and stereotypes associated with the group as a whole.
2. *Increased complexity of intergroup perceptions.* This form of generalization involves a change in the perceived heterogeneity of category structure. Instead of perceiving the out-group category as a relatively homogeneous social group, the individual comes to recognize variability among category members. Attitudes toward the category as a whole may not be altered, but affect and stereotypes are differentiated among various "sub-types" of the general category.
3. *Decategorization.* In this form of generalization, the meaningfulness of the category itself is undermined. Based on the frequency or intensity of exposure to individual members of a social group, the utility of category membership as a basis for identifying or classifying new individuals is reduced. (p. 316)

Each of these forms of generalization deserves brief discussion.

CHANGE IN ATTITUDES TOWARD THE GROUP AS A WHOLE

Many people assume that if we have contact with members of other groups, our attitudes toward those groups will become more positive. This, however, is not necessarily the case. Contact can promote better relations between groups or increase hostility between groups. The question that needs to be answered is when does contact lead to better relations between groups?

Walter Stephan (1985) isolates 13 characteristics of the contact situation that facilitate positive attitude change toward a social group to occur as a result of our individual contact with specific strangers:

1. Cooperation within groups should be maximized and competition between groups should be minimized.
2. Members of the ingroup and the outgroup should be of equal status both within and outside the contact situation.
3. Similarity of group members on nonstatus dimensions (beliefs, values, etc.) appears to be desirable.
4. Differences in competence should be avoided.
5. The outcomes should be positive.
6. Strong normative and institutional support for the contact should be provided.
7. The intergroup contact should have the potential to extend beyond the immediate situation.
8. Individuation of group members should be promoted.
9. Nonsuperficial contact (e.g., mutual disclosure of information) should be encouraged.
10. The contact should be voluntary.
11. Positive effects are likely to correlate with the duration of the contact.
12. The contact should occur in a variety of contexts with a variety of ingroup and outgroup members.
13. Equal numbers of ingroup and outgroup members should be used. (p. 643)

This list is long, but Stephan points out that it is incomplete. If we want to reduce our prejudice or ethnocentrism, we must make sure that our contact with strangers meets as many of these conditions as possible.

INCREASED COMPLEXITY OF INTERGROUP PERCEPTIONS

This form of generalization involves seeing the social category as heterogeneous, rather than homogeneous. Stated differently, we can increase the complexity of our intergroup perceptions by recognizing how members of a social category are different. Think of the social groups males and females. Are all males and all females the same? Obviously, the answer is no. We see differences among males and females and place them in subcategories. Females, for example, may categorize males into "male chauvinists" and "feminists."

Increasing the complexity of our intergroup perceptions is consistent with Langer's (1989) notion of mindfulness. As you may recall from Chapter 1, one aspect of becoming mindful of our communication is the creation of new categories. Creating new categories for Langer means differentiating among the individuals within the broad social categories we use. This means increasing the number of "discriminations" we make—using specific rather than global labels (e.g., a person with a lame leg, rather than a "cripple"). When we are mindful of differences among the members of the various outgroups with whom we communicate, our expectations are based on the subcategories, not the broader social category.

DECATEGORIZATION

Decategorization occurs when we communicate with strangers based on their individual characteristics rather than the categories in which we place them (i.e., communication is mainly interpersonal, not mainly intergroup). To accomplish this, we must differentiate individual strangers from their groups. Differentiation alone, however, is not sufficient for decategorization or personalization to occur.

When we personalize or decategorize our interactions with strangers, personal identity takes on more importance than social identity.

To illustrate this distinction, consider the statement "Janet is a nurse." This description can be psychologically represented in one of two ways. It could mean that Janet is subordinate to (i.e., a specific instance of) the general category of nurses. Or it could mean that being a nurse is subordinate to (i.e., a particular characteristic of) the concept of Janet. The former interpretation is an example of category-based individuation, and the later is an example of personalization. (Brewer & Miller, 1988, p. 318)

The difference lies in how we process the information. If we focus on the strangers' personal identities, we can decrease the degree to which their social identities affect our expectations.

❑ Ethical Issues in Communicating With Strangers

At the outset of this chapter, I indicated that our expectations have a "should" component. The should aspect of our expectations are derived from our ethical systems. I conclude this chapter by discussing ethical issues in communicating with strangers.

MORAL RELATIVISM

We are living in a time of "moral skepticism." Charles Taylor (1992), for example, points out that many people today are *not* sure that it is valid to make moral judgments. One reason people may have trouble making ethical judgments is that they have extended the descriptive theory of cultural relativity to the domain of ethics. The theory of cultural relativism asserts that the behavior of people in different cultures can be understood only in the context of those cultures. Stated differently, if we want to understand the behavior of people in other cultures, we have to do it from their frame of reference. Many of the early writers discussing cultural relativism, however, incorporated the idea of tolerance in their discussions of cultural relativism. Melville Herskovits (1950), for example, maintains that cultural relativism "is a philosophy which in recognizing the values set up by every society to guide its own life, lays stress on the dignity in every body of custom, and on the need for tolerance of conventions though they may differ from one's own" (p. 76).

Alison Renteln (1988) points out that incorporating tolerance in the theory of cultural relativity was due to the time in which the theory was developed; "cultural relativism was introduced in part to combat . . . racist, Eurocentric notions of progress" (p. 37); for example, viewing people from the Third World as savages or primitive. John Barnsley (1972) contends, however, that it is necessary to draw a distinction between the evaluative and descriptive aspects of ethical relativity:

> [Cultural] relativism . . . asserts the factual diversity of customs, of moral beliefs and practices. . . . The thesis itself, however, is purely a factual one. . . . Ethical relativism proper, on the other hand, is an evaluative thesis, affirming that the value of actions and the validity of moral judgments are dependent upon their sociocultural context. The two theses are logically distinct, though not unrelated. (pp. 326-327)

In other words, saying that ethics develop out of culture and vary across cultures (cultural relativism) is different from saying that valid moral judgments can only be made within a particular cultural context (ethical relativism).

Peter Berger argues recognizing cultural relativity

> does not, of course, free the individual from finding his [or her] own way morally. That would be another instance of "bad faith," with the objective fact of relativity being taken as an alibi for the subjective necessity of finding those single decisive points at which one engages one's whole being. (Cited by Barnsley, 1972, p. 355)

Even if we accept cultural diversity, we must still make ethical judgments in our interactions with people from other groups. Like Berger, Renteln (1988) contends that cultural relativism "does not force its adherents to foreswear moral criticism" (p. 63).

We cannot avoid making ethical judgments. There is no meta-ethic to guide our moral judgments, but there may be cultural universals that can be used. David Bidney (1968), for example, suggests that there may be universals regarding prohibitions against activities such as treason, murder, rape, and incest because "in all cultures the perpetuation of society takes precedence over the life of the individual" (p. 545).

Sissela Bok (1989) suggests areas where there may be cultural universals in ethical behavior:

> Of the four, two are the widely acknowledged curbs on violence and deceit. . . . To cement agreement about how and to who those curbs apply, and to keep them from being ignored or violated at will, a third constraint—on breaches of valid promises, contracts, laws, and treaties—is needed.
>
> Whether expressed in religious or secular form, these three values are shared by every civilization, past and present. Any community, no matter how small or disorganized, no matter how hostile toward outsiders, no matter how cramped its perception of what constitutes, say, torture, has to impose at least *some* internal curbs on violence, deceit, and betrayal in order to survive. But because persons acting clandestinely easily bypass or ignore these constraints, a fourth is necessary on excessive secrecy. (pp. 81-82)

Bok's list of moral constraints are not the only possible basis for making ethical judgments but do provide a basis for the development of a set of ethical principles that we can use in our own life.

Charles Taylor (1992) points out that in making moral judgments we have to balance individual and community needs. Individuals have a right to define themselves however they want, but they must do this in dialogue (discussed in Chapter 7) with others. Taylor contends that to make valid moral judgments about other cultures, we must first seriously study the other cultures so that we understand them.

DIGNITY AND INTEGRITY

Dignity and integrity play a large role in ethical behavior. *Dignity* involves a minimal level of self-respect (Pritchard, 1991). It refers to feeling worthy, honored, or respected as a person. Being moral involves maintaining our own sense of dignity, and maintaining others' sense of dignity as well. Lynne McFall (1987) defines *personal integrity* as involving a set of principles that we uphold even under adverse circumstances for the right reasons. We do not have to agree with another person's principles to say that he or she has integrity. For us to have personal integrity, the principles that we uphold must be "ones that a reasonable person might take to be of great importance" (p. 11).

Michael Pritchard (1991) contends that personal integrity reflects our view of what is important. Personal integrity is linked closely to moral integrity. *Moral integrity* requires "a somewhat unified moral stance. . . . Those with moral integrity can be expected to refuse to compromise moral standards for the sake of personal expediency" (Pritchard, 1991, p. 90). The "Aspen Declaration on Character Education" isolated six core values that make up a unified moral stance: (a) respect, (b) responsibility, (c) trustworthiness, (d) caring, (e) justice and fairness, and (f) civic virtue and citizenship.[14] With respect to moral integrity, it is important to recognize that

> when morality conflicts with other considerations, morality should prevail. Contemporary philosophers refer to this as the *overridingness* of morality. . . . The overridingness of morality need require only that one's conduct be limited to what is morally acceptable. That is, one should not choose immoral or morally objectionable courses of action over those that are morally acceptable. (Pritchard, 1991, pp. 225-226)

The overridingness of morality must be a major concern any time we communicate with strangers.

Behaving in a moral fashion requires that we respect others and their moral views (Gutmann, 1992). We do not have to agree with others' views of morality, we only have to see their views as based on a moral system. Amy Gutmann (1992) contends that if people disregard the views of others, they are *not* worthy of respect. This view has clear implications for what often is referred to as *hate speech* (i.e., speech that puts down others because of their membership in a group). Gutmann argues that there is "no virtue in misogyny, racial or ethnic hatred" (p. 22). She goes on to point out that racist and anti-Semitic remarks (hate speech) are *not* defensible on moral grounds.[15] "Hate speech violates the most elementary moral injunction, to respect the dignity of all human beings" (p. 23). William Galston (1991) takes a similar position when he says that the language of rights is morally incomplete. To say that "I have a right to do X" [e.g., engage in hate speech] is not to conclude that "X is the right thing for me to do." . . . Rights give reasons to others not to interfere with me in the performance of the protected acts; however, they do not in and of themselves give me sufficient reason to perform the acts. There is a gap between rights and rightness that cannot be closed without a richer moral vocabulary—one that involves principles of decency, duty, responsibility, and the common good, among others. (p. 8)

Amitai Etzioni (1993) suggests that our rights are limited by the rights of others; we can do what we want only if it does not harm others.

Gutmann (1992) contends that we have a moral obligation to respond when we hear others engage in hate speech. Etzioni concurs arguing that *"if we care about attaining a higher level of moral conduct than we now experience, we must be ready to express our moral sense"* (p. 36). This does not mean that we should not disagree with members of other groups. We can and should articulate our disagreements with others in a respectful fashion.

MORAL INCLUSION-EXCLUSION

As indicated in Chapter 1, "moral exclusion occurs when individuals or groups are perceived as *outside the boundary in which moral values, rules, and considerations of fairness apply.* Those who are morally excluded are perceived as nonentities, expendable, or undeserving; consequently, harming them appears acceptable, appropriate, or just" (Optow, 1990, p. 1). Susan Optow (1990) argues that there are three attitudes associated with being morally inclusive. First, people who are morally inclusive assume that considerations of fairness apply to other people. Second, people who are morally inclusive are willing to provide a share of community resources to others who need them. Third, people who are morally inclusive are willing to make sacrifices to help others. Many moral philosophers (e.g., Nozick, 1974) suggest that considerations of fairness and principles of morality should be applied to members of the human species. Others (e.g., Regan, 1983) believe that the boundary for moral behavior should be cognitive awareness.

This criteria extends the boundary of moral behavior to many mammals (e.g., dolphins, whales, dogs). Still others (e.g., Stone, 1974) suggest that the boundary of moral behavior should extend to inanimate objects (e.g., the planet, plants).

Optow (1990) isolates two major factors that lead us to behave in a morally exclusive fashion. When we are engaged in group *conflict*, for example, ingroup cohesiveness is high, but at the same time concern for fairness for members of outgroups is low. Another factor that contributes to moral exclusiveness is *feeling unconnected* to the other person or group. When we feel connected to others in any way, we feel attraction and empathy and engage in helpful behavior toward others. These behaviors are morally inclusive. When we see someone within our moral community (i.e., those we believe should be treated morally) harmed, we perceive an injustice to have taken place. If we harm others in our moral community, we will feel shame, guilt, remorse, or self-blame. When we see someone outside our moral community harmed, we may not perceive that their rights are violated and we may not be concerned. When this occurs, we are being morally exclusive.

Moral exclusion can take many forms. It can range from slavery, genocide, political repression, and violations of human rights to failing to recognize undeserved suffering in others. The Holocaust during World War II and the My Lai massacre during the Vietnam War are examples of severe moral exclusion. Moral exclusion, however, occurs in everyday interactions, too. If we distance ourselves from others psychologically, ignore our responsibility to others, or glorify violence, we are being morally exclusive.

Table 3.6 contains a questionnaire designed to help you determine how morally inclusive you are. Take a few minutes to complete it before you continue reading.

Scores on the questionnaire range from 10 to 50. The higher your score on the assessment in Table 3.6, the more morally inclusive you are. The ideal score on this questionnaire is 50. Very few people, however, score this high. We can, nevertheless, choose to increase our moral inclusiveness. This requires that we be mindful when we find ourselves making judgments of others.

Table 3.6 Assessing Your Moral Inclusiveness

The purpose of this questionnaire is to assess your moral inclusiveness. Respond to each statement indicating the degree to which you agree or disagree: "Strongly Disagree" (answer 1), "Disagree" (answer 2), "Sometimes Disagree and Sometimes Agree" (answer 3), "Agree" (answer 4), and "Strongly Agree" (answer 5).

_____   1. Everyone should be treated fairly.
_____   2. There are people who do not deserve my respect.
_____   3. All people have a right to be treated with dignity.
_____   4. I do not make sacrifices to foster others' well being.
_____   5. Moral values apply equally to everyone.
_____   6. I am not morally obligated to treat everyone with respect.
_____   7. I apply the same rules to my friends and enemies.
_____   8. It is not my responsibility to help those who need assistance.
_____   9. All forms of life should be treated with reverence.
_____ 10. There are conditions (other than in a declared war) under which it is acceptable to harm others.

To find your score, first reverse your responses for the even-numbered items (i.e., if you wrote 1, make it 5; if you wrote 2, make it 4; if you wrote 3, leave it as 3; if you wrote 4, make it 2; if you wrote 5, make it 1). Next, add the numbers next to each statement. Scores range from 10 to 50. The higher your score, the more moral inclusive you are.

SOURCE: Based on Optow's (1990) discussion of moral exclusion.

To summarize, changing our attitudes toward outgroups, increasing the complexity of our intergroup perceptions, and decategorization can all change our expectations of strangers. To create positive expectations and improve our relations with members of other groups, we need to use all three processes simultaneously. Changing our expectations of strangers is necessary for us to communicate effectively with them. To improve our communication effectiveness, we also need to understand how we make sense of strangers' behavior. This is the topic of the next chapter.

❑ Notes

1. Burgoon and Hale (1988) do not limit their statement to this group; I do.
2. See Stephan and Stephan (1989) for several citations to support this claim.

3. This quote is from an afterword to a book for first-grade teachers published in the early 1970s. Unfortunately, I lost the reference to the book in which it appeared.

4. Lukens (1978) isolated the first three distances. Gudykunst and Kim (1984) extended her work to include the last two distances.

5. The survey was conducted in October and November 1992 by Martilla & Kiley with a margin of error of plus or minus three percent. It was reported in the *Los Angeles Times*, June 12, 1993, p. A25.

6. This statement may be limited to conduct in the presence of "educated" individuals. In Chapter 1, I quoted Spike Lee (1990) as saying "racism is fashionable today." I believe that both statements are "true" in specific contexts.

7. For excellent examples, see the Frontline video "Racism 101" or issues of newsmagazines that focused on this topic in the first six months of 1990.

8. Blanchard et al. (1991) actually use the term racism. I believe that their results will extend to any form of prejudice.

9. See Vassiliou, Triandis, Vassiliou, and McGuire (1972) for a complete discussion of the complexity of stereotypes.

10. These conclusions are supported by Mullen and Johnson's (1993) research.

11. For a recent review of research on categorization and category representations, see Messick and Mackie (1989); for a current review of stereotypes and communication, see Hewstone and Brown (1986); see Jussim, Coleman, and Lerch (1987) for a summary of the major theories of stereotyping.

12. Many of the ideas presented in this section were first brought to my attention in Kellermann (1993).

13. See Giles, Mulac, Bradac, and Johnson (1987) for a review of research on accommodation.

14. Reported in *World Monitor*, October 1992, pp. 6-7.

15. I am *not* arguing that racist remarks fall outside the Constitutional protection for speech. Rather, I am arguing that they violate standards of morality.

4

Attributing Meaning
to Strangers' Behavior

In the previous chapter, I discussed how our expectations affect our communication behavior. In this chapter, I extend this analysis by looking at the way we make sense of our world—our perceptions and attributions. I begin by looking at the perception process. Next, I examine the individual and social attribution processes and isolate factors that lead us to make errors in attributions. I also discuss the role of cultural and personality factors in the attribution process. I conclude by looking at ways we can improve the accuracy of our perceptions and attributions.

❏ The Perception Process

Our perception involves our awareness of what is taking place in the environment. There are three critical aspects of our perceptions that influence our communication with strangers: perceptions are selective; perceptions involve categorization; and rigid categories inhibit effective communication. I begin by looking at the selective nature of perception.

PERCEPTIONS ARE SELECTIVE

If we had to pay attention to *all* of the stimuli in our environment, we would experience information overload. In the interest of not overloading ourselves with too much information, we limit our attention to those aspects of the other person or the situation that are essential to what we are doing (Bruner, 1958). We might, for example, perceive the color of a person's skin, but not notice its texture. Alan Watts (1966) points out that

> to notice is to select, to regard some bits of perception, or some features of the world, as more noteworthy, more significant than others. To these, we attend, and the rest we ignore—for which reason . . . attention is at the same time ignore-ance (i.e., ignorance) despite the fact that it gives us a vividly clear picture of what we choose to notice. Physically, we see, hear, smell, taste, and touch innumerable features that we never notice. (p. 29)

Our perceptions of other people also are highly selective.

Gregory Bateson (1979) points out that the process of selecting information from our environment and forming images takes place unconsciously. We do not consciously decide on the things to which we pay attention. We are conscious of our perceptions (what we see), but we need to keep in mind that what we see is manufactured in our brain. What we see does not really exist because "all experience is subjective" (Bateson, 1979, p. 31). Our presuppositions and expectations influence the cues that we select from the environment and what we see (expectations are discussed in detail below).

William Ittelson and Hadley Cantril (1954) point out that our perceptions are always a function of our interaction with specific people in specific situations. We react to people based on the way we perceive them in the interaction, *not* as entities independent of our interaction with them. Each of our perceptions are unique; they are based on our culture, our ethnicity, our sex, our background experiences, and our needs. Our perceptions overlap with those of others to the extent that we share common experiences (e.g., culture). Although our perceptions are based on our interactions with others, we tend to mistakenly assume that our perceptions are "real" and external to ourselves.

> *Our perceptions are always a function of our interaction with specific people in specific situations.*

The problems for our communication with others arise because we mistakenly assume that we perceive and observe others in a unbiased fashion. But our perceptions are highly selective and biased. Our past experiences are one source of bias in our perceptions. If, for example, our mother was quiet before she exploded and got angry with us, we may perceive that others are getting angry when they are quiet. Our previous experiences with a particular person also can bias our perception of her or his current behavior. Our emotional states also bias our perceptions. Our moods provide a lens through which we interpret our own and others' behavior. Other biases in our perceptions are a function of the categorization process and our expectations.

PERCEPTIONS INVOLVE CATEGORIZATIONS

When we select information from the environment we need to organize it in some way. We try to find meaningful patterns. We do this by putting things or people into categories. Categorization is a fundamental aspect of thought. It allows "us to structure and give coherence to our general knowledge about people and the social world, providing typical patterns of behavior and the range of likely variation between types of people and their characteristic actions and attributes" (Cantor, Mischel, & J. Schwartz, 1982, p. 34).

When we categorize something, we group objects (people or things) by aspects they have in common and ignore aspects they do not have in common. Our categorizations are based on only selected aspects of the thing or person. In categorizing, we have to ignore some aspects in order to classify a person or thing. Once we have created the category, we assume that things within the category are similar and that things in different categories are different. To illustrate, we can classify photographic film as black and white or color, but in doing this we ignore other important qualities of film—its speed, say. With respect to people, we might classify a person as depressed (as opposed to not depressed), but in so doing we ignore other qualities of the person. Once formed, however, the category influences how we respond to the person.

When we categorize things or people we draw distinctions among them and create boundaries between categories. "Things assume a distinctive identity only through being differentiated from other things, and their meaning is always a function of the particular mental compartment in which we place them" (Zerubavel, 1991, p. 3). Once the categories are formed, we tend to take them for granted and assume there are gaps between them. These gaps enhance our viewing the categories as separate and distinct. It is important to keep in mind that we created the categories in the first place and that the gaps between the categories are a function of the way we created the categories.

RIGID CATEGORIES INHIBIT ACCURATE PERCEPTIONS

Creating gaps between the categories we form is a natural part of the perceptual process. What creates problems in communication is the rigidity with which we maintain the boundaries between categories. Eviatar Zerubavel (1991) points out that

> the most distinctive characteristic of the rigid mind is its unyielding, obsessive commitment to the mutual exclusivity of mental entities. The foremost logical prerequisite of a rigid classification is that a mental item belongs to no more than one category. . . . The rigid mind cherishes sharp, clear-cut distinctions among mental entities. (p. 34)

People with rigid categories try to classify each thing and person into a single category. When something does not clearly fit one category, it threatens the cognitive structure of a person with a rigid category system. Forcing things or people into mutually exclusive categories biases our perceptions. People with rigid category systems experience anxiety or fear when confronted with something or someone that cannot be categorized (Zerubavel, 1991).

If we hold our categories rigidly, we do not recognize individual variations within our categories or consider recategorizing someone based on new information. If our categories are rigid, we may categorize someone as disabled, for example, and then see *all* disabled people as alike. All disabled people, however, are not alike. To communicate effectively with someone who is disabled, we must be able to recognize how he or she is like other disabled people *and* how she or he is different from other disabled people. Similarly, if our categories are rigid, we might categorize someone as depressed and refuse to consider reclassifying the person, even when confronted with consistent evidence that he or she is not depressed.

We draw boundaries and categorize people to make sense of the world. We draw a boundary between ourselves and others, for example, so that we will feel distinct. We not only have a need to be distinct, but we also have a need to feel connected. If we draw a rigid boundary between ourselves and others, we will be very lonely. If we do not draw a sufficient boundary between ourselves and others, on the other hand, we will have little sense of self (e.g., low self-esteem). Balancing our needs for distinction (autonomy) and connection requires that we have flexible categories. "Flexibility entails the ability to be both rigid and fuzzy. Flexible people notice structures yet feel comfortable destroying them from time to time" (Zerubavel, 1991, p. 120). If our mental structures are flexible and elastic, we can "break away from the mental cages in which we so often lock ourselves" (p. 122). Having flexible categories is necessary to be mindful and communicate effectively. If we know we have rigid categories, we can choose to be more flexible when we are mindful of our communication.

When we are mindful, one thing we can do to overcome the biases in our perceptions is to look for exceptions. Michelle Weiner-Davis (1992) points out that once we recognize a single exception, it helps us to stop our cognitive distortions due to either/or thinking. To illustrate, if we categorize a stranger as not talkative, or quiet, we would try to think of times that he or she is talkative. When we recognize that there are times that she or he is talkative, we will not view him or her in exactly the same way (i.e., she or he is not always quiet). This change in perceptions will lead to more accurate perceptions of the other person.

⊐ The Attribution Process

Attributions are our attempts to explain others' behavior. Our attributions are based on both individual and social characteristics. When we make attributions on automatic pilot, we make errors, especially when we communicate with strangers. I begin our discussion of attributions by looking at how we explain the behavior of members of our ingroup.

INDIVIDUAL ATTRIBUTIONS

Fritz Heider (1958) raises the question of how we make sense of our own and others' behavior and how our interpretations shape our responses to behavior. He believes that we act as naive or intuitive scientists when we are trying to make sense of the world. Briefly, Heider suggests that we are motivated by practical concerns such as our need to simplify and comprehend our environment, and to predict others' behavior. To meet these needs, we try to get beneath external appearances to isolate stable underlying processes, which he called dispositional properties. Heider contends that others' motives are the dispositions we use most frequently in giving meaning to our experiences. He also points out that it is not our experiences per se, but our interpretations of our experiences that constitute our "reality."

Harold Kelley (1967) extends Heider's work by trying to explain when we attribute behavior to internal causes and when we attribute it to external causes. He argues that when observing others' behavior we attempt to make attributions about the effect of the environment on their behavior by ruling out individual explanations for the behavior. We organize our observations into a cube with three dimensions: person × object × situation. In the *person* dimension, we compare the person engaging in the behavior with others. Do other people engage in the same behavior as the person being observed? We are trying to find out the degree to which there is *consensus* on the behavior across people. In the *object* dimension, we compare the different objects of the person's behavior. Does the person behave the same way toward different people or objects? Here we are looking for whether the object of the person's behavior is *distinctive*. In the *situation* dimension, we vary the context in which the behavior occurs. Does the person behave the same in different situations? The focus here is on whether there is *consistency* across time and location of the behavior. We then use a covariation principle to assess the degree to which the behavior occurs in the presence and absence of the various causes.[1]

It may appear that the attribution process takes a long time, but in actuality, we go through this analysis very quickly when we have complete information. Kelley (1972) argues that in the presence of incomplete data, we infer meaning based on our preconceptions about how specific causes are associated with specific effects. Our causal schemata permit "economical and fast attributional analysis, by providing a framework within which bits and pieces of information can be fitted in order to draw reasonably good inferences" (p. 152).

There are several biases that affect our attribution processes. First, we have a tendency to overestimate the influence of personal, dispositional characteristics and underestimate the influence of situational factors when we make attributions. This is called the *fundamental attribution error* (Ross, 1977). Second, there is an *egocentric bias*—our tendency to see our own behavior as normal and appropriate (Kelley, 1967). We explain others' behavior that is different as a function of their personal dispositions. Third, we use an *ego-protective bias* when we tend to attribute our success to personal dispositions and our failures to situational factors (Kelley, 1967). Fourth, we tend to stop searching for interpretations of behavior once we have a relevant and reasonable interpretation (*premature closure;* Taylor & Fiske, 1978). Fifth, we have a tendency to overemphasize negative information about others' behavior (*principle of negativity;* Kanouse & Hanson, 1972).

SOCIAL ATTRIBUTIONS

Heider's (1958) and Kelley's (1967) explanations of the individual attribution process do not take into account that we are members of social groups. It is necessary to look at the influence of group memberships on the attribution process. When group membership is taken into consideration, the process is called social attributions. *Social attributions* are concerned with how members of one social group explain the behavior of their own members and members of other social groups.

Miles Hewstone and Joseph Jaspars (1984) isolate three propositions regarding the social nature of attributions:

1. Attribution is social in origin (e.g., it may be created by, or strengthened through, social interaction, or it may be influenced by social information).
2. Attribution is social in its reference or object (e.g., an attribution may be demanded for the individual characterized as a member of a social group, rather than in purely individual terms; or for a social outcome, rather than any behavior as such).
3. Attribution is social in that it is common to the members of a society or group (e.g., the members of different groups may hold different attributions for the same event). (pp. 379-380)

Hewstone and Jaspars argue that we enhance our social identities when we make social attributions. They also point out that our social attributions usually are based on the social stereotypes we share with other members of our ingroups. Our social attributions, however, can also be based on our ethnocentrism or other intergroup attitudes.

Miles Hewstone and Rupert Brown (1986) contend that when we perceive ourselves and others in individual terms (e.g., our personal identities generate our behavior) or we see an outgroup member as atypical, we tend to make person-based attributions. Person-based attributions, in turn, lead us to look for personal similarities and differences between us and the other person. When we perceive ourselves and others as members of groups (e.g., our social identities generate our behavior), we tend to make category-based attributions. Category-based attributions then lead us to look for differences between our ingroup and the relevant outgroup.

The nature of the attributions we make are important and influence our relations with members of other groups. When members of different groups are working together and fail at their task, members of the ingroup usually blame the outgroup for the failure. Attributions like this do not help to improve intergroup relations and can, in fact, have a negative influence. If ingroup members are somehow prevented from blaming the outgroup for the failure, cooperation that results in failure does not result in increased bias toward the outgroup (Worchell & Norwell, 1980).

THE ULTIMATE ATTRIBUTION ERROR

Thomas Pettigrew (1979) proposes that the *ultimate attribution error* is "a systematic patterning of intergroup misattributions shaped in part by prejudice" (p. 464). He points out that our tendency to attribute behavior to dispositional characteristics is enhanced when a member of an outgroup is perceived to engage in negative behavior. When members of an outgroup engage in what is perceived to be positive behavior, in contrast, our tendency is to treat the person as an "exception to the rule" and we discount dispositional explanations for the behavior. We therefore attribute the behavior to situational factors.

When our expectations are confirmed by others' behavior, we rely on others' dispositions associated with our stereotype of their group and do not bother to consider other explanations for the behavior (Pyszczynski & Greenberg, 1981). When others do not confirm our expectations, we tend to attribute their behavior to external factors (Stephan & Rosenfield, 1982).

With respect to the ultimate attribution error, Pettigrew (1978) concludes that across-group perceptions are more likely than within-group perceptions to include the following:

1. For acts perceived as antisocial or undesirable, behavior will be attributed to personal, dispositional causes. Often these internal causes will be seen as innate characteristics, and role requirements will be over-looked. ("He shoved the white guy, because blacks are born violent like that.")

2. For acts perceived as prosocial or desirable, behavior will be attributed either: (a) to the situation—with role requirements receiving more attention ("Under the circumstances, what could the cheap Scot do, but pay the check?"); (b) to the motivational, as opposed to innate, dispositional qualities ("Jewish students make better grades, because they try so much harder"); or (c) to the exceptional, even exaggerated "special case" individual who is contrasted with his/her group—what Allport (1954) called "fence-mending" ("She is certainly bright and hardworking—not at all like other Chicanos" [sic]). (p. 39)

It is very likely that we will make the ultimate attribution error when communicating on automatic pilot. To reduce the possibility of making this error when making attributions about the behavior of strangers, we must be mindful of our interpretations of their behavior.

⊐ Personality Factors Influencing Our Attributions

Our personalities influences the way we make attributions. Two personality characteristics, category width and uncertainty orientation, affect the flexibility of our cognitive systems. These characteristics are discussed in this section.

CATEGORY WIDTH

"Category width refers to the range of instances included in a cognitive category" (Pettigrew, 1982, p. 200).[2] To illustrate, is a pane of glass in the wall that is one inch wide and 12 feet high a window? A narrow categorizer would probably say no, whereas a wide categorizer would probably say yes. Wide categorizers have more latitude than narrow categorizers in what they include in a category. Richard Detweiler (1978) points out that category width "is a term used to describe the amount of discrepancy tolerable among category members—how similar do things have to be to be called by the same name? A narrow categorizer might put only highly similar things in the same category, whereas a broad categorizer might put more discrepant things in the same category" (p. 263).

Pettigrew (1982) suggests that individual differences in category width are related to more general information processing strategies people use. Broad categorizers, for example, tend to perform better than narrow categorizers on tasks that require holistic, integrated information processing. Narrow categorizers, in comparison, tend to perform better than broad categorizers on tasks that require detailed, analytic information processing. Milton Rokeach (1951) believes that broad categorizers include concepts like Buddhism, Capitalism, Christianity, Democracy, Judaism, and Socialism in the same category (e.g., beliefs or doctrines), whereas narrow categorizers do not. Rokeach also contends that narrow categorizers are more ethnocentric than broad categorizers. Narrow categorizers also "react more to change, seek less prior information, and are more confident of their performances" than broad categorizers (Pettigrew, 1982, p. 207).

Category Width and Intergroup Attributions. Detweiler (1975) studied how category width influences the attributions European Americans make about people who are culturally similar (another European American) or culturally dissimilar (a person from Haiti) who engage in either positive or negative behavior. Narrow categorizers

> assume that the effects of behavior of a person from another culture tell all about the person, even though he [or she] in fact knows nothing about the actor's [or actress's] cultural background. He [or she] seems to make strong judgments based on the positivity or negativity of the effects of the behavior as evaluated from his [or her] own cultural viewpoint. Contrarily, when making attributions to a person who is culturally similar, the narrow [categorizer] seems to view the similarity as overshadowing the behavior. Thus, positive effects are seen as intended, and negative effects are confidently seen as unintended. (p. 600)

Narrow categorizers therefore may have trouble making accurate attributions about messages from both people who are culturally similar and people who are culturally dissimilar.

When making attributions about a culturally dissimilar person, a wide categorizer

> seems to assume that he [or she] in fact doesn't know enough to make "usual" attributions. Thus, behaviors with negative effect result in less confident and generally more neutral attributions when judgments are made about a person from a different culture. Conversely, the culturally similar person who causes a negative outcome is rated relatively more negatively with greater confidence by the wide [categorizer], since the behavior from one's own cultural background is meaningful. (p. 600)

Wide categorizers thus are more likely than narrow categorizers to search for the appropriate interpretation of a culturally dissimilar person's behavior.

Assessing Your Category Width. Table 4.1 contains a questionnaire designed to help you assess your category width. Take a couple of minutes and complete it now.

Scores on the questionnaire range from 10 to 50. The higher your score, the broader your categories. The important thing to keep in mind is that lower scores suggest that you have a tendency to judge the behavior of people who are different using your own group's standards. Narrow categorizers need to recognize that they will assume that they have sufficient information to make an attribution about people who are different when they do not. This assumption in turn will lead them to make inaccurate attributions about the behavior of people from different cultures or ethnic groups. These tendencies, however, can be managed cognitively by becoming mindful when narrow categorizers communicate with people who are different.

UNCERTAINTY ORIENTATION

Uncertainty orientation influences whether or not we try to gather information about others that needs to be discussed before

Table 4.1 Assessing Your Category Width

The purpose of this questionnaire is to help you to assess your category width. Respond to each of the statements by indicating the degree to which the statement is true regarding how you typically think about yourself. When you think about yourself, is the statement "Always False" (answer 1), "Usually False" (answer 2), "Sometimes True and Sometimes False" (answer 3), "Usually True" (answer 4), or "Always False" (answer 5)?

_____ 1. I do well on tasks that require integrated information processing.
_____ 2. I do well on tasks that require detailed information processing.
_____ 3. Things can be very dissimilar and share a common quality and I will use the same label to describe them.
_____ 4. I make strong judgments about others.
_____ 5. I do well on tasks that require holistic information processing.
_____ 6. I am confident that I perform well in social situations.
_____ 7. I try to make sure I have sufficient information before judging others.
_____ 8. I do well on tasks that require analytic information processing.
_____ 9. I try to obtain a lot of information before making decisions.
_____ 10. I react negatively to change.

To find your score, first reverse the responses for the even-numbered items (i.e., if you wrote 1, make it 5; if you wrote 2, make it 4; if you wrote 3, leave it as 3; if you wrote 4, make it 2; if you wrote 5, make it 1). Next, add the numbers in front of each statement. Scores range from 10 to 50. The higher your score, the wider your categories.

SOURCE: Adapted from Pettigrew's (1982) description of category width.

addressing skills. Our orientation toward uncertainty is based on the degree to which we have an open or closed mind. People with an open mind "need to know and understand" themselves and others (Rokeach, 1960, p. 67). People with a closed mind, in contrast, "need to ward off threatening aspects of reality" (p. 67). This often is accomplished by ignoring new information made available.

Defining Uncertainty Orientation. With respect to uncertainty orientation, Richard Sorrentino and Judith Ann Short (1986) point out

> that there are many people who simply are not interested in finding out information about themselves or the world, who do not conduct causal searches, who could not care less about comparing themselves with others, and who "don't give a hoot" for resolving

discrepancies or inconsistencies about the self. Indeed, such people (we call them certainty oriented) will go out of their way not to perform activities such as these (we call people who *do* go out of their way to do such things uncertainty oriented). (pp. 379-380)

Uncertainty oriented people are interested in reducing uncertainty, whereas certainty oriented people try to avoid looking at uncertainty when it is present.

Uncertainty oriented people integrate new and old ideas and change their belief systems accordingly.[3] They evaluate ideas and thoughts on their own merit and do not necessarily compare them with others. Uncertainty oriented people want to understand themselves and their environment. The more uncertainty oriented we are, the more likely we are willing to question our own behavior and its appropriateness when communicating with strangers. Also, the more uncertainty oriented we are, the more we would try to gather information about strangers so we can communicate effectively with them.

Certainty oriented people, in contrast, like to hold on to traditional beliefs and have a tendency to reject ideas that are different. Certainty oriented people maintain a sense of self by not examining themselves or their behavior.

Assessing Your Uncertainty Orientation. If you are reading this book by choice and have gotten this far, you probably are relatively uncertainty oriented (this may not hold if you are reading it for a class and are going to be tested on it). The questionnaire in Table 4.2 is designed to help you assess your certainty-uncertainty orientation. Take a few minutes and complete it now.

Scores on the questionnaire range from 10 to 50. The higher your score, the more uncertainty oriented you are. The thing to keep in mind is that the less uncertainty oriented you are (or the more certainty oriented you are), the greater the potential misunderstandings you may have when you communicate with people who are different. If you are highly certainty oriented (i.e., you got a low score on the questionnaire), you have a lot of misunderstandings and do not know about them or care about them if you do recognize them. Sorrentino and Short (1986) talk about

Table 4.2 Assessing Your Uncertainty Orientation

The purpose of this questionnaire is to help you assess your orientation toward uncertainty. Respond to each statement indicating the degree to which it is true regarding the way to typically respond: "Always False" (answer 1), "Usually False" (answer 2), "Sometimes False and Sometimes True" (answer 3), "Usually True" (answer 4), or "Always True" (answer 5).

_____ 1. I do not compare myself with others.
_____ 2. If given a choice, I prefer to go somewhere new rather than somewhere I've been before.
_____ 3. I reject ideas that are different than mine.
_____ 4. I try to resolve inconsistencies in beliefs I hold.
_____ 5. I am not interested in finding out information about myself.
_____ 6. When I obtain new information, I try to integrate it with information I already have.
_____ 7. I hold traditional beliefs.
_____ 8. I evaluate people on their own merit without comparing them to others.
_____ 9. I hold inconsistent views of myself.
_____ 10. If someone suggests an opinion that is different than mine, I do not reject it before I consider it.

To find your score, first reverse the responses for the odd-numbered items (i.e., if you wrote 1, make it 5; if you wrote 2, make it 4; if you wrote 3, leave it as 3; if you wrote 4, make it 2; if you wrote 5, make it 1). Next, add the numbers next to each statement. Scores range from 10 to 50. The higher your score, the greater your uncertainty orientation.

SOURCE: Based on Sorrentino and Short's (1986) description of uncertainty orientation.

uncertainty orientation as a personality trait, but I believe our orientation can be managed, at least in part, if we are mindful when we communicate.

❑ Culture and Misattributions

The cultural and ethnic norms and rules for communication we learned as children often contribute to misunderstandings when we communicate with people who are different. It is not possible for me to discuss the full range of areas where misunderstandings might occur in a short book like this. I therefore have chosen to try to illustrate how misunderstandings occur by linking them to two of the dimensions of cultural variability discussed in Chapter 2. Understanding how individualism-collectivism and low- and high-context communication affect our attributions can help us to make appropriate attributions when we communicate with people from different cultures.

INDIVIDUALISM-COLLECTIVISM

Members of collectivistic cultures are group oriented and they strongly identify with their ingroups. In individualistic cultures, emphasis is placed on the self. The differences in the group- or self-orientation often lead to misinterpretations of the behavior of members of other cultures in the formation and development of interpersonal relationships between members of individualistic and collectivistic cultures.

To begin, consider the use of personal pronouns in individualistic and collectivistic cultures. A member of a collectivistic culture who identifies with the group, for example, may use the pronoun "we" when stating a personal opinion. A member of an individualistic culture would perceive such a statement as being about something that the group may do or believe, but not necessarily the speaker's opinion. This misinterpretation will result in misunderstanding if the cultural differences in use of personal pronouns is ignored.

Another example of how differences in individualism-collectivism can lead to misunderstanding involves how face is negotiated. *Face* is defined as the public self-image (Ting-Toomey, 1988). Face can be based on our need for inclusion or our need for autonomy. Further, we can have a concern for our own face or a concern for another's face. Problems in communication may occur when there is a difference in interpretation of the face concern being used. In collectivistic cultures, the concern for face is predominately other oriented. In individualistic cultures, the concern is self-oriented. Misunderstandings may occur when individualists fail to give face to collectivists when they interact.

The issue of giving face, especially to people with higher status, is important in collectivistic cultures. When people from individualistic cultures violate this expectation, it can have major consequences for a relationship. Richard Brislin and his associates (1986) present an example of this in the context of business negotiations between individuals in Japan and the United States:

> Phil Downing . . . was involved in the setting up of a branch of his company that was merging with an existing Japanese counterpart. He seemed to get along very well with the executive colleagues assigned to work with him, one of whom had recently been elected chairman of the board when his grandfather retired. Over several weeks discussion, they had generally laid out some working policies and agreed on strategies that would bring new directions needed for development. Several days later . . . the young chairman's grandfather happened to drop in. He began to comment on how the company had been formed and had been built up by the traditional practices, talking about some of the policies the young executives had recently discarded. Phil expected the new chairman to explain some of the new innovative and developmental policies they had both agreed upon. However, the young man said nothing; instead, he just nodded and agreed with his grandfather. Phil was bewildered and frustrated . . . and he started to protest. The atmosphere in the room became immediately tense. . . . A week later the Japanese company withdrew from the negotiations. (pp. 155-156)

The young chairman of the Japanese company was giving his grandfather face by agreeing with him. This did not, however, negate any of the negotiations he had with Phil. Phil obviously did not understand this. By protesting and disagreeing with the grandfather, Phil not only failed to give face to the grandfather, he threatened the grandfather's face. The young chairman, therefore, decided not to do business with Phil.

Face issues also can lead to misunderstanding in interethnic encounters in the United States. In the European American middle-class subculture, for example, refusing to comply with a directive given by a superior is attributed as a face-threatening act. In the African American subculture, however, "stylin' " includes refusing to comply as part of a verbal game. This can be a problem when European American teachers interact with African American students and neither understands the others' communication style:

The [European American] teachers, not realizing the play argument was a salient speech event in the children's speech community, took literally the child's refusal to comply, often with disastrous results for the child's reputation. Such children can be seen as recalcitrant and possibly emotionally disturbed [by European American teachers]. (Erickson, 1981, pp. 6-7)

For effective communication to occur in situations like this at least one of the participants must be mindful.

LOW- AND HIGH-CONTEXT COMMUNICATION

Peter Ehrenhaus (1983) argues that members of cultures where high-context messages predominate are sensitive to situational features and explanations, and tend to attribute others' behavior to the context, situation, or other factors external to the individual. Members of cultures in which low-context messages predominate, in contrast, are sensitive to dispositional characteristics and tend to attribute others' behavior to characteristics internal to the individual (e.g., personality). Individuals use the information that they believe is important when interacting with members of other cultures. Because individuals' explanations are based on their own cultural presuppositions, there is a likelihood misattributions will occur. Members of cultures in which low-context messages predominate, for example, tend not to emphasize situational factors enough when explaining behavior of members of cultures in which high-context messages predominate. Members of cultures in which high-context messages predominate, in contrast, tend not to emphasize factors internal to the individual enough when trying to explain the behavior of members of cultures in which low-context messages predominate.

Another area where misunderstandings may occur in communication between members of low- and high-context cultures is in the directness of speech used. As indicated in Chapter 1, members of cultures where low-context communication predominates tend to use a direct style of speech. Members of cultures in which high-context communication predominates, in contrast, tend to use an indirect style of speech. The problems when people from low- and high-context cultures interact is illustrated in

Deborah Tannen's (1979) study of Greek-U.S. communication. Tannen (1979) notes that Greeks tend to employ an indirect style of speech and interpret others' behavior based on the assumption that they also are using the same style. North Americans, in contrast, use a direct style of speech and assume others are using it also.

Tannen observes that when Greeks and North Americans communicate there often are misunderstandings due to these differences in style of speech. Tannen (1975) reports a conversation between a husband (nonnative speaker [NNS] of English who learned indirect rules) and a wife (native speaker [NS] using direct communication styles) that illustrates these differences:

> **NS (wife):** Bob's having a party. Wanna go?
> **NNS (husband):** OK
> **NS:** (later) Are you sure you wanna go?
> **NNS:** OK, let's not go. I'm tired anyway.

In this conversation the husband interpreted the wife's questions as an indirect indication that she did not want to go.

Tannen (1979) points out that overcoming misunderstandings due to direct-indirect style differences is difficult because "in seeking to clarify, each speaker continues to use the very strategy which confused the other in the first place" (p. 5). To resolve the misunderstandings, obviously one of the people involved must recognize that the differences in style are creating the problem, try to accurately interpret the other person's messages, and then shift her or his style of speech.

Misattributions also result from the way people try to reduce uncertainty using low- and high-context messages, particularly in initial interactions with strangers. To illustrate, consider how uncertainty is reduced in the United States and Japan. In the European American middle-class subculture, people try to obtain information about others' attitudes, feelings, and beliefs to reduce uncertainty. In Japan, where high-context messages are emphasized, on the other hand, people must know others' status and background in order to reduce uncertainty and know which version of the language to use (there are different ways to speak to people who are "superiors," "equals," and "inferiors").[4] This leads Japanese to introduce themselves by saying things like "'I belong to Mitsubishi Bank.' and immediately asking . . . 'What is your job?', 'How old are you?', and 'What is the name of your company?'" (Loveday, 1982, pp. 4-5). These questions are designed to gather the information necessary for a Japanese to communicate with a stranger. They are, however, perceived as "rude" and "nosey" by middle-class European Americans.

❏ Improving the Accuracy of Our Attributions

If we recognize that our perceptions of and attributions for strangers' behavior may be in error, we need to try to improve our accuracy. There are at least three communication skills that are useful in increasing our accuracy: perception checking, active listening, and feedback. These skills are discussed in this section.

PERCEPTION CHECKING

If two people are communicating it is likely that they are perceiving what is going on differently. Much of the time when we communicate small differences in perceptions are not problematic. At times, however, even small differences in perceptions can lead to ineffective communication. If others do not directly tell us what they are thinking or feeling, our perceptions can be inaccurate. When this occurs, perception checking is a valuable skill to have among our communication skill resources.

The Perception-Checking Skill. The purpose of perception checking is to send the relational message that we want to understand the other person's thoughts or feelings. Perception checking provides us with an opportunity to make sure our interpretation of the other person's behavior is what he or she meant before we act. Perception checking helps reduce uncertainty for the person doing the perception checking. Checking perceptions also can reduce anxiety for both people involved because it helps each recognize that their need for a shared view of the world is being met. Perception checking therefore increases the likelihood that we will communicate effectively.

Perception checking involves two processes. First, we have to describe what we think the other person's thoughts and/or feelings are. In doing this, we *must* refrain from evaluating the other person's thoughts or feelings. Second, we need to ask the other person if our perceptions are accurate. An example of a perception check would be "You look happy. Are you?" This statement describes our perception of the other person's feelings without any evaluation, and it asks the other person if our perception is correct. If we are not sure what the person feels we can still check our perceptions. To illustrate, the statement "I'm not sure from your expression whether you are hurt or angry. Which is it?" is a form of perception check.

Sometimes we may think we are checking our perceptions when we actually aren't. If we do not describe our perceptions without evaluation and ask if they are correct, we are not checking our perceptions. Only asking a question is not perception checking. "Are you angry with me?" and "Why are you mad at me?" are not perception checks. Speaking for the other person also is not checking our perceptions. If we said, "You're always depressed," we are not checking our perception. If we said "You look depressed. Are you?" we would be checking our perceptions. Also if we express a judgment we are not checking our perceptions. If someone expressed a feeling and we said "Why on earth would you feel that way?" we would not be checking our perception. We would be judging the other person's feeling.

There are a few important things to keep in mind about perception checking. If the person doing the perception checking does not change his or her perceptions when the other person says "No. I'm not feeling . . . ," then the perception check will not improve the quality of communication. Rather, it will inhibit the possibility of effective communication. The reason for this is that the other person will interpret the relational message being transmitted as the person doing the perception checking does not want to understand her or his feelings.

The person responding to the perception check also has a responsibility for the quality of the communication taking place. For communication to be effective, the person responding to the perception check needs to tell the truth. If someone says to us, "You appear angry. Are you?" we need to tell the truth. If we are angry and say no, then our anger will still influence the way we communicate. If we say no, then we have a responsibility to act as though we are not angry for communication to be effective.

Using Perception Checks. Checking our perceptions is *not* something most of us do in our everyday communication. Using this skill in your everyday communication with others may feel awkward at first because we do not have a script for perception checking. The more you do it, however, the more natural it will become. Also, the more you engage in perception checking, the more likely you will develop a script for doing it, and the more likely that it will become one of your resources for communication when you are on automatic pilot.

Perception checking is one of the simplest and most powerful techniques we can use to improve the quality of our communication. I am not suggesting that you use perception checking all of the time. Use it when you think that there is a chance that your perceptions may not be accurate or when it is important that you base your behavior on accurate perceptions. Also, it is important to keep in mind that perception checking involves direct communication and therefore has an individualistic bias. If you are an individualist communicating with a collectivist, it is important to keep in mind that collectivists may not feel comfortable answering direct questions. In this case, you may have to ask your perception checking questions indirectly.

LISTENING EFFECTIVELY

Carol Roach and Nancy Wyatt (1988) point out that listening is not a natural activity, it is not a passive activity as most of us assume, and most of us are not very skilled listeners. Hearing is natural, automatic process, whereas listening is the "process of discriminating and identifying which sounds are meaningful or important to us and which aren't" (p. 2). Successful listening, therefore, is a purposive activity (i.e., it requires that we are mindful). More specifically, "real listening involves taking in new information and checking it against what you already know, selecting important ideas from unimportant ideas, searching for categories to store the information in (or creating categories), and predicting what's coming next in order to be ready for it" (p. 4). Most of us need practice to be able to accomplish this.

Assessing Your Listening. Table 4.3 contains an assessment designed to help you assess your typical listening behavior. Take a few minutes to complete it now.

Scores on this questionnaire range from 10 to 50. The higher your score, the better listener you are. If your score is low, you can choose to listen more effectively when you are mindful of your communication behavior. When we are mindful, we need to try to engage in active listening.

Active Listening. Many writers recommend that we engage in active or empathic listening.[5] Carl Rogers (1980), for example, believes in entering "the private perceptual world of the other and becoming thoroughly at home in it. It involves being sensitive, moment by moment, to the changing felt needs which flow in this other person" (p. 142). There are three sets of interrelated skills involved in active listening: attending skills, following skills, and comprehending skills.[6]

Attending skills involve the ways that we attend to the person speaking. One thing we need to do is indicate to the speaker that we are involved in the conversation. This is accomplished by our body posture. If we are leaning backward with our arms crossed, the speaker will probably assume that we are not involved. If, in contrast, we lean forward and face the speaker, he or she will probably assume we are listening. Eye contact also is important. In the European American subculture "it involves focusing one's eyes softly on the speaker and occasionally shifting the gaze from his [or her] face to other parts of the body" (Bolton, 1990, p. 181). Attending requires that we give the other person our undivided

Table 4.3 Assessing Your Listening Behavior

The purpose of this questionnaire is to assess your listening behavior. Respond to each statement indicating the degree to which it is true regarding the way you generally listen: "Always False" (answer 1), "Usually False" (answer 2), "Sometimes False and Sometimes True" (answer 3), "Usually True" (answer 4), and "Always True" (answer 5).

_____ 1. I have a difficult time separating important and unimportant ideas when I listen to others.

_____ 2. I check new information against what I already know when I listen to others.

_____ 3. I have an idea what others will say when I listen to them.

_____ 4. I am sensitive to the other person's feelings when I listen to them.

_____ 5. I think about what I am going to say next when I listen to others.

_____ 6. I focus on the process of communication that is occurring between me and the other person when I listen to them.

_____ 7. I cannot wait for others to finish talking so I can take my turn.

_____ 8. I try to understand the meanings that are being created when I communicate with others.

_____ 9. I focus on determining whether others understand what I said when they are talking.

_____ 10. I ask others to elaborate when I am not sure what they mean.

To find your score, first reverse your responses for the odd-numbered items (i.e., if you wrote 1, make it 5; if you wrote 2, make it 4; if you wrote 3, leave it as 3; if you wrote 4, make it 2; if you wrote 5, make it 1). Next, add the numbers next to each statement. Scores range from 10 to 50. The higher your score, the better your listening behavior.

attention. To do this, the environment in which we are communicating needs to be nondistracting.

Following skills indicate to the other person that we are trying to understand her or his perspective. The first thing we need to do is give the other person time to speak. The other person needs time to decide whether she or he wants to talk and to decide what to say. This often requires that we be silent more than we would like. We also need to indicate to the other person that we are interested in what he or she has to say. We could begin, for example, by checking our perceptions and then asking the person to tell us more about his or her views. We can invite the other person to talk by saying "I'm interested in what you have to say" or "would you like to talk about it?" When we are listening we need to let the other person know we are paying attention and encourage her or him to continue speaking. This can be accomplished by saying things like "mm-hmm," "oh," "I see," and so forth.

Comprehending skills involve ways that we can understand the other person better. Perception checking (discussed earlier) is one method that we can use to better comprehend what others are saying. Another way we can make sure we are understanding the other person is to *paraphrase* what the other person is saying in our own words. By restating what the other person says in our own words, we ensure that we have not misinterpreted the other person's position. This can easily be accomplished by saying something like "I want to make sure I understand what you're saying . . . " The other thing we can do to increase our understanding is to use *probing questions*—questions designed to find out who, what, when, where, why, and how. We need to be careful, however, when we ask questions. If we ask too many questions, we end up dealing with our own agenda rather than understanding the other person.

Active listening can help us better understand others if we listen without presupposing any particular outcome and focus on what is being said as well as how it is being said in the conversation we are having. Stated differently, we must stop the internal monologue (e.g., thinking about what we are going to say next) that is going on in our heads (Howell, 1982).

Active listening obviously lengthens the amount of time it takes to have a conversation. There are other potential problems with the approach that stem from the fact that it is not the way we normally listen. Because most of us do not use active listening regularly, we do not have a script to guide us in active listening. Our initial attempts at active listening, therefore, may feel awkward. This is natural and to be expected. The more we practice active listening, however, the more natural it will feel. When we use active listening, others may wonder what is happening when we ask them to "say more" or when we paraphrase what they said. Whether or not they cooperate will have a lot to do with our attitude. If we demonstrate that we really want to understand them and are not just playing some game, it will increase the likelihood they will cooperate.

Active listening is a simple way to increase the effectiveness of our communication. Using this skill with members of other groups can help us better understand how group differences affect our communication.

FEEDBACK

We seek feedback from others and provide feedback on their communication when there is uncertainty present (Ashford & Cummings, 1983). *Feedback* refers to "the response listeners give to others about their behavior. . . . Feedback from others enables us to understand how our behavior affects them, and allows us to modify our behavior to achieve our desired goals" (Haslett & Ogilvie, 1988, p. 385). Feedback may be verbal or nonverbal. Affective or evaluative feedback tends to be given nonverbally, whereas cognitive or content feedback tends to be given verbally (Zajonc, 1980).

By paying attention to the feedback we receive and using it effectively, we engage in "a series of diminishing mistakes—a dwindling series of under-and-over corrections converging on the goal" (K. Deutsch, 1968, p. 390). To the extent that we use feedback effectively, we converge toward mutual understanding and shared meanings. If we do not receive feedback and use it effectively, however, we diverge from shared meanings and misunderstandings occur.

Guidelines for Giving Feedback. Beth Haslett and John Ogilvie (1988) provide concrete suggestions for giving effective feedback in the middle-class European American subculture. First, feedback should be direct and specific, and be supported by evidence (e.g., a rationale needs to be given). Indirect and vague feedback generally is not effective with people in the United States (especially in the middle-class subculture). Second, the issue on which the feedback is given needs to be separated from the person. Avoid judging the person being given feedback. Third, present the situation on which feedback is being given as a mutual problem (e.g., do not blame the other person for screwing up). Fourth, do

not overload someone with negative feedback; mix negative feedback with positive feedback. Fifth, provide the feedback at a time
close to the occurrence, but at a time the other person will be
receptive. If I am emotionally upset and unable to control my
anger, for example, it will not do any good to give me feedback
until I have calmed down. Sixth, deliver feedback in an assertive,
dynamic, responsive, and relaxed style. Finally, be trustworthy,
fair, credible, and preserve the other person's public image when
you give feedback.

There are three other things to keep in mind when giving
feedback. First, when we give feedback we need to use "I" statements. "I" statements are statements giving our own thoughts
and feelings. Second, we should focus our feedback in the "here
and now." If we bring up the past, it hinders the effectiveness of
our feedback. Third, the feedback we give others must be our
own. We need to avoid giving others feedback from third parties.
We cannot use "I" statements to give third party feedback.

Giving Intergroup Feedback. The suggestions for providing feedback outlined here are based on research with European Americans in the United States. Modifications are necessary when such
persons deal with others. Feedback always has to be appropriate
to the time, person, and our relationship with the other person.
When giving intergroup feedback, we also need to take into
consideration the other person's group memberships. How would
feedback be given in her or his group?

To illustrate, assume that I (a European American male) want
to present feedback to a Japanese male friend with whom I am
communicating in Japan. If I am direct in the feedback that I give
my friend, he may perceive my feedback as a threat to his public
image (i.e., it may threaten his face). The reason for this is that
Japanese try to preserve harmony in relations with friends. To
accomplish this, they use an indirect style of communication. If I
am direct and he perceives this as a threat, my feedback will be
ineffective. To provide culturally sensitive feedback, I have to be
indirect in the way I give it. If we are in the United States speaking
English, I can be more direct than if we are in Japan speaking
Japanese.

❏ Notes

1 Kelley (1972) uses an analysis of variance statistical analogy to explain this process.

2. See Pettigrew (1982) for a summary of the findings from over 100 studies of category width.

3. This summary is drawn from Sorrentino and Short (1986).

4. For a complete discussion of the cultural differences in how uncertainty is reduced, see Gudykunst and Ting-Toomey (1988).

5. See, for example, Roach and Wyatt (1988) and C. Rogers (1980).

6. My discussion is drawn in part from the work of Robert Bolton (1990).

Exchanging Messages
With Strangers

In the previous two chapters I examined our expectations for strangers' behavior and how we make sense of strangers' behavior. The focus of these chapters was on how we interpret strangers' messages to us. The focus of this chapter is on the messages we give to strangers. To place our intergroup messages in context, I begin by looking at cultural differences in language usage. Following this, I look at language usage in intergroup contexts. I conclude this chapter by examining those things we can do to improve the quality of the messages we transmit to strangers.

❏ Cultural Differences in Language Usage

Culture and language are highly interrelated. Our culture influences the language we speak, and how we use our language influences our culture. My focus in this section is on how our culture influences our use of language. I begin by looking at differences in beliefs about talk. Following this, I examine the use of direct and indirect messages. Next, I examine how topics are managed in conversations. I conclude this section with an overview of how culture influences the way we persuade others.

BELIEFS ABOUT TALK AND SILENCE

Beliefs about talk refer to our evaluations of the functions of talk and silence. There are many different beliefs about talk that we can hold. We can, for example, see talk as more important than silence. We also can hold different beliefs about the nature of the talk in which we engage. To place these various beliefs in context, I begin with how culture influences the importance we place on talk.

Importance of Talk. John Wiemann, Victoria Chen, and Howard Giles (1986) contend that European Americans see talk as more important and enjoyable than native-born Chinese or Chinese Americans. European Americans are more likely than the other two groups to initiate conversations with others and to engage in conversations when opportunities present themselves. Chinese Americans are more likely to engage in these activities than native-born Chinese. European Americans also see talk as a means of social control, whereas native-born Chinese see silence as a control strategy.

Harry Triandis (cited in Giles, N. Coupland, & Wiemann, 1992) argues that the differences in beliefs about talk between Chinese and European Americans are due to individualism-collectivism:

> Individualists have a choice among many groups . . . to which they do belong, and usually belong to these groups because they volunteer. Collectivists . . . are born into a few groups and are more or less stuck with them. So, the collectivists do not have to go out of their way and exert themselves to be accepted, while individualists have to

work hard to be accepted. Hence, the individualists often speak more, try to control the situation verbally, and do not value silence. (p. 11)

This should not be taken to suggest that collectivists do not engage in small talk or gossip, because they do. Collectivists, however, do not see talk as important in developing relationships with others as individualists.

Silence. One belief about talk that we can hold is that silence is an important part of communication. In individualistic cultures like the United States, silence often is viewed as the opposite of sound. Many people in individualistic cultures have a low tolerance for silence; it is something to be filled in conversations.

Silence is viewed differently in collectivistic cultures. It is viewed as an important part of communication. Takie Sugiyama Lebra (1987), for example, isolates four meanings of what can be conveyed by silence in Japan: truthfulness, social discretion, embarrassment, and defiance. Lebra argues that Japanese view truth as occurring only in the inner realms. Activities regarding the outer self do not involve an individual's true feelings and therefore frequently involve distortion, deception, or "moral falsity." A person who speaks little is trusted more than a person who speaks a lot. Truthfulness emerges from silences, not words, in Japan. Silence also allows Japanese to be socially discreet. "Social discretion refers to silence considered necessary or desirable in order to gain social acceptance or to avoid social penalty" (Lebra, 1987, p. 347). At times, talking may be dangerous and require that the person tell the truth. In these instances, silence allows the person to avoid social disapproval. Silence also saves Japanese from embarrassment. Verbally expressing emotions to each other, for example, may cause a married couple to become embarrassed. A person also may indicate disagreement or anger with someone else by being silent.

Exaggeration. Not valuing talk and valuing silence is one belief about talk that we can hold. We also have beliefs about the nature of the talk in which people should engage. Should our talk be succinct, should it be elaborate, or should it be exaggerated?

The forms of assertion and exaggeration used in the Arabic language clearly illustrate the use of exaggeration in communication:

The built-in mechanism of assertion in language affects the Arabs' communication behavior in at least two ways. First, an Arab feels compelled to overassert in almost all types of communication because others expect him [or her] to. If an Arab says exactly what he [or she] means without the expected assertion, other Arabs may still think that he [or she] means the opposite. For example, a simple "No" by a guest to the host's request to eat more or drink more will not suffice. To convey the meaning that he [or she] is actually full, the guest must keep repeating "No" several times, coupling it with an oath such as "By God" or "I swear to God." Second, an Arab often fails to realize that others, particularly foreigners, may mean exactly what they say even though their language is simple. To the Arabs, a simple "No" may mean the indirectly expressed consent and encouragement of a coquettish woman. On the other hand, a simple consent may mean the rejection of a hypocritical politician. (Almaney & Alwan, 1982, p. 84)

The Arab proclivity to use verbal exaggerations is probably responsible for more diplomatic misunderstandings between the United States and Arab countries than any other single factor (Cohen, 1987).

Assessing Your Beliefs About Talk. Table 5.1 contains a questionnaire designed to help you assess your beliefs about talk and silence. Take a few minutes to complete it now.

Scores on the questionnaire range from 10 to 50. The higher your score, the more important you see talk to be in expressing your identity. Neither high nor low scores on this questionnaire are necessarily more desirable. It is important, however, to remember that if your score is high, you may have problems communicating with strangers who do not value talk as much as you do. Also, if you score is low, you may have problems communicating with people who value talk more than you do. Either way, to increase your effectiveness you must be mindful of your communication and recognize group-based differences in orientations toward talk and silence.

Table 5.1 Assessing Your Beliefs About Talk

The purpose of this questionnaire is to help you assess your beliefs about talk. Respond to each statement regarding the degree to which you agree or disagree with the statement. If you strongly disagree with the statement, answer 1; if you disagree, answer 2; if you neither agree or disagree, answer 3; if you agree, answer 4; if you strongly agree, answer 5.

_____ 1. I enjoy talking when I find myself in social situations.
_____ 2. I do not enjoy small talk.
_____ 3. I try to break the ice by talking when I first meet others.
_____ 4. I view people who are reticent positively.
_____ 5. I could talk for hours at a time.
_____ 6. I do not enjoy talking with others.
_____ 7. I think that untalkative people are boring.
_____ 8. I do not trust the words people use when they talk.
_____ 9. I judge people by how well they speak.
_____ 10. I do not talk when I have nothing important to say.

To obtain your score, first reverse the answers you gave to the even-numbered items (i.e., if you answered 1, make it a 5; if you answered 2, make it a 4; if you answered 3, leave it a 3; if you answered 4, make it a 2; if you answered 5, make it a 1). Once you have reversed the even-numbered items, add the responses for the items. Your score will range from 10 to 50. The higher your score, the more you value talk as a way of communicating.

DIRECT VERSUS INDIRECT LANGUAGE USAGE

When we want to assert ourselves as unique persons (individualism), we must be direct so that others will know where we stand. To tell others who they are, individualists must be direct. If, on the other hand, our goal is to maintain harmony in the ingroup (collectivism), we cannot be direct because we might offend another member of the ingroup. To maintain harmony, collectivists need to be cautious and indirect.

Cultural Differences in Direct Language Usage. Roichi Okabe (1983) contends that analytic thinking tends to predominate in the United States, whereas synthetic thinking tends to predominate in Japan. *Analytic thinking* involves looking at parts rather than focusing on the whole. *Synthetic thinking,* in contrast, involves trying to grasp things in their totality, in their suchness. Constructing low-context messages requires analytic thinking, whereas constructing high-context messages involves synthetic thinking. Analytic thinking leads to the use of linear logic when talking or writing because it is necessary to specify how the parts are related to each other. Synthetic thinking leads to a more dotlike logic. "The speaker organizes his or her ideas in a stepping-stone mode: The listener is supposed to supply what is left unsaid" (Okabe, 1983, p. 29).

Okabe (1983) illustrates cultural differences in direct and indirect forms of communication by further comparing the United States and Japan:

> Reflecting the cultural value of precision, [U.S.] Americans' tendency to use explicit words is the most noteworthy in their communicative style. They prefer to employ such categorical words as "absolutely," "certainty," and "positively." . . . The English syntax dictates that the absolute "I" be placed at the beginning of the sentence in most cases, and that the subject-predicate relation be constructed in an ordinary sentence. . . . By contrast, the cultural assumptions of interdependence and harmony require that Japanese speakers limit themselves to implicit and even ambiguous use of words. In order to avoid leaving an assertive impression, they like to depend more frequently on qualifiers such as "maybe," "perhaps," "probably," and "somewhat." Since Japanese syntax does not require the use of a subject in a sentence, the qualifier-predicate is the predominant form of sentence construction. (p. 36)

These differences often are manifested even when Japanese speak in English and North Americans speak in Japanese.

Language use in Puerto Rico (a collectivistic, high-context culture) shares many commonalities with the Asian cultures. Marshall Morris (1981) draws five generalizations about the use of discourse in Puerto Rico:

1. In Puerto Rican society, one's place and one's sense of oneself depends on an even, disciplined, and unthreatening style of behavior.

2. In language one must take great care not to put oneself or others at risk, and one must reduce the risk of confrontation to the lowest degree possible. This implies a systematic blurring of meaning—that is, imprecision and indirectness.

3. This implies a constant problem of interpretation, testing, probing, second-guessing, and investigation, but conducted indirectly.
4. The personal value of the individual—and so the validity of his [or her] words—will be determined by what he [or she] actually *does*, not what he [or she] says.
5. Information does not come in discrete "bits," but as complex indicators of fluid human relationships, the "bits" being inextricable from the constant, implicit negotiation of meaning. (pp. 135-136)

As with other forms of indirect communication, what is not said may be as important as what is said in Puerto Rico.

Indirectness in Individualistic Cultures. Before proceeding, it is important to recognize that indirectness occurs in individualistic cultures like the United States too. The reasons for indirectness in individualistic cultures like that of the United States, however, appear to be different than that in collectivistic cultures. John Condon (1984) quotes a professional interpreter in Japan as saying that

[U.S.] Americans can be just as indirect as the Japanese, but they are indirect about different things, and being indirect carries a different meaning. [U.S.] Americans are usually indirect when something very sensitive is being discussed or when they are nervous about how the other person might react. Whenever [U.S.] Americans are indirect, I suspect that *something* is going on!
    Japanese indirectness is a part of our way of life. It is not because we are such kind and considerate people that we worry so about other's reactions. It is just that we know our own fates and fortunes are always bound up with others. I think you can value directness when you value individualism, or when you are with people you know and trust completely. (pp. 43-44)

North Americans are indirect at times and Japanese also are direct (most frequently in close friendships).

Assessing Your Direct and Indirect Tendencies. Table 5.2 contains a questionnaire designed to help you assess your tendency to use direct or indirect forms of communication. Take a few minutes to complete it now.

Table 5.2 Assessing Your Direct and Indirect Communication Style

---

The purpose of this questionnaire is to help you assess your tendency to be direct or indirect when you communicate. Respond to each statement regarding the degree to which you agree or disagree with the statement. If you strongly disagree with the statement, answer 1; if you disagree, answer 2; if you neither agree or disagree, answer 3; if you agree, answer 4; if you strongly agree, answer 5.

_____ 1. I hint at what I want when I communicate.
_____ 2. I can talk about personal information with most people.
_____ 3. I am able to recognize subtle and indirect messages easily.
_____ 4. I often try to persuade others when I communicate with them.
_____ 5. I qualify my language (e.g., use "maybe," "perhaps") when I communicate.
_____ 6. I avoid ritualistic forms of communication when I talk with others.
_____ 7. I focus on what others are not saying more than what they are saying when we communicate.
_____ 8. I openly disagree with others when I communicate.
_____ 9. I expect others to infer my opinion when we communicate.
_____ 10. I am not ambiguous when I communicate with others.

To obtain your score, first reverse the answers you gave to the odd-numbered items (i.e., if you answered 1, make it a 5; if you answered 2, make it a 4; if you answered 3, leave it a 3; if you answered 4, make it a 2; if you answered 5, make it a 1). Once you have reversed the odd-numbered items, add the responses for the items. Your score will range from 10 to 50. The higher your score, the more you are direct when you communicate; the lower your score, the more indirect you tend to be.

Scores on the questionnaire range from 10 to 50. The higher your score, the more direct your communication. As with beliefs about talk, neither high nor low scores are necessarily desirable. It is important to remember, however, that if your score is high or low you may have problems communicating with someone who has the opposite tendency. If you find yourself in this situation, you need to be mindful of your communication and try to figure out how to adapt your communication to communicate more successfully (adapting communication is discussed in more detail in the next chapter).

TOPIC MANAGEMENT AND TURN TAKING IN CONVERSATIONS

The ways that we take turns and manage topics in conversations also differ across cultures. Individualism-collectivism influences topic management and turn distribution in conversations.[1] Japanese (collective), for example, "take short turns, distribute their turns relatively evenly, and continue to distribute their turns evenly regardless of who initiates a topic" (Yamada, 1990, p. 291). North Americans (individualists), in contrast, "take long monologic turns, distribute their turns unevenly, and the participant who initiates a topic characteristically takes the highest proportion of turns in that topic" (p. 291). Collectivists organize topics interdependently, whereas individualists organize topics independently.

> *Collectivists organize topics interdependently, whereas individualists organize topics independently.*

The way we manage conversations also is affected by individualism-collectivism. Collectivists use verbal and nonverbal complementary expressions and repetition to support others when they speak and maintain negotiations. Individualists, in contrast, use less synchronizing behaviors and repetition. Individualists tend to use feedback devices (e.g., questions, comments) to indicate they are attentive, whereas collectivists tend to use back-channeling (e.g., brief utterances that make conversation flow smoothly) to accomplish this purpose. To illustrate, when North American "speakers orient attention, they focus on the specific topical content. Japanese speakers only value the emphatic interactional behavior and tend to consider the message exchange secondary" (Hayashi, 1990, p. 188).

Collectivists send backchannel signals to the person with whom they are communicating more than individualists (e.g., White, 1989). Backchannel signals are the verbalizations we use to tell the other person that we are listening. To the extent that people are competent in using the backchanneling techniques of other cultures when speaking their language, effective communication is facilitated (LoCastro, 1987).

PERSUASIVE STRATEGIES

Another important aspect of verbal communication that varies across cultures is how we try to persuade others. Members of collectivistic cultures take the context into consideration and select strategies that are appropriate to the context. Members of individualistic cultures, in contrast, focus on the person they are trying to persuade and use strategies that may be perceived as socially inappropriate (Gudykunst & Ting-Toomey, 1988).

To illustrate the differences in persuasive strategy selection, consider Randy Hirokawa and Akira Miyahara's (1986) comparison of the strategies managers in corporations in the United States and Japan use to persuade their subordinates in two situations. The first situation involves the manager trying to persuade consistently tardy employees to change their behavior. Japanese managers indicate that they appeal to the employees' duty (e.g., "It is your duty as a responsible employee of this company to begin work on time."). North American managers prefer to threaten the employees (e.g., "If you don't start reporting to work on time, I will have no choice but to dock your pay.") or to give an ultimatum (e.g., "If you can't come to work on time, go find yourself another job.").

The second situation involves how the manager persuades employees to give their ideas and suggestions to the manager. Japanese managers prefer to use altruistic strategies (e.g., "For the sake of the company, please share your ideas and suggestions with us.") or appeal to duty (e.g., "Remember that it is your duty as a good company employee to suggest how we can improve the overall performance of the company."). North American managers prefer to make direct requests (e.g., "I want you to feel free to come to me with any ideas you have for improving the company."), to make promises (e.g., "Don't hesitate to offer ideas and suggestions because we always reward good suggestions."), or to ingratiate themselves with the employees (e.g., "You are one of our best people and I really value your judgment, so please feel free to come to me with ideas you have.").

❏ Language Usage in Communicating With Strangers

Cross-cultural variations in languages and verbal communication styles influence how people from different cultures communicate. There also are language variations within cultures that influence the way we communicate. Each of us, for example, speaks a *dialect*. "Dialect refers to all the differences between varieties of a language, those in pronunciation, word usage, and syntax" (Chaika, 1982, p. 132). Sometimes the difference between language and dialect is not clear-cut. Elaine Chaika (1982) points out that

> political boundaries, in themselves, often determine whether two speech varieties will be considered different languages or not. For instance, some varieties of Swedish and Norwegian are mutually comprehensible, but they are considered different languages because they are separated by national borders. Conversely, the so-called dialects of Chinese are as different as French from Italian, but being spoken in one country they are not considered different languages. (p. 133)

Chaika (1982) argues that how we speak is tied closely to how we define ourselves. In highly mobile cultures like the United States, "speech is likely to be the most reliable determiner of social class or ethnic group" (p. 139).

There are several aspects of language and dialect usage that are important in understanding our communication with strangers. Our attitudes toward other languages and dialects influence how we respond to others, whether we learn other languages, when we use other languages or dialects, and whether we accommodate to people with whom we are communicating. I begin the discussion of language usage in communicating with strangers by looking at attitudes toward language usage.

LANGUAGE ATTITUDES

The language or dialect we speak influences how others judge us and whether they are willing to help us. The dialect we speak influences whether others will help us (Gaertner & Bickman, 1971). People speaking a standard dialect are more likely to receive help on the phone than people speaking an ethnic dialect. Speakers using a standard dialect also are rated higher on competence, intelligence, industriousness, and confidence than speakers using a nonstandard dialect (see Bradac, 1990, for a review). Our language attitudes are influenced by our stereotypes, the situation in which the language is used, and our social class. Our social class also influences language attitudes. Speaking properly

> is a matter of great concern to the educated middle class, which above all wishes to be identified as educated. Its members' being recognized as those to be listened to hinges strongly on language. When people say they want to know the right way to speak, they do not mean the right way to communicate their ideas, but rather the right way to announce that those ideas are to be respected, to be listened to. (Chaika, 1982, p. 239)

Class differences in language usage were outlined in Chapter 2. Our language attitudes can be characterized in terms of two interrelated dimensions, standardization and vitality:

> Standardization is the more static dimension, referring to the extent to which norms for correct usage . . . have been codified, adopted, and promoted for a particular variety. This might be accomplished through the compilation of dictionaries and grammars while the acceptance of a variety may be advanced by elites and government. . . . Vitality is the more dynamic dimension, reflecting the range and importance of functions served by language varieties . . . and the social pressures toward shift in language use. (Ryan, Hewstone, & Giles, 1984, pp. 143-144)

Changes in our language attitudes are due mostly to changes in perceived vitality (Ryan et al., 1984). Vitality refers to the range and importance of the functions of our language or dialect for communication (Giles et al., 1977). As we perceive the vitality of a language or dialect increasing, we view its use more positively.

SECOND-LANGUAGE COMPETENCE

There are numerous explanations of second-language learning (see Gardner, 1985, for reviews of major theories), but only the intergroup model takes into consideration the intergroup factors relevant to second-language learning. Howard Giles and Jane Byrne (1982) argue that second-language learning cannot be explained unless the relations between the groups are taken into consideration. Peter Garrett, Howard Giles, and Nikolas Coupland

(1989) isolate factors that contribute to members of a "minority" group learning the language of the "dominant" group.

If members of minority groups identify weakly with their group or do not view language as an important part of their identity, they are likely to try to learn the dominant language. If members of minority groups view their language as an important part of their identity, they will try to learn the dominant language to the extent that it does not threaten their identity. Further, if members of minority groups perceive few alternatives to their "subordinate" status and view the chance of it changing as small, they will try to learn the dominant language. They will also try to learn the dominant language if they perceive cognitive alternatives to their status and realize that these can be met by learning the dominant language.

Members of minority groups will try to learn the dominant language to the extent that they perceive the boundaries between their group and the dominant group to be soft and open. If they believe that learning the dominant language will help them be accepted in the dominant group, they will try to learn the language. Members of minority groups will try to learn the dominant language to the extent that they derive satisfactory social identities from other group memberships. That is, they are members of other social categories that provide them with satisfactory identities. If members of minority groups perceive the vitality of their group to be low, they will attempt to learn the dominant group language. They also will try to learn the dominant language if they believe learning it will contribute to the vitality of their ingroup.

In addition to the intergroup factors, Garrett et al. (1989) isolate sociolinguistic factors that contribute to second-language learning. First, the more similar the dominant language and the majority language, the more likely members of minorities are to learn the dominant language. Second, there must be exposure to the dominant language for it to be learned (e.g., members of the minority group must have contact with speakers of the dominant language). Third, members of the minority group need to have the opportunity to use the dominant language in a variety of contexts.

COMMUNICATION ACCOMMODATION

Henri Tajfel (1978) suggests that when we interact with strangers, we compare ourselves on a number of value dimensions with the strangers. Our intergroup social comparisons lead us to search for characteristics of our own group that will enable us to differentiate ourselves favorably from the outgroup. Such positive ingroup distinctiveness not only allows us personal satisfaction in our group membership, but it also helps us form a positive social identity. Applying this psychological process to speech behavior, Howard Giles (1973) describes the tendency to accentuate (e.g., emphasize) linguistic difference as *speech divergence.* Some individuals in interaction with others shift their speech in their desire for their listeners' social approval. One tactic, consciously or unconsciously conceived, is for them to modify their speech in the direction of the listeners' speech patterns, a process Giles terms *speech convergence.*

Howard Giles and his colleagues (1977) suggest that when members of a subordinate group accept their inferior status, they attempt to converge into the dominant group socially and psychologically by means of speech convergence. If, on the other hand, members of subordinate groups consider their inferior status to be illegitimate and the intergroup situation to be unstable, they seek psychological distinctiveness by redefining their group attributes in a socially and psychologically more favorable direction. This can be accomplished linguistically by accentuating ingroup characteristics by means of speech divergence using the group's dialect, accent, jargon, or other form of speech variation.

We have a tendency to react favorably to outgroup members who linguistically converge toward us (Giles & Smith, 1979). This, however, is not always the case. Giles and Byrne (1982) point out that as an outgroup's members begin to learn the speech style of our ingroup, we may diverge in some way to maintain our linguistic distinctiveness. Our reaction to outgroup members' speech convergence depends on the intent we attribute to the outgroup members. If we perceive their intent to be positive, we evaluate their convergence positively.

Our evaluation of outgroup members' language usage in conversations is based on situational norms in the initial stages of conversations and on interpersonal accommodation later in the conversation (Genesse & Bourhis, 1982). Richard Bourhis (1985) argues that following situational norms is the strategy we use most frequently in early stages of hostile intergroup encounters. In later stages of conversations, however, we adopt strategies based on our goals, our desire to assert our group identity, and our affective response to the other person.

Howard Giles and colleagues (1986) argue that communication convergence is a function of a speaker's desire for (a) social approval, (b) high communication efficiency, (c) shared self- or group presentation, and (d) an appropriate identity definition. For communication convergence to occur, there also needs to be a match between the speaker's view of the recipient's speech style and the actual style used, and the specific speech style used must be appropriate for both speaker and recipient. Divergence, in contrast, is a function of the speaker's desire (a) for a contrastive self-image, (b) to dissociate from the recipient, (c) to change the recipient's speech behavior, and (d) to define an encounter in intergroup terms. Divergence also occurs when recipients use a speech style that deviates from a norm that is valued and consistent with the speaker's expectations regarding the recipient's performance. If strangers accommodate to our communication style and we perceive their intent to be positive, it will reduce our uncertainty and anxiety in communicating with them.

CODE SWITCHING

The code (i.e., language or dialect) we use is, in part, a function of the vitality of the languages or dialects involved, and our desire to accommodate to the person with whom we are communicating.[2] There are also normative factors that contribute to our code choice. Immigrants in the United States, for example, use English in public formal settings, but their native language in informal, nonpublic settings. Similarly, the topic of conversation affects the code used. Immigrants tend to use their native language when discussing stressful or exciting topics and when discussing life in the native country. Using the first language to discuss life in the native country reinforces cultural heritage and fills a need to "identify with compatriots" (Chaika, 1982, p. 239).

In addition to the topic of conversation and the setting, people may switch languages to show warmth and group identification (Gumperz & Hernandez-Chavez, 1972). Recall Richard Rodriguez's explanation of the effect of speaking in Spanish on his feelings of being bonded to his family presented in the ethnic identity section of Chapter 2. We might also switch codes to increase the distance between ourselves and others (Scotton, 1993). Chaika (1982) points out that people sometimes switch codes for emphasis or to see if a stranger belongs to the ingroup. She argues that

> the switch from one language to another, in itself, has meaning. No matter what else a switch means, it reinforces bonds between speakers. Such switching can obviously only occur between those who speak the same language. It may be done in the presence of nonspeakers as a way of excluding them, just as jargon may. (p. 238)

The language or dialect people select thus reinforces their social identities.

❑ Improving the Quality of Our Messages

There are several things we can do to improve the quality of the messages we transmit to strangers. We must, for example, adapt our messages to the person interpreting them (this is discussed in the next chapter). We also need to avoid being aggressive. Rather, we need to construct messages that are assertive, confirming, and inclusive.

BEING ASSERTIVE, NOT AGGRESSIVE

Dominic Infante (1987) defines *verbal aggressiveness* as "the tendency to attack the self-concepts of individuals instead of, or in addition to, their positions on topics of communication" (p. 164). All verbal aggressiveness involves a hostile response to others, but not all hostility involves attacking others' self-concepts. A verbally aggressive message is one designed to cause others pain or to make them think less favorably about themselves. We sometimes refer to these messages as put-downs. We are *not* necessarily conscious of our intention to put down others when we are verbally aggressive.

Infante (1988) points out that what is considered to be verbally aggressive depends on the individuals involved, who is observing the behavior, and the culture in which the interaction takes place. We may intend to be verbally aggressive, but the person with whom we are communicating may not perceive the message as aggressive. Alternatively, we may *not* intend to be verbally aggressive, but the person with whom we are communicating perceives that he or she is being attacked.

Infante (1988) isolates several ways that we can be verbally aggressive: (a) character attacks, (b) competence attacks, (c) background attacks, (d) physical appearance attacks, (e) insults, (f) maledictions (speaking evil of others), (g) teasing, (h) ridicule, (i) profanity, (j) threats, and (k) nonverbal indicators (e.g., shaking a clenched fist, giving "the finger," rolling eyes, deep sigh). Infante contends that we should not underestimate our use of verbal aggressiveness. Engaging in verbal aggressiveness can lead to (a) damaged self-concepts, (b) hurt feelings, (c) anger, (d) irritation, (e) embarrassment, (f) relationship deterioration, (g) relationship termination, and (h) physical violence (Infante, 1988).

There are at least four causes of verbal aggression (Infante, 1988). First, verbal aggressiveness may be due to a mental disorder. Repressed hostility, for example, can lead to verbal aggressiveness. Second, feelings of disdain for others may cause us to be verbally aggressive. If we do not like others, we may be aggressive in our communication with them. This issue is discussed in more detail in the section on moral inclusiveness in Chapter 3. Third, we may have been socialized to be aggressive. Males in the United States, for example, are taught "to be competitive, forceful, dominant, and aggressive. Females have been taught to be more submissive, less assertive, nice, and nonaggressive" (Infante, 1988, p. 26). Fourth, verbal aggressiveness may be due to a lack of skills for handling disagreements. This issue will be examined in more detail when I discuss managing conflict in the last chapter.

Although aggressive communicators usually achieve their goals, the person with whom they are aggressive does not, and this person frequently feels hurt, defensive, or humiliated (Alberti & Emmons, 1986). The alternative to aggressiveness is assertiveness. *Assertiveness* involves communicating in a way that indicates that we are standing up for our rights, but not trampling on the rights of others (Alberti & Emmons, 1986). Assertive communicators act in their own best interests, and they state their opinions and express their feelings directly and honestly. They express themselves in a way that is personally satisfying and socially effective.

Verbally, assertiveness involves (a) stating our wants, (b) honestly expressing our feelings, (c) using objective words (e.g., describing others' behavior, not interpreting it; this process is discussed in detail in the next chapter), (d) using direct statements of what we mean, and (e) using "I" messages (e.g., "I felt angry," not "You made me angry"; Bloom, Coburn, & Pearlman, 1975). Nonverbally, assertiveness involves attentive listening behavior (discussed in Chapter 4 on listening) and communicating care for the other person (Bloom et al., 1975).

When we are assertive we need to own our own messages. One way to do this is speaking for ourselves using "I" messages. We speak for ourselves when we use personal pronouns like "I," "my," and "mine." When we indicate that "I think..." or I feel...," we are clearly owning our own thoughts and feelings. When we use the generic "you," or words like "some people" instead, it is not clear whose ideas are being expressed.

It is important to recognize that what constitutes assertive behavior is "*person-and-situation specific*" (Alberti & Emmons, 1986). How we perceive assertive behavior depends on the sex and the culture of the communicator. When males and females engage in exactly the same assertive behavior, males often are evaluated more positively (e.g., in terms of likability, attractiveness, and competence) than females (Stewart, Stewart, Friedley, & Cooper, 1990). In some collectivistic cultures (e.g., Japan, Korea), reticence (e.g., nonassertiveness) is prized.[3] What is perceived as assertive behavior in the United States might be perceived as aggressive behavior in some collectivistic cultures. This suggests that individualists need to adapt their assertive messages when communicating with collectivists to be effective. The adaptations necessary, however, depend on the specific individuals communicating. Individualists, for example, may have to use a more indirect, rather than direct, style of communication. They also would need to understand that when collectivists say "We think . . . ," they may really mean "I think." Similarly, collectivists need to adapt their behavior to communicate effectively with individualists. They will need to be more assertive than they are when communicating with other collectivists.

BEING CONFIRMING

Martin Buber (1958) contends that confirmation is the most fundamental human need. *Confirmation* is "the process through which individuals are recognized, acknowledged, and endorsed" (Laing, 1961, p. 83). Confirming messages involve four components: (a) recognizing the other person, (b) responding to the other person's messages, (c) accepting the other person's experiences as real, and (d) indicating to the other person a willingness to be involved with her or him (Sieburg, 1975). The relationship component of confirming messages implies three meanings: (a) "You exist," (b) "I acknowledge your way of experiencing," and (c) "We are relating" (Sieburg, 1975, pp. 4-10).

Disconfirmation occurs when others are denied, their experiences are denied, or their significance is denied (Cissna & Sieburg, 1981). Characteristics of disconfirming communication include (a) not recognizing the other person, (b) not acknowledging a relationship with the other person, (c) not accepting the other person's experiences, and (d) denying the validity of the other person's experiences (Cissna & Sieburg, 1981). The relationship component of disconfirming messages sends three relational meanings: (a) "You do not exist," (b) "I do not acknowledge your experiences," and (c) "We are not relating."

We confirm or disconfirm others by the words we choose to use when we talk to them and the way that we say what we do. Our relational messages define the relationship between us and others. We often are not aware of how others interpret our relational messages. We may not intend to send a disconfirming message, but the other person may interpret what we say or how we say it to be disconfirming. This can be especially problematic in our communication with strangers because they may interpret the relational component of our messages differently than we do. We need to make sure that our messages are interpreted as confirming by strangers. This requires us to be mindful of our communication and watch for signs that strangers may be interpreting our messages as disconfirming.

CREATING INCLUSIVE MESSAGES

As indicated in the previous section, the words we use can disconfirm others. The words we use also influence how we think about members of other groups. If we consistently use male terms and pronouns to refer to people in different occupations (e.g., the physician, he . . . ; policeman), for example, it affects the way we think about the occupations to which we refer.[4] To illustrate, if we use the term "mailman," for example, we will think of all people who deliver the mail as men. This obviously is not the case. Women deliver the mail too. The inclusive term we can use instead of mailman is "mail carrier." By inclusive language I am referring to language that makes everyone feel included. This may seem like a small thing, but our language usage clearly influences our attitudes toward and thoughts about particular groups.

Consistently using male pronouns disconfirms women. There also are many ethnic stereotypes we use in our everyday language (e.g., "Jew someone down") that disconfirm members of the ethnic groups involved and idioms referring to disabilities (e.g., "the blind leading the blind") that disconfirm disabled people. To be confirming when we communicate with members of different groups we need to avoid the use of these terms and idioms. We all use noninclusive language in our everyday communication. To the extent that we can minimize our use of noninclusive language, we can be more confirming to others. To the extent that we use inclusive language, we can decrease the influence of our stereotypes on our communication.

Being inclusive also involves referring to strangers in a way that they want to be called. Sometimes we try to avoid the use of group labels when we talk about or to members of other ethnic groups. One reason for this is that we may want to down-play group differences. This strategy works well when we are interacting with members of other groups who do not identify strongly with their group. Playing down group differences, however, does not work well when we are interacting with members of other groups who identify strongly with their group. Another reason we may try to avoid the use of group labels is that we may want to try to focus on similarities rather than differences. This strategy never works well. To communicate effectively with others we must understand both the differences and the similarities between us and them. If we focus exclusively on the similarities, the differences become all the more problematic when they arise (I discuss the issue of similarities and differences in more detail in the next chapter).

Rather than ignoring group labels, it is important for us to understand how members of other groups want us to refer to them. I do *not* mean to suggest that we should use politically correct labels. We must, however, support others' self-concepts if we want to develop closer relationships with them (this issue is discussed in more detail in Chapter 7). Calling others what they want to be called and recognizing their group memberships is part of supporting their self-concepts.

❏ Notes

1. The examples presented are drawn from Japanese-U.S. American conversations, but I believe these patterns will generalize to other collectivistic and individualistic cultures.

2. See Gudykunst, Ting-Toomey, Hall, and Schmidt (1989) and Sachdev and Bourhis (1990) for sources for the arguments made here.

3. In some collectivistic cultures, aggressive behavior may be prized in some situations (e.g., *machismo* in Latin cultures leads to aggressive behavior toward females by males being acceptable).

4. See the references in Chapter 3 in my discussion of sexism.

6

Being Perceived
as a Competent Communicator

The purpose of this chapter is to look at what it means to be perceived as a competent communicator in intergroup encounters. I begin by defining perceived communication competence. Following this, I examine the three components of perceived competence: motivation, knowledge, and skills.

❑ Defining Perceived Competence

John Wiemann and James Bradac (1989) point out that in everyday usage competence implies adequate, sufficient, and/or suitable. Given this usage, we see people who get by and manage to avoid the pitfalls and traps of communication as competent communicators. Misinterpreting others' messages is one of the major pitfalls or traps in the communication process. If we consistently misinterpret others' messages, our communication is not adequate

159

or sufficient; effective communication requires that misunderstandings are minimized.[1]

Suitability implies that our communication is appropriate; we communicate in ways that meet the minimum contextual requirements of the situation in which we find ourselves. There are at least three aspects of the context that are important in determining appropriateness:

1. The verbal context, that is, making sense in terms of wording, of statements, and of topic
2. The relationship context, that is, the structuring, type and style of messages so that they are consonant with the particular relationship at hand
3. The environmental context, that is, the consideration of constraints imposed on message making by the symbolic and physical environments (Wiemann & Backlund, 1980, p. 119)

Our perceptions of competence vary across contexts. Former President Reagan, for example, is perceived as very competent when delivering canned speeches (i.e., he is called the "great" communicator). At the same time, President Reagan is not perceived as highly competent in answering questions extemporaneously at news conferences.

COMPETENCE AS IMPRESSIONS

Our view of our communication competence may not be the same as that of the person with whom we are communicating. I, for example, might see myself as a very competent communicator, but when you and I interact you may perceive me as incompetent. An observer might have still a different perception of my competence. Understanding communication competence, therefore, minimally requires that we take into consideration our own and the other person's perspective.

If we can have different views of our competence than the people with whom we are communicating, then competence is an impression we have of ourselves and others. Stated differently, "competence is not something intrinsic to a person's nature or behavior" (Spitzberg & Cupach, 1984, p. 115). There are several implications of this view of competence:

> First, competence does not actually reside in the performance; it is an *evaluation* of the performance by someone. . . . Second, the fact that *someone* is making the evaluation means that it is subject to error, bias, and judgment inferences; different judges using the same criteria may evaluate the performance differently. Third, since the evaluation always must be made with reference to some set of implicit or explicit *criteria*, the evaluation cannot be understood or validated without knowledge of the criteria being employed; thus, the same performance may be judged to be competent by one standard and incompetent by another. (R. McFall, 1982, pp. 13-14)

This view of competence clearly suggests that the specific skills we have do not ensure that we will be perceived as competent in any particular interaction. Our skills, however, do increase the likelihood that we are able to adapt our behavior so that others see us as competent (Wiemann & Bradac, 1989).

If people from different cultures use the same criteria (e.g., appropriateness) to judge a person's competence, they may still evaluate the same performance differently. Consider the example at the end of Chapter 4 of the Japanese asking "How old are you?" during an initial interaction with a North American. Another Japanese observing this interaction would likely evaluate the Japanese speaker's question as appropriate. The North American who is asked the question, in contrast, is likely to see the question as inappropriate.

The standards people use to judge competence also vary across cultures. Raymonde Carroll (1988), for example, argues that the French value animated conversations that are fast moving with frequent interruptions. Often, the speakers ask questions and do not wait for answers. North Americans, however, prefer fuller answers to questions, less interruptions, and more continuity in the conversation than the French. The French may interpret North American conversation and readiness to discuss serious topics in social gatherings as inappropriate (and incompetent) because in France serious conversations occur in contexts other than social situations and require a strong commitment between individuals.

North Americans, however, may view the French style of frequent interruptions and short answers to their questions as inappropriate and therefore incompetent.

COMPONENTS OF COMPETENCE

Brian Spitzberg and William Cupach (1984) isolate three components of communication competence: motivation, knowledge, and skills. *Motivation* refers to our desire to communicate appropriately and effectively with others. Of particular importance to the present analysis is our motivation to communicate with people who are different. *Knowledge* refers to our awareness or understanding of what needs to be done in order to communicate appropriately and effectively. *Skills* are our abilities to engage in the behaviors necessary to communicate appropriately and effectively.

We may be highly motivated and lack the knowledge or the skills necessary to communicate appropriately and effectively. We also may be motivated and have the knowledge necessary, but not the skills. If we are motivated and have the knowledge and skills, this still does not ensure that we will communicate appropriately or effectively. There are several factors that may intervene to affect our behavior. We may, for example, have a strong emotional reaction to something that happens. Our emotional reaction in turn may cause us to "act out" a script we learned earlier in life that is dysfunctional in the situation in which we find ourselves. To illustrate, consider a European American who is served snake in another culture. He or she is likely to have a strong negative reaction to eating this meat. If the person is unable to control his or her emotional reaction cognitively, there is little chance that she or he will behave in a way that is perceived as competent by people in the other culture.

It is also possible that the environment may influence our ability to use the knowledge or skills we have. To illustrate, although I view myself as a person who can adjust to other cultures relatively easily, the environment in Calcutta, India, affected my ability to use my knowledge and skills. I had such a strong emotional reaction to the poverty I saw (e.g., people searching through garbage for food, large numbers of people sleeping in the street) that I was not able to use my knowledge or skills to adapt.

The person with whom we are communicating may also be a factor in our ability to be perceived as competent. If the other person communicates with us in a way that suggests we are not competent, we will in all likelihood act in an incompetent fashion.[2] It is also possible that we may act appropriately and effectively without actually having the knowledge necessary to engage in the behaviors by imitating the behavior of another person. This can work when communicating with people who are different when we do not have sufficient knowledge of the other person's group, but it is not the best strategy. I agree with John Wiemann and Clifford Kelly (1981) that "knowledge without skill is socially useless, and skill cannot be obtained without the cognitive ability to diagnose situational demands and constraints" (p. 290).

Our motivation, knowledge, and skills interact with outcomes of our interactions with others to yield perceptions of competence. I have mentioned two outcomes—appropriateness and effectiveness—already. Other potential outcomes include, but are not limited to, interpersonal attraction, trust, satisfaction with our communication, the development of interpersonal relationships (i.e., intimacy), managing conflict, adapting to other cultures, and building community. The remainder of this chapter is devoted to the three components of competence. The final chapter is devoted to applications of these ideas to developing intimate relationships, managing conflict, and building community with strangers.

❏ Motivation

Jonathan H. Turner (1988) suggests that certain basic needs motivate us to interact with others. *Needs* are "fundamental states of being in humans which, if unsatisfied, generate feelings of deprivation" (p. 23). The needs that serve as motivating factors are: (a) our need for a sense of security as a human being, (b) our need for a sense of predictability (i.e., I trust you will behave as I think you will); (c) our need for a sense of group inclusion; (d) our need to avoid diffuse anxiety; (e) our need for a sense of a common shared world; (f) our need for symbolic/material gratification; and (g) our need to sustain our self-conceptions. We vary in the degree to which we are conscious of our various needs. We are the least conscious of the first three, moderately conscious of the fourth, and the most conscious of the last three.

Each of our needs, separately and in combination, influences how we want to present ourselves to others, the intentions we form, and the habits or scripts we follow.[3] The needs also can influence each other. Anxiety, for example, can result from not meeting our needs for group inclusion, predictability, security, or sustaining our self-conceptions. Turner argues that our overall level of motivational energy is a function of our level of anxiety produced by these four needs. Three of these needs are critical in our communication with strangers and warrant further discussion.

NEED FOR PREDICTABILITY

One of the major reasons that we are not motivated to communicate with members of other groups is that we often do not see their behavior as predictable. J. H. Turner (1988) contends that we "need to 'trust' others in the sense that, for the purposes of a given interaction, others are 'reliable' and their responses 'predictable'" (p. 56). When others' behavior is predictable, we feel that there is a rhythm to our interactions with others. When others' behavior is not predictable, there is no rhythm to our interaction and we experience diffuse anxiety.

If we do not feel a part of interaction taking place (i.e., our need for inclusion is not met), we will have a difficult time seeing others' behavior as predictable. One reason we may not feel part of the interaction is that we have learned communication rules different from those of people from other groups and we often follow our own rules, even when communicating in the others' language. If Japanese follow their cultural norms regarding silence in conversations when speaking English, for example, North Americans will feel that the rhythm of the conversation is off and they will not feel part of the conversation taking place.

If we do not recognize that predictability will be lower when we are getting to know a person from another group, the low level of predictability will decrease our motivation to communicate. One way that we can deal with this problem is to be mindful when we communicate with members of other groups. When we are mindful, we need to remind ourselves that the lack of predictability may not be due to the other person; rather, there may be group differences influencing our communication. After recognizing this, we can try to gather information that will help us understand what is happening and thus increase the predictability of others' behavior.

NEED TO AVOID DIFFUSE ANXIETY

J. H. Turner (1988) views *anxiety* as a "generalized or unspecified sense of disequilibrium" (lack of balance) (p. 61). Anxiety stems from feeling uneasy, tense, worried, or apprehensive about what might happen. It is an emotional (affective) response to situations based on a fear of negative consequences (Stephan & Stephan, 1985). Turner argues that feelings of anxiety stem from deprivations in meeting our needs for security, predictability, group inclusion, and self-confirmation. He contends that if we have not meet our needs for security, predictability, and group inclusion, the focus of our behavior is in trying to deal with the anxiety associated with not meeting these needs. Because we are not highly aware of our needs for security, predictability, and group inclusion, however, we have a hard time pinpointing the source of the anxiety. The net result is that "considerable interpersonal energy can be devoted to meeting these needs as they grope around for a solution to their often vague feelings of discomfort" (p. 63).

Anxiety is an important motivating factor in intergroup encounters. If anxiety is too high, we avoid communicating with members of other groups in order to lower our anxiety. To be motivated to communicate with members of other groups, we have to manage our anxiety if it is too high or too low. This requires that we be mindful. When we are mindful, there are several things they can do to manage our anxiety. I discuss these techniques in the section on ability to manage anxiety later in this chapter.

NEED TO SUSTAIN OUR SELF-CONCEPTIONS

Another consequence of high anxiety is that our need to sustain our self-conceptions becomes important (J. H. Turner, 1988). Sustaining our self-conceptions is much more difficult, however, when we communicate with members of other groups than when we communicate with members of our own groups. Our self-conceptions are made up of the various identities we have that are our theories of ourselves:

> Identity, like any theory, is both a *structure,* containing the organized contents of experience, and an active *process* that guides and regulates one's thoughts, feelings, and actions. . . . It influences how information is perceived, processed, and recalled . . . it acts as a script to guide behavior . . . and it contains the standards against which one's behavior can be compared and evaluated. (Schlenker, 1986, p. 24)

Our self-conceptions thus influence how we communicate with others and our choice (conscious and unconscious) of those with whom we form relationships.

J. H. Turner (1988) contends that we try to maintain our self-conceptions, even going to the point of using defense mechanisms (e.g., denial) to maintain our views of ourselves. Our need for self-concept support directly influences our communication. Donald Cushman, Barry Valentinsen, and David Dietrich (1982), for example, suggest that we are attracted to others who have the ability to support our self-conceptions. Perceiving that others support our self-conceptions is necessary if we are going to form or maintain an interpersonal relationship with them.

One of the problems in intergroup encounters can be that one or both of the communicators perceives that the other person does not support his or her self-conceptions. If we are communicating on automatic pilot, we are likely to respond negatively in this situation. When we are mindful of our communication, however, we can recognize that members of other groups might emphasize different aspects of their self-conceptions from those we stress. Individualists, for example, stress their personal identity, whereas collectivists emphasize social identities. Failure to support each others' self-conceptions may not be due to lack of concern, but rather a failure to understand group differences in what each considers to be important aspects of the self. To illustrate, Japanese are likely to ask questions about North Americans' social identities when North Americans expect questions about their personal identity. If North Americans perceive this as lack of self-concept support, they will not be motivated to interact with Japanese. If North Americans are mindful of their communication, however, they can recognize that this is just a cultural difference. This interpretation should not have a negative effect on North Americans' motivation to communicate with Japanese.

APPROACH-AVOIDANCE TENDENCIES

Most us spend the vast majority of our time interacting with people who are relatively similar to us. Our actual contact with people who are different is limited; it is a novel form of interaction (T. Rose, 1981). If our attempts to communicate with strangers are not successful and we cannot easily get out of the situations in which we find ourselves, then our unconscious need for group inclusion becomes unsatisfied. This leads to anxiety about ourselves and our standing in a group context (J. H. Turner, 1988). One way we deal with this anxiety is to retreat into known territory and limit our interactions to people who are similar. At the same time, most of us want to see ourselves as nonprejudiced and caring people. We may, therefore, want to interact with strangers to sustain our self-concept. Holding both attitudes at the same time is not unusual. The combination of our need to avoid diffuse anxiety and our need to sustain our self-conceptions often leads us to an approach-avoidance orientation toward intergroup encounters.[4]

The questionnaire in Table 6.1 is designed to help you assess your tendency to approach or avoid interacting with strangers. Take a few minutes to complete it now.

Table 6.1 Assessing Your Approach-Avoidance Tendencies

The purpose of this questionnaire is to help you assess your tendency to approach or avoid contact with strangers. Respond to each of the statements by indicating the degree to which the statement is true regarding how you typically think about yourself. When you think about yourself, is the statement "Always False" (answer 1), "Usually False" (answer 2), "Sometimes True and Sometimes False" (answer 3), "Usually True" (answer 4), or "Always True" (answer 5)?

_____ 1. I have the opportunity to meet people who are different regularly.
_____ 2. I am highly anxious when I have to communicate with people from other groups.
_____ 3. I think close relations with people who are different is desirable.
_____ 4. I avoid interacting with people from other groups when possible.
_____ 5. I enjoy interacting with members of other groups.
_____ 6. I would object if someone in my family married a person who is different from us.
_____ 7. I try to encourage social relations with people who are different.
_____ 8. I am never sure how to behave when I interact with people from other groups.
_____ 9. I have tried to develop friendships with people who are different.
_____ 10. I do not feel secure when I interact with people from other groups.

To find your score, first reverse the responses for the even-numbered items (i.e., if you wrote 1, make it 5; if you wrote 2, make it 4; if you wrote 3, leave it as 3; if you wrote 4, make it 2; if you wrote 5, make it 1). Next, add the numbers next to each statement. Scores will range from 10 to 50. The higher your score, the more willing you are to approach people who are different.

SOURCE: Adapted in part from Hofman (1985).

Scores on the questionnaire range from 10 to 50. The higher your score, the greater your tendency to approach strangers. The important thing to remember is that if your score is low, you can consciously manage your anxiety and consciously decide to interact with strangers.

❑ Knowledge

Misunderstandings can occur for a variety of reasons when we communicate with strangers. We may not transmit our message in a way that it can be understood by others, strangers may misinterpret what we say, or both situations can occur simultaneously. The problems that occur may be due to our or stranger's pronunciation, grammar, familiarity with the topic being discussed, familiarity with the other person, familiarity with the other person's native language, fluency in the other person's language, or social factors (Gass & Varonis, 1984). If we are familiar with or fluent in other people's language, for example, we can usually understand them better when they speak our language than if we know nothing about their language.

Generally speaking, the greater our cultural and linguistic knowledge and the more our beliefs overlap with the strangers with whom we communicate, the less the likelihood there will be misunderstandings. Lack of linguistic and cultural knowledge contributes to misunderstandings because we "listen to speech, form a hypothesis about what routine is being enacted, and then rely on social background knowledge and co-occurrence expectations to evaluate what is intended and what attitudes are conveyed" (Gumperz, 1982, p. 171).

The knowledge component of communication competence refers to our awareness of what we need to do to communicate in an appropriate and effective way. This includes a specific awareness of the skills discussed in the next section and how they can be used when communicating with strangers. When communicating with strangers, we also need to have knowledge about the other person's group. My focus in this section therefore is on how we can gather information about strangers and their groups so that we can interpret their messages accurately. Although my focus is on gathering information about strangers, the processes outlined apply equally to gathering information about people who are similar to us.

KNOWLEDGE OF HOW TO GATHER INFORMATION

Charles Berger (1979) isolates three general types of strategies we can use to gather information about others and reduce our uncertainty about them and the way they will interact with us: passive, active, and interactive strategies. To illustrate this process, assume that we want to find out about Yuko, a Japanese to whom we have just been introduced. Although I am using an intercultural example, the strategies discussed can be used to gather information about anyone.

When we use *passive strategies* we take the role of "unobtrusive observers" (i.e., we do not intervene in the situation we are observing). Obviously, the type of situation in which we observe Yuko influences the amount of information we gain about her. If we observe Yuko in a situation where she does not have to interact with others, we will not gain much information about her. Situations in which she is interacting with several people at once, in contrast, allow us to make comparisons of how Yuko interacts with the different people.

If we know any of the people with whom Yuko is interacting, we can compare how Yuko interacts with the people we know and how she might interact with us. It also should be noted that if other Japanese are present in the situation, we can compare Yuko's behavior with theirs to try to determine how she is similar to and different from other Japanese.

There is one other aspect of the situation that will influence the amount of information we obtain about Yuko's behavior. If the situation is a formal one, her behavior is likely to be a function of the role she is filling in the situation and we will not learn much about Yuko as an individual. Informal situations where behavior is not guided by roles or social protocol, on the other hand, may provide more useful information about Yuko's behavior.

The preceding examples all involve our taking the role of an observer. The *active strategies* for reducing uncertainty require us to do something to acquire information about Yuko without actually interacting with her. One thing we could do to get information about Yuko is to ask questions of someone who knows her. When we ask others about someone we need to keep in mind that the information we receive may not be accurate. The other person may intentionally give us wrong information or the other person may not really know Yuko well.

We can also gather information about other groups by asking people who have had contact with those groups or gathering information from the library. In this example, we could gather information on Japan by questioning someone we know who has lived in Japan, reading a book on Japanese culture, or completing a Japanese cultural assimilator (a programmed learning course that teaches the reader about the Japanese culture). This would give us information about Yuko's cultural background and allow us to make cultural predictions about her behavior. Again, we need to keep in mind that our informant may or may not have good information about Japan and that Yuko may or may not be a typical Japanese.

This raises the issue of how we can select good informants to learn about other groups. People who have a lot of informal social contact with members of the other group, for example, are better informants than people who have little informal contact or even a lot of contact in formal settings. We also would be well off to select informants who have been successful in their interactions with members of other groups. To illustrate, if there are two members of our group who have frequent contact with the group in which we are interested, we would select the one who appears to be most successful in interacting with members of the other group (based on our observations of both persons' interactions or their reports of their interactions).

When we use active strategies to gather information we do not actually interact with the people about whom we are trying to gather information. The *interactive strategies* of verbal interrogation (question asking) and self-disclosure, in contrast, are used when we interact with the other person.

One obvious way we can gather information about others is to use *interrogation;* that is, ask them questions. When we are interacting with someone from our own group, there are limitations to this strategy that have to be kept in mind. First, we can ask only so many questions. I am not sure of what the exact number is, but I always know when I have asked too many. Second, our questions must be appropriate to the nature of the interaction we are having and the relationship we have with the other person.

When we are communicating with strangers, the same limitations are present, and there are others. The number and type of questions that strangers consider acceptable may not be the same as what we consider acceptable (recall the example of the questions the Japanese asked in the previous chapter). Strangers also may not be able to answer our questions, especially if our questions deal with why they behave the way they do (the ultimate answer to "why" questions is "because!" or "that is the way we do it here"). When interacting with strangers there is also the added problem of our not wanting to appear stupid or be rude. We therefore often avoid asking strangers questions.

If we can overcome our fear of looking stupid, asking questions is an excellent way to gather information about strangers. Generally speaking, strangers will probably respond in a positive way as long as they perceive that our intent is to learn about them personally or their group and *not* to judge them.[5]

The other way we can gather information about another person when interacting with her or him is through *self-disclosure*—telling the other person new information about ourselves.[6] Self-disclosure works as an information gathering strategy because of the reciprocity norm.[7] Essentially, the reciprocity norm states that if I do something for you, you will reciprocate and do something for me. The reciprocity norm appears to be a cultural universal; it exists in all cultures.[8]

In conversations between people who are not close (i.e., people we meet for the first time, acquaintances), we tend to reciprocate and tell similar information about ourselves to that which the other person tells us. If I disclose my opinion on a topic when you and I are talking, you will probably tell me your opinion on the same topic. There will, however, be some differences when we communicate with strangers rather than people from our own group. The topics that are appropriate to be discussed, for example, vary from culture to culture and ethnic group to ethnic group. If we self-disclose on a topic and a stranger does not reciprocate, there is a good chance we have found an inappropriate topic of conversation in that person's group. Because the timing and pacing of self-disclosure varies across cultures and ethnic groups, it is also possible that our timing is off or we have tried to self-disclose at an inappropriate pace.

KNOWLEDGE OF GROUP DIFFERENCES

Many people assume that to communicate effectively with members of other groups, we should focus only on similarities. This, however, is not necessarily the case. If members of another group strongly identify with their group, they will feel that their self-concepts are not being confirmed if we focus only on similarities. This is true whether the other person comes from a different culture, ethnic group, disability group, age group, or social class. To communicate effectively we must understand real differences between our group and strangers' groups. We often are aware of differences based on our ethnocentrism, prejudice, sexism, ageism, and stereotypes. These differences, however, may not be real (e.g., our stereotypes may not be accurate or the person may be an atypical member of his or her group).

Recognizing differences often facilitates effective communication. Lerita Coleman and Bella DePaulo (1991), for example, point out that

> there is evidence to suggest that [nondisabled] people would rather work and socialize with disabled people who acknowledge their disability than with those who do not acknowledge it. . . . Although acknowledgement of the disability on the part of the disabled person does not always lead to acceptance . . . it does reduce uncertainty and tension and enhances the attractiveness of the disabled person. Interactions proceed less problematically when a disabled person "appropriately" self-discloses about the disability. (p. 82)

A similar argument can be made for other group differences.

To communicate effectively, we need to be aware of the actual differences that exist between our group and other groups, and between ourselves and other individuals. One way we can isolate these actual differences is to learn all we can about other groups (e.g., become an expert on another culture or ethnic group). This approach, however, is not practical. How can we be experts on all of the groups that the strangers with whom we have contact are members? Obviously, we cannot.

When we are communicating with people from other cultures, we can use the dimensions of cultural variability discussed in Chapter 2 to develop a preliminary understanding of the real differences between our culture and another culture. To illustrate, Tsukasa Nishida and I (Gudykunst & Nishida, 1994) isolate several cultural differences that would help North Americans better understand Japanese communication:

1. Recognizing that Japan is a collectivistic culture where people conceptualize themselves as interdependent with one another. This leads to an emphasis on *wa* (harmony) in the ingroup, as well as an emphasis on *enryo* (reticence) and *amae* (dependence) in interactions with others. The importance of *wa* also leads to drawing a distinction between *tatemae* (what is stated in public) and *honne* (what is truly believed).

2. High-context messages are used more frequently in Japan than low-context messages. This leads to an emphasis on indirect forms of communication, as opposed to an emphasis on direct forms of communication in the United States. *Sasshi* (the ability to guess) is necessary to understand indirect messages.

3. Japan is a high uncertainty avoidance culture. This leads to an emphasis on rituals and the specification of relatively clear rules in most communication situations. People who deviate from the rules are viewed as dangerous and therefore are avoided whenever possible.

4. Japan is a high power distance culture. This leads to an emphasis on status (e.g., position, age) in communication. Power distance also leads to an emphasis on *on* and *giri* (obligations) in relationships between individuals in Japan.

5. Japan is a highly masculine culture. This leads to an emphasis on communicating with members of the same sex and separation of the sexes in many social situations.

These five conclusions are not all-inclusive, but they summarize the way the major dimensions of cultural variability influence Japanese communication.

Broad generalizations like those isolated here can help us understand the differences between ourselves and members of another culture if the person from the other culture is a relatively typical member of her or his culture. To communicate effectively with a specific stranger, however, we must go a step further and try to understand personal differences between us.

Table 6.2 Assessing Your Knowledge of Another Group

The purpose of this questionnaire is to help you assess your knowledge of another culture or ethnic group. The statements in this questionnaire contain a blank space. Think of a specific culture or ethnic group when you are reading the statements. Respond to each statement by indicating the degree to which the statement is true regarding your knowledge: "Always False" (answer 1), "Usually False" (answer 2), "Sometimes True and Sometimes False" (answer 3), "Usually True" (answer 4), or "Always True" (answer 5).

____	1. I understand the norms of _____.
____	2. I do not understand how _____ manage conflict.
____	3. I understand the customs of _____.
____	4. I do not understand how _____ support each others' self-conceptions.
____	5. I understand the values of _____.
____	6. I do not understand how _____ persuade each other.
____	7. I understand the communication rules of _____.
____	8. I do not understand how _____ comfort each other.
____	9. I understand the language (or dialect) of _____.
____	10. I do not understand how _____ joke with each other.

To find your score, first reverse your answers for the even-numbered items (i.e., if your answered 1, make it a 5; if you answered 2, make it a 4; if you answered 3, leave it as 3; if you answered 4, make it a 2; if you answered 5, make it a 1). Once you have reversed the even-numbered items, add the numbers your wrote next to each statement. Scores range from 10 to 50. The higher your score, the greater your knowledge of the group.

Table 6.2 contains a questionnaire designed to help you assess your knowledge about another group. To complete the questionnaire you need to think of a specific group (e.g., another culture or ethnic group). Take a couple of minutes to complete the questionnaire now.

Scores on the questionnaire range from 10 to 50. The higher your score, the greater your understanding of the other group. The thing to keep in mind is that the higher your score, the less likely it is you will misinterpret messages you receive from members of this group. If your score is relatively low, it suggests that you might want to try to better understand the other group to help you communicate more effectively with members of this group.

KNOWLEDGE OF PERSONAL SIMILARITIES

Although understanding differences is important, we also have to understand similarities if we are going to develop relationships with strangers. Understanding similarities at the group level is important, but finding similarities at the individual level is critical if we want to develop a relationship with a stranger (this issue is discussed in more detail in the next chapter). Isolating similarities requires that we be mindful of our communication.

One way we can be mindful is by creating new categories. One way to create new categories is to develop subcategories of a broader category (e.g., separating Chicanos and Chicanas from Mexican Americans in our stereotype of people of Mexican descent). The smaller our categories, the more effectively we can communicate with people in the category. We create new categories when we consciously search for similarities we share with strangers rather than focusing only on differences. Does the person from the other group, for example, have children who go to the same school as ours? Does he or she belong to the same social clubs we do? Does she or he experience frustrations similar to ours in her or his professional and personal life? Does he or she have similar worries about his or her family? The first two questions search for shared group memberships, whereas the second two focus on shared values, attitudes, or beliefs.

Robert Bellah, Richard Madsen, William Sullivan, Ann Swidler, and Steven Tipton (1985) point out that we need to seek out commonalities because "with a more explicit understanding of what we have in common and the goals we seek to attain together, the differences between us that remain would be less threatening" (p. 287). Finding commonalities requires that we be mindful of our prejudices. "Racism and sexism and homophobia and religious and cultural intolerance . . . are all ways of denying that other people are the same kind as ourselves" (Brodie, 1989, p. 16).

The position that Bellah and his associates advocate vis-à-vis cultural and ethnic differences is consistent with Langer's (1989) contention that

because most of us grow up and spend our time with people like ourselves, we tend to assume uniformities and commonalities. When confronted with someone who is clearly different in one specific way, we drop that assumption and look for differences. . . . The mindful curiosity generated by an encounter with someone who is different, which can lead to exaggerated perceptions of strangeness, can also bring us closer to that person if channeled differently. (p. 156)

Langer suggests that once individuals satisfy their curiosity about differences, understanding can occur. She therefore argues that what is needed is a way to make mindful curiosity about differences not taboo. One way that each of us can contribute to the acceptance of mindful curiosity is by accepting others' questions about us and our groups as "requests for information" until we are certain there is another motivation.

KNOWLEDGE OF ALTERNATIVE INTERPRETATIONS

Effective communication requires that we minimize misunderstandings or maximize the similarity in the ways messages are interpreted. To accomplish this, we must recognize that there are many ways that messages can be interpreted, and often these interpretations involve evaluations of others' behavior. There are at least three interrelated cognitive processes involved here: description, interpretation, and evaluation. To communicate effectively it is necessary to distinguish among these three processes. By *description* I mean an actual report of what we have observed with the minimum of distortion and without attributing social significance to the behavior. Description includes what we see and hear and is accomplished by counting or recording observations. To clarify these processes, consider the following example:

Description
Kim stood six inches away from me when we talked.

This statement is descriptive in nature. It does not attribute social significance to Kim's behavior; it merely tells what the observer saw. If we attribute social significance to this statement, or make an inference about what we saw, we would be engaged in *interpretation*. In other words, interpretation is what we think about what we see and hear. The important thing to keep in mind is that multiple interpretations can be made for any particular description of behavior. Returning to our example, we have the following:

Description
Kim stood six inches away from me when we talked.

Interpretations
Kim is aggressive.
Kim violated my personal space.
Kim likes me.

Each of these interpretations can have several different evaluations. *Evaluations* are positive or negative judgments concerning the social significance we attribute to behavior: whether or not we like it. To illustrate this, we can use the first interpretation given above:

Interpretation
Kim is aggressive.

Evaluations
I like that; Kim stands up for her- or himself.
I don't like that; Kim should not violate my rights by standing so close.

Of course, several other evaluations could be made, but these two are sufficient to illustrate potential differences in evaluations that can be made regarding any one interpretation.

If we are unable to distinguish among these three cognitive processes, it is likely that we will skip the descriptive process and jump immediately to either interpretation or evaluation when confronted with different patterns of behavior. This leads to misattributions of meaning and thus to ineffective communication. Being able to distinguish among the three processes, on the other hand, increases the likelihood of our seeing alternative interpretations, thereby increasing our ability to effectively communicate. Differentiating among the three processes also increases the likelihood of our making more accurate predictions of others' behavior. If we are able to describe others' behavior, we can make more accurate predictions because we are able to see alternative interpretations of behavior patterns.

If we do not separate descriptive and interpretive processes, misunderstandings are inevitable. When we communicate on automatic pilot we usually interpret others' behavior without describing it. Our interpretation is based on our cultural, ethnic, and social-class upbringing. Our interpretation of someone's behavior, however, may be very different from what he or she intended by the behavior. When we think there might have been a misunderstanding, we need to stop and describe the behavior in question. Then we need to look for alternative interpretations. After we have thought of some alternative interpretations, we can ask the other person which interpretation is correct (using the perception-checking skill discussed in Chapter 4). If we cannot ask the other person, we can make an educated guess as to what the other person meant based on our knowledge of the other person or the groups of which she or he is a member. Separating descriptions and interpretations, as I am suggesting here, requires that we be mindful.

❏ Skills

The skills necessary to communicate effectively and appropriately with strangers are those that are directly related to reducing our uncertainty and anxiety.[9] Reducing anxiety requires at least three skills: ability to be mindful, ability to tolerate ambiguity, and ability to manage anxiety. Reducing uncertainty minimally requires three skills: ability to empathize, ability to adapt our behavior, and the ability to make accurate predictions and explanations of others' behavior (the first two skills are necessary to develop the third).

ABILITY TO BE MINDFUL

By now it should be clear that I believe becoming mindful is an important aspect of communicating effectively with strangers.

We must be cognitively aware of our communication if we are to overcome our tendency to interpret strangers' behavior based on our own frame of reference. Because I have discussed mindfulness at length throughout the book, I will not go into great detail here. There is, however, one point I want to reiterate. Namely, we are seldom highly mindful of our communication.

When we interact with strangers, we become somewhat mindful of our communication. Our focus, however, is usually on the outcome ("Will I make a fool of myself?") rather than the process of communication. As you will recall, however, focusing on the outcome does not facilitate effective communication. For effective communication to occur we must focus on the process.

Even when we communicate with people close to us, we are not mindful of the process. Mihaly Csikszentmihalyi (1990) contends that

> there are few things as enjoyable as freely sharing one's most secret feelings and thoughts with another person. Even though this sounds commonplace, it in fact requires concentrated attention (mindfulness), openness, and sensitivity. In practice, the degree of investment of psychic energy in a friendship is unfortunately rare. (p. 188)

He goes on to argue that we must control our own life if we want to improve our relationships with others. Such control requires that we be mindful.

The questionnaire in Table 6.3 is designed to help you assess how mindful you are when you communicate. This is a difficult idea to assess. To complete the questionnaire you must think about your communication (i.e., become mindful of it). This will lead you to overestimate how mindful you actually are when you communicate. The questionnaire, nevertheless, will give you a rough idea of where you fall with respect to being mindful if you try to answer the questions based on your normal patterns of communication. Take a few minutes to complete it now.

Scores on the questionnaire range from 10 to 50. The higher your score, the more mindful you are when you communicate. Keep in mind that your score probably is inflated because you were mindful when you completed the questionnaire. Also remember that mindfulness is a skill that we can control. If your

Table 6.3 Assessing Your Mindfulness

The purpose of this questionnaire is to help you assess your ability to be mindful when you communicate. Respond to each statement by indicating the degree to which it is true regarding the way you normally communicate: "Always False" (answer 1), "Usually False" (answer 2), "Sometimes False and Sometimes True" (answer 3), "Usually True" (answer 4), or "Always True" (answer 5).

_____ 1. I pay attention to the situation and context when I communicate.

_____ 2. I think about how I will look to others when I communicate with them.

_____ 3. I seek out new information about the people with whom I communicate.

_____ 4. I ignore inconsistent signals I receive from others when we communicate.

_____ 5. I recognize that the person with whom I am communicating has a different point of view from mine.

_____ 6. I use the categories in which I place others to predict their behavior.

_____ 7. I can describe others with whom I communicate in great detail.

_____ 8. I am concerned about the outcomes of my encounters with others.

_____ 9. I try to find rational reasons why others may behave in a way I perceive negatively.

_____ 10. I have a hard time telling when others do not understand me.

To find your score, first reverse the responses for the even-numbered items (i.e., if you wrote 1, make it 5; if you wrote 2, make it 4; if you wrote 3, leave it as 3; if you wrote 4, make it 2; if you wrote 5, make it 1). Next, add the numbers next to each statement. Scores range from 10 to 50. The higher your score, the more mindful you are when you communicate.

SOURCE: Based on Langer's (1989) description of mindfulness.

score is low, you can train yourself to be more mindful about your communication.

ABILITY TO TOLERATE AMBIGUITY

Tolerance for ambiguity implies the ability to deal successfully with situations, even when a lot of information needed to interact effectively is unknown. Brent Ruben and Daniel Kealey (1979) point out that

the ability to react to new and ambiguous situations with minimal discomfort has long been thought to be an important asset when adjusting to a new culture. . . . Excessive discomfort resulting from being placed in a new or different environment—or from finding

Table 6.4 Assessing Your Tolerance for Ambiguity

The purpose of this questionnaire is to help you assess your orientations toward ambiguity. Respond to each statement indicating the degree to which it is true regarding the way you typically respond: "Always False" (answer 1), "Usually False" (answer 2), "Sometimes False and Sometimes True" (answer 3), "Usually True" (answer 4), or "Always True" (answer 5).

____ 1. I am not comfortable in new situations.
____ 2. I deal with unforeseen problems successfully.
____ 3. I experience discomfort in ambiguous situations.
____ 4. I am comfortable working on problems when I do not have all of the necessary information.
____ 5. I am frustrated when things do not go the way I expected.
____ 6. It is easy for me to adjust in new environments.
____ 7. I become anxious when I find myself in situations where I am not sure what to do.
____ 8. I am relaxed in unfamiliar situations.
____ 9. I am not frustrated when my surroundings are changed without my knowledge.
____ 10. I am comfortable in situations without clear norms to guide my behavior.

To find your score, first reverse the responses for the odd-numbered items (i.e., if you wrote 1, make it 5; if you wrote 2, make it 4; if you wrote 3, leave it as 3; if you wrote 4, make it 2; if you wrote 5, make it 1). Next, add the numbers next to each statement. Scores range from 10 to 50. The higher your score, the greater your tolerance for ambiguity.

the familiar environment altered in some critical ways—can lead to confusion, frustration and interpersonal hostility. Some people seem better able to adapt well in new environments and adjust quickly to the demands of the changing milieu. (p. 19)

Ruben and Kealey's research indicates that the greater our tolerance for ambiguity, the more effective we are in completing task assignments in other cultures.

Our tolerance for ambiguity affects the type of information we try to find out about others. People with a low tolerance for ambiguity try to gather information that supports their own beliefs. People with a high tolerance for ambiguity, in contrast, seek objective information from others (McPherson, 1983). Objective information is necessary to understand strangers and accurately predict their behavior.

The questionnaire in Table 6.4 is designed to help you assess your tolerance for ambiguity. Take a couple of minutes and complete it now.

Scores on the questionnaire range from 10 to 50. The higher your score, the greater your tolerance for ambiguity. If your score is low, you can still consciously choose to not panic in ambiguous situations if you are mindful.

ABILITY TO MANAGE ANXIETY

As indicated earlier, the amount of anxiety we experience when we communicate with strangers influences our motivation to communicate with them. If our anxiety is above our maximum threshold or below our minimum threshold, we will not be able to communicate effectively. If anxiety is too high, we will be too preoccupied with managing our anxiety to communicate effectively. If it is too low, we will not have enough adrenaline flowing to want to communicate.

Helen Kennerley (1990) isolates two general issues in managing anxiety: (a) controlling bodily symptoms and (b) controlling worrying thoughts or cognitive distortions. There are several physical symptoms associated with anxiety. When we are highly anxious we might experience respiratory problems (e.g., difficulty in breathing), palpitations of the heart, dry mouth, muscular tension, or a tension headache.

To manage our anxiety, Hugh Prather (1986) suggests the most important thing we can do is break away from the situation in which we feel anxious. This might mean leaving the room or mentally withdrawing for a short period of time. Once we have withdrawn, we need to calm ourselves and remember that our anxiety is not going to harm us. We can allow our anxious feelings to pass and then return to the situation.

If our anxiety does not dissipate quickly, we need to do something that will restore our calm. We can use various techniques to control the physical symptoms associated with our anxiety. These include, but are not limited to, yoga, hypnotism, meditation, and progressive muscular relaxation (i.e., relaxing the various muscle groups in our bodies in a systematic fashion). Respiratory control also can be used to manage the physical symptoms of anxiety. One way to practice controlled breathing is to sit up straight and concentrate on your breathing. Mindfully draw in a long breath and focus on your inhaling. Then let out the breath, focusing on your exhaling.

We can control our worrying thoughts by overcoming our cognitive distortions. When we interpret our own and others' behavior our perceptions often are distorted because of the ways we think about our feelings and behavior. David Burns (1989) isolates ten forms of cognitive distortions that influence the ways we interpret behavior: (a) all-or-nothing thinking; (b) overgeneralizations; (c) mental filters; (d) discounting the positive and focusing only on the negative; (e) jumping to conclusions; (f) magnification, or making problems bigger than they are; (g) emotional reasoning; (h) "should" statements (e.g., I should be a better person); (i) labeling; and (j) blaming ourselves or others. To overcome our worrying thoughts, we need to be mindful of our communication. When we are mindful, we need to replace the worrying thoughts with a rational response. Unless we stop distorting our thought processes, we will *not* be able to manage our anxiety consistently over long periods of time.

ABILITY TO EMPATHIZE

The one skill that most consistently emerges in discussions of effectively communicating with strangers is empathy. Robert Bell (1987) argues that *empathy* is multifaceted, involving cognitive (thinking), affective (feeling), and communication components:

> Cognitively, the empathic person takes the perspective of another person, and in so doing strives to see the world from the other's point of view. Affectively, the empathic person experiences the emotions of another; he or she *feels* the other's experiences. Communicatively, the empathic individual signals understanding and concern through verbal and nonverbal cues. (p. 204)

The cognitive, affective, and communication components are highly interrelated and all must be present for others to perceive that we are being empathic.

Empathy involves (a) carefully listening to others, (b) understanding others' feelings, (c) being interested in what others say, (d) being sensitive to others' needs, and (e) understanding others' points of view (Hwang, Chase, & Kelley, 1980). Although these indicators of empathy include verbal components, we tend to rely on nonverbal behavior more than verbal behavior when we interpret others' behavior as empathic (Bell, 1987).

Sympathy is often confused with empathy. When we are *empathic*, we imagine how the other person is feeling; when we are *sympathetic*, we imagine how we would feel in the other person's situation.[10] Milton Bennett (1979) argues that the "Golden Rule"—"Do unto others as you would have them do unto you"—which many people are taught as children involves a sympathetic response to others, not an empathic response. He proposes that we follow the "Platinum Rule"—"Do unto others as they would have you do unto them"—which involves an empathic response. This is a reasonable approach as long as what others want done unto them does not violate our basic moral principles or universally accepted principles of human rights. Ethics was discussed in Chapter 3.

Table 6.5 contains a questionnaire designed to help you assess your ability to display empathy. Take a few minutes to complete it now.

Scores on the questionnaire range from 10 to 50. The higher your score, the greater your empathy. If your score is on the low side, remember that you can increase your tendency to display empathy if you are mindful of your communication.

ABILITY TO ADAPT

To gather information about and adapt our behavior to strangers requires that we are flexible in our behavior.[11] As suggested in the discussion of knowledge, we must be able to select strategies that are appropriate to gather the information we need about strangers in order to communicate effectively with them. This requires that we have different behavioral options for gathering information open to us. Do we sit back and watch the other person

Table 6.5 Assessing Your Empathy

The purpose of this questionnaire is to help your assess your ability to empathize. Respond to each statement by indicating the degree to which the statement is true regarding the way you typically communicate with others. When you think of your communication, is the statement "Always False" (answer 1), "Usually False" (answer 2), "Sometimes False and Sometimes True" (answer 3), "Usually True" (answer 4), or "Always True" (answer 5).

_____ 1. I try to understand others' experiences from their perspectives.
_____ 2. I follow the "Golden Rule" ("Do unto others as you would have them do unto you") when communicating with others.
_____ 3. I can "tune in" to the emotions others are experiencing when we communicate.
_____ 4. When trying to understand how others feel, I imagine how I would feel in their situation.
_____ 5. I am able to tell what others are feeling without being told.
_____ 6. Others experience the same feelings as I do in any given situation.
_____ 7. When others are having problems, I can imagine how they feel.
_____ 8. I find it hard to understand the emotions others experience.
_____ 9. I try to see others as they want me to.
_____ 10. I never seem to know what others are thinking when we communicate.

To find your score, first reverse the responses for the even-numbered items (i.e., if you wrote 1, make it 5; if you wrote 2, make it 4; if you wrote 3, leave it as 3; if you wrote 4, make it 2; if you wrote 5, make it 1). Next, add the numbers next to each statement. Scores range from 10 to 50. The higher your score, the more you are able to empathize.

---

or go interact with him or her? Which strategy will provide the information we need to know to communicate effectively?

We also must be able to adapt and accommodate our behavior to people from other groups if we are going to be successful in our interactions with them. Robert Duran's (1983) conceptualization of communicative adaptability is consistent with the perspective used here. He argues that *communication adaptability* involves: "1) The requirement of both cognitive (ability to perceive) and behavioral (ability to adapt) skills; 2) Adaptation not only of behaviors but also interaction goals; 3) The ability to adapt to the requirements posed by different communication contexts; and 4) The assumption that perceptions of communicative competence reside in the dyad" (p. 320).

Harry Triandis and colleagues (1988) provide suggestions for how individualists and collectivists might want to consider adapting their behavior and ways of thinking when communicating with each other. *For individualists to communicate more effectively with collectivists,* Triandis and his associates suggest that individualists (a) recognize that collectivists pay attention to group memberships and use group memberships to predict collectivists behavior; (b) recognize that when collectivists group memberships change, their behavior changes; (c) recognize that collectivists are comfortable in vertical, unequal relationships; (d) recognize that collectivists see competition as threatening; (e) recognize that collectivists emphasize harmony and cooperation in the ingroup; (f) recognize that collectivists emphasize face (public self-image) and help them preserve their face in interactions; (g) recognize that collectivists do not separate criticism from the person being criticized and avoid confrontation whenever possible; (h) cultivate long-term relationships; (i) be more formal than usual in initial interactions; and (j) follow collectivists' guidance in disclosing personal information.

For collectivists to interact effectively with individualists, Triandis and his associates suggest that collectivists (a) recognize that individualists' behavior cannot be predicted accurately from group memberships; (b) recognize that individualists will be proud of their accomplishments and say negative things about others; (c) recognize that individualists are emotionally detached from their ingroups; (d) recognize that individualists prefer horizontal, equal relationships; (e) recognize that individualists do not see competition as threatening; (f) recognize that individualists are not persuaded by arguments emphasizing harmony and cooperation; (g) recognize that individualists do not form long-term relationships and that initial friendliness does not indicate an intimate relationship; (h) recognize that individualists maintain relationships when they receive more rewards than costs; (i) recognize that individualists do not respect others based on position, age, or sex as much as collectivists; and (j) recognize that outgroups are not viewed as highly different from the ingroup. Suggestions also could be based on the other dimensions of cultural variability presented in Chapter 2.

Often the adaptations we make when interacting with strangers do not improve the effectiveness of our communication (see, for example, the discussion of communicative distance in Chapter 3). "Adjustments majority speakers make when speaking to minority members often give the impression that the speaker is patronizing and distant and, in turn, affect the recipients' behavior and conversational style" (Kraut & Higgins, 1984, p. 114). If strangers perceive we are patronizing they will become defensive, and communication cannot be effective when one of the individuals is defensive. To be more effective we must adapt our messages to the specific person with whom we are communicating. Others understand our messages better when they are constructed for them than when we do not adapt our messages.[12]

One important aspect of adapting our behavior is the ability to speak another language (or at least use phrases in another language). If we always expect strangers to speak our language, we cannot be effective in communicating with them. Ernest Boyer (1990), chair of the Carnegie Endowment for Teaching, points out that we "should become familiar with other languages and cultures so that [we] will be better able to live, with confidence, in an increasingly interdependent world" (p. B4).

Harry Triandis (1983) points out that the importance of speaking another language depends, at least in part, on where we are:

In some cultures foreigners are expected to know the local language. A Frenchman [or woman] who arrives in the United States without knowing a word of English, or an American who visits France with only a bit of French, is bound to find the locals rather unsympathetic. For example, I have found a discrepancy between my friends' and my own experience in Paris. Their accounts stress discourtesy of the French, while I have found the French to be quite courteous. I suspect the difference is that I speak better French than the majority of visitors and am therefore treated more courteously. In contrast, in other cultures the visitor is not expected to know the local language. In Greece, for example, one is not expected to know the language although a few words of Greek create delight, and increase by order of magnitude (a factor of ten) the normal hospitable tendencies of that population. (p. 84)

Some attempt at using the local language is necessary to indicate an interest in the people or culture.

The need to adapt our behavior is not limited to speaking another language. If I (a European American male) am communicating with someone from another culture who wants to stand closer to me than I want him or her to stand (e.g., someone from a Latin or Arab culture), I have two options if I am mindful of my communication. First, I can try to enforce my own interpersonal distance (e.g., the other person should stand at least at arm's length from me). If the other person keeps trying to establish her or his distance, however, he or she will dance me around the room (i.e., the other person moves forward, I move back, to regain the distance that is comfortable for him or her, the other person again moves closer). If I am not mindful of my communication, this is what is likely to occur. Alternatively, I can choose to use a different pattern of behavior. I can decide to stand closer to the other person than I would if I was communicating with someone from my own culture. This option will, in all likelihood, lead to more effective communication. When people are following different norms, at least one of the parties has to adapt for effective communication to occur.

You may be asking yourself, why do I have to adapt? Why doesn't the other person adapt, especially if he or she is a foreigner in the United States? The other person could adapt, and people from other cultures visiting or living in the United States usually do to some extent. As members of the human community, nevertheless, we have to make choices about whether and when to adapt to others. I believe that if we know what can be done to improve the chances for effective communication, have the skills to do what needs to be done, and choose not to adapt our communication, we have to take responsibility for misunderstandings that occur as a result. There are obviously situations where this principle may not hold. If the behavior required, for example, goes against our moral standards or violates another's human rights, some other option must be found.

The questionnaire in Table 6.6 is designed to help you to assess your ability to adapt your behavior. The questionnaire obviously does not tap all aspects of how we might adapt our behavior. It

Table 6.6 Assessing Your Ability to Adapt Your Behavior

The purpose of this questionnaire is to help you assess your ability to adapt your behavior. Respond to each statement by indicating the extent to which it is true of your normal patterns of communication: "Always False" (answer 1), "Usually False" (answer 2), "Sometimes False and Sometimes True" (answer 3), "Usually True" (answer 4), or "Always True" (answer 5).

_____ 1. I adapt my behavior to the person with whom I am communicating.
_____ 2. I use the same nonverbal communication with everyone.
_____ 3. I am able to modify how I present myself to others.
_____ 4. I do not adapt my language to the way the person with whom I am communicating is speaking.
_____ 5. I adapt my behavior to the situation in which I find myself once I know what behavior is required.
_____ 6. I tend to use one communication style all of the time.
_____ 7. I can modify the way I come across to others, depending on how I want them to see me.
_____ 8. I am not very flexible in the ways I communicate.
_____ 9. I communicate differently with acquaintances and with close friends.
_____ 10. I insist that others communicate with me on my terms.

To find your score, first reverse your answers to the even-numbered items (i.e., if you wrote 1, make it 5; if you wrote 2, make it 4; if you wrote 3, leave it as 3; if you wrote 4, make it 2; if you wrote 5, make it 1). Next, add the numbers you wrote next to each statement. Scores range from 10 to 50. The higher your score, the greater your ability to adapt your behavior.

SOURCE: Ideas for some of the items are drawn from Lennox and Wolfe's (1984) ability to modify self-presentations scale.

does, however, cover the major areas needed to communicate effectively with people who are different. Take a few minutes to complete it now.

Scores on the questionnaire range from 10 to 50. The higher your score, the more flexible you are in your behavioral repertoire. The important thing to keep in mind if you do not have a high score is that you can increase your behavioral flexibility with practice. Once you understand what behavior is necessary in a particular situation (i.e., have the necessary knowledge), you can become mindful of your communication and decide to try out the behavior. Who knows, you may find that you like it. If you do not like the behavior or find it unethical, however, you will have to find an alternative way to respond.

ABILITY TO MAKE ACCURATE PREDICTIONS AND EXPLANATIONS

The final important skill is the ability to make accurate predictions and explanations of others' behavior. If we can empathize, have the ability to adapt our communication, and we are mindful, we can gather the information necessary to reduce uncertainty. Reducing uncertainty requires that we be able to describe others' behavior, select accurate interpretations of their messages, accurately predict their behavior, and be able to accurately explain their behavior.

Rachel Karniol (1990) points out that we assume that others' thoughts, feelings, and behavior are rule governed. If we do not make such an assumption we could not ever predict others' thoughts, feelings, or behavior. The problem with the accuracy of our predictions is that we only know a limited number of rules that we can use to understand others' thoughts, feelings, and behavior. As we may not know the rules that strangers are using, we assume that they are the same as ours when we are on automatic pilot. To understand the rules that others are using to guide their thoughts, feelings, and behavior, we must be mindful. When we are mindful, we can be empathic and use active listening to try to understand others' rules. Once we understand the rules strangers are using, we can make accurate predictions and explanations of their behavior.

When we are on automatic pilot, our predictions and explanations for others' behavior are based on our stereotypes, attitudes, and previous experiences with the individuals involved. We may be highly confident of our predictions and explanations when we are on automatic pilot, but our predictions and explanations may *not* be accurate. If our predictions are based only on our stereotypes of another person's group, for example, our predictions will not be accurate if our stereotypes are inaccurate or the person is not typical of his or her group. Accurate predictions or explanations of strangers' behavior requires that we use cultural, social, and personal information.

To make accurate predictions and explanations, we must be able to gather accurate information about others. When our anxiety is too high we are not able to gather accurate information about others (Wilder & Shapiro, 1989). If our anxiety is too low, we also will have problems gathering accurate information about others. To gather accurate information, we must mindfully manage our anxiety so that it is below our maximum threshold and above our minimum threshold. The accuracy of our predictions and explanations for strangers' behavior also is dependent upon our knowledge of group differences, our knowledge of similarities, and our knowledge of alternative interpretations. Our accuracy also is effected by our expectations. If we expect the interactions to be negative, for example, our anxiety will be high, probably above our maximum thresholds, and we will not be able to make accurate predictions or explanations. We also are better able to make accurate predictions and explanations if our needs (see motivation section of this chapter) have been met.

Another factor that influences the accuracy of our predictions and explanations is our view of our ingroups and outgroups. We tend to view our ingroups as being more differentiated than outgroups. The more familiar we are with outgroups, however, the greater our perceived differentiation of the outgroups (Linville, Fisher, & Salovey, 1989). The more variability we perceive in outgroups, the less our tendency to treat all members in a similar negative fashion (Johnstone & Hewstone, 1991). The variability we perceive in outgroups provides information about the strangers with whom we are communicating and thus increases the accuracy of our predictions.

The more variability we perceive in outgroups, the less our tendency to treat all members in a similar negative fashion.

Our perceptions of strangers' intentions toward us also affect the accuracy of our predictions and explanations of their behavior. We tend to be more accurate, for example, in perceiving others' intentions when they are negative than when they are positive. "Intentions to convey hostility are perceived more accurately than intentions to convey positive feelings" (Bodenhausen, Gaelick, & Wyer, 1987, p. 159). Our accuracy in interpreting others' intentions also is lower if we have been dissatisfied with our previous

Table 6.7 Assessing Your Ability to Accurately Predict and Explain Others' Behavior

---

The purpose of this questionnaire is to help you assess your ability to accurately predict and explain the behavior of people from other groups. Respond to each statement by indicating the degree to which the statement is true with respect to your communication with either a particular group of people *or* a specific person from another group. When you communicate with people who are different, is the statement "Always False" (answer 1), "Usually False" (answer 2), "Sometimes True and Sometimes False" (answer 3), "Usually True" (answer 4), or "Always True" (answer 5),

_____   1. I can make accurate predictions regarding the behavior of _____.
_____   2. I cannot accurately predict how _____ will behave when we have a disagreement.
_____   3. I can accurately explain the values of _____.
_____   4. I do not understand how _____ see themselves when we communicate.
_____   5. I can accurately explain the behavior of _____ to others.
_____   6. I do not understand the attitudes _____ hold.
_____   7. I can accurately interpret the messages I receive from _____.
_____   8. I often make errors in attributions when I am trying to understand the behavior of _____.
_____   9. I can accurately describe the behavior of _____.
_____ 10. I cannot tell when _____ misinterprets messages I transmit.

To find your score, first reverse your answers to the even-numbered items (i.e., if you wrote 1, make it 5; if you wrote 2, make it 4; if you wrote 3, leave it as 3; if you wrote 4, make it 2; if you wrote 5, make it 1). Next, add the numbers you wrote next to each of the statements. Scores range from 10 to 50. The higher your score, the greater your understanding of people who are different.

---

interactions with them than if we have been satisfied with our previous interactions (Bodenhausen et al., 1987).

The questionnaire in Table 6.7 is designed to help you assess your ability to accurately predict and explain the behavior of people who are different when you communicate with them. Take a couple of minutes and complete the questionnaire now.

The scores on the questionnaire range from 10 to 50. The higher your score, the more accurate your predictions and explanations. The more accurate your predictions and explanations are, the more effective your communication will be. The questionnaire in Table 6.7 is designed to assess *either* your ability to accurately predict and explain the behavior of a group of people *or* your ability to accurately predict and explain the behavior of a specific person. When you first completed the questionnaire you focused on either a group or specific person. I suggest that before reading the next chapter you take the time to complete the questionnaire in Table 6.7 a second time, focusing on a person if you initially completed it for a group or focusing on a group if you initially thought of a specific person. Obviously, you can complete the questionnaire for many different groups or individuals.

To conclude, I have discussed the factors that contribute to our being perceived as a competent communicators—our motivation, knowledge, and skills—in this chapter. In the final chapter, I apply these ideas to managing conflict, developing relationships, acting in an ethical manner, and building community with strangers.

❏ Notes

1. Spitzberg and Cupach (1984) use the term effectiveness to refer to task outcomes (e.g., goal achievement).
2. Watzlawick, Beavin, and Jackson (1967), for example, point out that the way members of a family communicate with each other can create mental illness.
3. J. H. Turner (1988) uses different labels for some of the terms (including the needs). He uses the ethnomethods, for example, to refer to what I call habits or scripts. I believe my terms capture the essence of his idea, but are not as full of academic jargon.
4. Spitzberg and Cupach (1984) also talk about approach avoidance as a factor in motivation. They, however, assume that it is a basic orientation to any encounter rather than deriving it from more basic needs as I am here.
5. Langer (1989) notes that there appear to be "taboo" questions. I believe, however, that most of the taboos are in our minds.
6. Berger (1979) actually isolates a third interactive strategy, deception detection, that I am not discussing.
7. See Gouldner (1960) for an extensive discussion of the reciprocity norm.
8. There are some differences in how it is manifested in different cultures. See Gudykunst and Ting-Toomey (1988) for a detailed discussion.
9. The theory on which the book is based (Gudykunst, 1988, 1993) suggests that effectiveness and adaptation are a function of reducing uncertainty and anxiety. Other variables (e.g., expectations) affect our level of uncertainty and anxiety and are not linked directly to effectiveness. Gao and Gudykunst (1990) tested this assumption in an adaptation context and it was supported. There are numerous other skills that could be discussed if I did not select the skills based

on the theory. There is some overlap between those selected on the basis of the theory and atheoretically derived lists of skills. Ruben (1976), for example, listed seven skills: (a) empathy, (b) tolerance for ambiguity, (c) display of respect, (d) interaction posture, (e) orientation to knowledge, (f) role behavior, and (g) interaction management.

10. These differences also can be explained in terms of situational (sympathy) versus individual (empathy) role taking. See Karniol (1990) for a discussion.

11. The way I am talking about behavioral flexibility is very similar to Lennox and Wolfe's (1984) notion of ability to modify self-presentations (which is a subscale in their revised self-monitoring scale). Spitzberg and Cupach (1984) included Snyder's (1974) notion of self-monitoring as a skill in communication competence. I have not called this self-monitoring or ability to modify self-presentations because I think the idea of behavioral flexibility is more general. The concepts, however, are interrelated.

12. See Kellermann (1993) for research to support this claim.

7

Applying Our Knowledge and Skills

I examined the factors that contribute to perceptions of our competence in communicating with strangers in the preceding chapter. In this chapter, I discuss three areas in which we can apply our knowledge and skills. I begin by looking at how we can manage conflict with strangers constructively. Next, I examine how we develop intimate relationships with strangers. I then discuss how we can apply our knowledge and skills for resolving conflict and developing interpersonal relationships to building community with strangers.

❏ Managing Conflict

Conflict is inevitable in any relationship: it is going to happen whether we want it to or not. Many of us nevertheless view conflict negatively. Conflict itself, however, is not positive or negative. How we manage the conflicts we have, in contrast, can have positive or negative consequences for our relationships.

Kenneth Thomas (1983) defines dyadic *conflict* as "the process which begins when one party perceives that the other has frustrated, or is about to frustrate, some concern of his" or hers (p. 891). This definition covers a broad range of phenomena. Conflicts can arise from instrumental (i.e., differences in goals or practices) or expressive (i.e., tension, often gen-

Conflict is inevitable in any relationship.

era ted from hostile feelings) sources (Olsen, 1978). To place the discussion of intergroup conflict in context, I begin by looking at cultural and ethnic differences in managing conflict.

CULTURAL AND ETHNIC
DIFFERENCES IN CONFLICT

Instrumental and expressive conflicts arise in all cultures. There are, however, cultural differences in the sources people tend to perceive as the major cause of conflict. People in individualistic cultures, for example, usually interpret the source of conflicts as being instrumental in nature. If the conflict is instrumentally based, people can argue over task-oriented issues and remain friends. People in collectivistic cultures, in contrast, tend to see conflict arising from expressive sources (Ting-Toomey, 1985). If the person and the issue are not separated, it is difficult to have open disagreement without one or both parties losing face.

Stella Ting-Toomey (1988) argues that people in individualistic cultures prefer direct styles of dealing with conflict such as domination, control, or solution orientation. People in collectivistic cultures, on the other hand, prefer indirect styles of dealing with conflict that allow all parties to preserve face. They tend to use obliging and smoothing styles of conflict resolution or avoid the conflict all together. These differences are consistent with Dean Barnlund's (1975) description of conflict strategies in Japan and the United States. He suggests that people in the United States

> prefer to defend themselves actively, employing or developing the rationale for positions they have taken. When pushed they may resort to still more aggressive forms that utilize humor, sarcasm, or denunciation. Among Japanese, the reactions are more varied, but defenses tend to be more passive, permit withdrawal, and allow greater concealment. (p. 423)

Avoiding conflict in order to preserve face is not limited to the Japanese culture. Chinese, for example, would advise an executive to meet with an insulter and the target of the insult separately so that conflict between the two can be avoided. People in the United States, in contrast, would advise an executive to have a joint meeting so that the problem between the insulter and target of the insult can be resolved (Bond, Wan, Leung, & Giacalone, 1985). Similarly, Mexicans tend to avoid or deny that conflict exists, whereas people in the United States tend to use direct strategies to deal with it (e.g., McGinn, Harburg, & Ginsburg, 1973).[1]

Most, if not all, of the cross-cultural studies comparing the United States with other cultures have focused on European Americans. There also are differences across ethnic groups in the United States.[2] Ting-Toomey (1986), for example, contends that African Americans prefer a controlling conflict resolution style, whereas European Americans prefer a solution-oriented style. Thomas Kochman's (1981) descriptions of African American and European American styles of communication are consistent with these findings.[3] He points out that

> where [European Americans] use the relatively detached and unemotional *discussion* mode to engage an issue, [African Americans] use the more emotionally intense and involving mode of *argument*. Where [European Americans] tend to *underestimate* their exceptional talents and abilities, [African Americans] tend to *boast* about theirs. (p. 106)

Kochman goes on to observe that African Americans favor forceful outputs (e.g., volume of voice), whereas European Americans prefer subdued outputs. African Americans interpret European Americans' subdued responses as lifeless and European Americans interpret African Americans' responses as in bad taste.

Kochman isolates several other areas where European Americans' and African Americans' styles of communication may be problematic when they communicate with each other, particularly in a conflict situation. One area of importance for dealing with conflict is how members of the two groups view their responsibilities for the others' sensibilities and feelings. He illustrates differences in this area by discussing differences in reactions to an assignment he gives in an interpersonal communication class. Students in the class are told to confront each other and comment on their perceptions of each other's style of communication. The student responses to the assignment divide basically along ethnic lines:

> Twelve of the fourteen [European American] students argued for the right of students *not* to hear what others might want to say about them—thus giving priority to the protection of individual sensibilities, those of others as well as their own, even if this might result in forfeiting their own chance to say what they felt. . . . The eight [African American] students and the remaining two [European American] students, on the other hand, argued for the rights of those students to express what they had to say about others even if the protection of all individual sensibilities would be forfeited in the process. On this last point, one [African American] woman said: "I don't know about others, but if someone has something to say to me, I want to hear it." (pp. 122-123)

Kochman argues that withdrawing the protection of sensibilities is seen as insensitive or cruel by European Americans, whereas African Americans see European Americans failing to say what they think as lack of concern for their real self.

Kochman points out that "the greater capacity of [African Americans] to express themselves forcefully and to receive and manipulate the forceful assertions of others gives them greater leverage in interracial encounters" (p. 126). When African Americans offend European Americans' social sensibilities, European Americans demand an apology. African Americans see this demand as weak and inappropriate. Part of the difference is in who is considered responsible when people are upset. When European Americans are upset, they tend to see the cause as the other person. African Americans, in contrast, see themselves as responsible for their feelings. African Americans "will commonly say to those who have become angry, '*Others* did not make you angry'; rather, 'You *let yourself* become angry'" (Kochman, 1981, p. 127).

The preceding examples are designed only to illustrate cultural and ethnic differences in the approaches to conflict. It is important to keep in mind that there are also differences within ethnic groups. Responses to Kochman's class assignment, for example, illustrated that some European Americans share the approach of his African American students. The differences should be due to the strength of the individuals' ethnic identities. In conflict situations, it is important to be aware of *potential* cultural or ethnic differences in the approach to conflict, but the focus in resolving the conflict has to be on being mindful of our communication and dealing with the other person as an individual.

ASSESSING HOW YOU MANAGE CONFLICT

Before discussing how to manage intergroup conflict, I want you to get a feel for how you typically manage conflict. The questionnaire in Table 7.1 is designed to help you assess how you manage conflict with strangers. Take a few minutes to complete it now.

Scores on the questionnaire range from 10 to 50. The higher your score, the greater your potential for successfully managing conflict with strangers. If your score is low, remember that managing conflict successfully requires that you be mindful of the *process* of our communication. When you mindfully try to manage intergroup conflict, you may want to keep the material discussed in the remainder of this section in mind.

MANAGING INTERGROUP CONFLICT

In many ways managing intergroup conflict is similar to managing conflict with members of our own groups. To successfully manage intergroup conflicts, however, requires that we adapt our behavior in at least two ways. First, we must take the other person's

Table 7.1 Assessing Your Management of Conflict

The purpose of this questionnaire is to help you assess your ability to success-fully manage conflict. Respond to each statement by indicating the degree to which it is true regarding how you manage conflict with strangers: "Always False" (answer 1), "Usually False" (answer 2), "Sometimes True and Sometimes False" (answer 3), "Usually True" (answer 4), or "Always True" (answer 5).

_____ 1. I respond emotionally when I have conflict with others.
_____ 2. I try to understand others with whom I am having a conflict.
_____ 3. If someone rejects my ideas during a conflict, I also reject theirs.
_____ 4. I act reliably (i.e., consistently) when trying to manage conflict with others.
_____ 5. I try to get others to agree with me when we have a conflict.
_____ 6. I balance emotion with reason when trying to manage conflicts with others.
_____ 7. I am not open to being persuaded when I have conflict with others.
_____ 8. I consult others before deciding on matters that affect them.
_____ 9. I am not as constructive as I could be when I have conflict with others.
_____ 10. I try to do what is best for the relationship, even if the person with whom I am having a conflict does not reciprocate.

To find your score, first reverse the responses for the odd-numbered items (i.e., if you wrote 1, make it 5; if you wrote 2, make it 4; if you wrote 3, leave it as 3; if you wrote 4, make it 2; if you wrote 5, make it 1). Next, add the numbers next to each statement. Scores range from 10 to 50. The higher your score, the greater your potential to successfully manage conflict with strangers.

SOURCE: Adapted from Fisher and Brown (1988).

group memberships into consideration. If the other person is a collectivist, for example, he or she may prefer to avoid the conflict. An individualist who thinks it is important to address the conflict needs to adapt his or her style of communication to accommodate to the collectivist (e.g., be more indirect than usual). We also must take the other person's group memberships into consideration in interpreting her or his messages. Second, we must be aware of how our expectations for members of the other person's group influences our communication. Our expectations (e.g., ethnocen-trism, prejudice, stereotypes) influence how we interpret the other person's messages when we are on automatic pilot. To success-fully manage conflict, we must set our group-based expectations aside, understand real group differences, and focus on understanding the other person's perspective on the conflict. To do this, we must be mindful. In this section, I outline ways we can manage intergroup conflict when we are mindful. I begin by looking at the climate we establish when we talk to the other person.

Supportive Climates. As indicated earlier, it is not conflict per se that is positive or negative. How we manage the conflict, however, can have positive or negative consequences for our relationships. In managing conflict with strangers or with people from our own groups, it is important that we establish what Jack Gibb (1961) calls a supportive climate.

The first characteristic of a supportive climate is *description* rather than evaluation. We cannot understand others if we evaluate them before we understand their positions. Using evaluative speech brings up defenses. Descriptive speech, in contrast, does not make the other person uneasy, and in addition, it allows us to find out how they are interpreting what is happening.

Taking a *problem orientation* is the second characteristic of a supportive climate. Defining a mutual problem and expressing a willingness to collaborate in finding a solution implies that we have no predetermined outcome we want to see. If we have a predetermined outcome in mind and try to force this outcome on the other person, we are trying to control them. Attempts to control others are inevitably met with resistance.

Being spontaneous, as opposed to being strategic, is the third characteristic of a supportive climate. If I appear to have a hidden motive and am acting in what appears a strategic way to you, it will arouse defensiveness in you. If you appear spontaneous and not strategic to me, on the other hand, I will not get defensive.

Empathy also is important in establishing a supportive environment. As indicated in the previous chapter, if I convey empathy in my communication with you, you will know that I am concerned with your welfare. If you appear neutral toward me, I will become defensive.

The fifth characteristic of a supportive climate is communicating that we are *equal.* If I talk in a way that you perceive as sounding superior, you will become defensive. If we truly want to manage conflicts with strangers, we must avoid communicating at Lukens's distances of indifference, avoidance, and disparagement and communicate at a distance of sensitivity or equality.

The final characteristic of a supportive climate is *provisionalism*. If I communicate to you that I am open to your viewpoint and willing to experiment with my behavior (i.e., try to change it if needed), you will not become defensive. If, on the other hand, I communicate in such a way that indicates that I think I am right and certain of my attitudes and behavior, you will become defensive.

Be Unconditionally Constructive. Roger Fisher and Scott Brown (1988) of the Harvard Negotiation Project recommend a similar approach for conducting negotiations. They begin with the assumption that one participant can change a relationship. If we change the way we react to others, they will change the way they react to us. The objective of change is developing "a relationship that can deal with differences" (p. 3). Achieving change requires that we separate relationship and substantive issues and pursue goals in each arena separately.

Fisher and Brown offer a prescriptive approach to effective negotiations. Stated most simply they believe that we should always be unconditionally constructive when dealing with others:

Do only those things that are both good for the relationship and good for us, whether or not they reciprocate:

1. *Rationality.* Even if they are acting emotionally, balance emotion with reason.
2. *Understanding.* Even if they misunderstand us, try to understand them.
3. *Communication.* Even if they are not listening, consult them before deciding on matters that affect them.
4. *Reliability.* Even if they are trying to deceive us, neither trust nor deceive them; be reliable.
5. *Noncoercive modes of influence.* Even if they are trying to coerce us, neither yield to that coercion nor try to coerce them; be open to persuasion and try to persuade them.
6. *Acceptance.* Even if they reject us and our concerns as unworthy of their consideration, accept them as worthy of our consideration, care about them, and be open to learning from them. (p. 38)

Few, if any, of us follow the six guidelines in our normal, everyday communication with others. In order to apply Fisher and Brown's guidelines, we must be mindful. As Keith Brodie (1989) points out, "what is unconscious is not within a person's control, but what is made conscious is available for human beings to understand, to change, or to reinforce" (p. 16).

Communicating to Manage Conflict. David Johnson (1986) suggests that the first step in managing conflicts is to *confront* the other person regarding the conflict. The goal of confronting the other person is to clarify and explore the issues surrounding the conflict. We should make the confrontation when we are sure that both parties are available to discuss the conflict (e.g., neither is emotionally upset, both have time). When we confront the other person we need to express our thoughts and feelings about the conflict and ask the other person to do the same. We should not try to manage the conflict when we confront the other person, but rather schedule a time when we can negotiate. To be effective, our confrontations need to be done in a way that does *not* increase the other person's anxiety or defensiveness and allows him or her to maintain her or his self-concept. This involves using the skills discussed throughout the book.

To successfully manage intergroup conflict we need to be *cooperative*, not competitive (M. Deutsch, 1973). This means that we need to define the conflict as a *mutual problem* that needs to be solved. When it is defined as a mutual problem to be solved, both parties can win instead of one party having to win and the other loose. In addition to defining the problem as mutual, we need to look for a *common definition of the problem.* If we do not agree on the definition of the problem, we cannot solve it. We also need to define the problem in the most limited way possible. If it is a big problem, we can break it down into smaller ones, and deal with the smaller ones one at a time.

In addition to cooperation, we need to try to communicate as effectively as possible. There are two sides to effective communication. First, we need to *adapt our messages* so that the other person can accurately interpret them. Second, we need to make sure that we *understand the other person.* This requires that our perceptions be as accurate as possible. We can decrease the distortions and biases in our perceptions by using the perception-checking and active-listening skills discussed in Chapter 4 and the empathy skill discussed in Chapter 6. When our perceptions are distorted, we will perceive that strangers have negative and hostile feelings toward us and not perceive the positive feelings they have. If we are not mindful, this can lead to a self-fulfilling prophecy of failure. If we do not understand the other person's position and she or he does not understand our position, there is no way we can find a solution acceptable to both of us. To successfully manage conflict, we must be able to accurately predict and explain strangers' behavior. We also have to make it clear to the other person that we are interested in finding a solution that is fair to both of us.

Recognizing similarities and not just focusing on differences is necessary to successfully manage conflict. If we focus only on differences between our position and that of the other person, we will never be able to manage the conflict. Finding a solution that will work for both of us requires that we see similarities in our positions and then build on these similarities. In defining the problem, we need to understand how our behavior has helped create the problem and make sure we understand the other person's position. To successfully manage conflicts, both parties must understand and see similarities in each other's positions and feelings.

To successfully manage conflicts we must be able to disagree with others and at the same time *confirm* them and their views of themselves. If we treat others as though they are not valued, they will become defensive and their anxiety will increase. Conflicts cannot be managed constructively when either party is defensive. Confirming the other person requires that we adapt our style of communication.

Stella Ting-Toomey (1994) provides suggestions as to how individualists and collectivists can adapt their behavior when they have a conflict. Individualists can make several adaptations that will increase the likelihood of success. First, individualists need to remember that collectivists use an interdependent self-construal. Their actions reflect on their ingroup and they have to take their ingroups into consideration in managing conflicts.

Second, individualists should try to deal with conflicts when they are small rather than allow them to become large issues and recognize that collectivists may want to use a third party to mediate the conflict. Third, individualists need to help the collectivists maintain face (public image) during the conflict. This means not humiliating or embarrassing collectivists in public. Fourth, individualists need to pay attention to collectivists' nonverbal behavior and implicit messages. Fifth, individualists need to actively listen when collectivists talk. Sixth, individualists need to use indirect messages more than they typically do; this means using qualifier words (e.g., maybe, possibly), being more tentative, and avoiding bluntly saying no. Seventh, Ting-Toomey suggests that individualists let go of conflict if collectivists do not want to deal with it (recall that avoiding is the preferred collectivist strategy).

Collectivists also need to make adaptations when dealing with individualists. First, collectivists need to recognize that individualists often separate the conflict from the person with whom they are having conflict. Second, collectivists need to focus on the substantive issues involved in the conflict. Third, collectivists need to use an assertive, rather than nonassertive, style when dealing with conflict. Fourth, collectivists need to be more direct than they usually are. This involves using more "I" statements and directly stating opinions and feelings. Fifth, collectivists need to provide verbal feedback to individualists and focus on the verbal aspects of communication more than they typically do. Sixth, collectivists need to recognize that individualists do not value silence in conversations. Seventh, collectivists need to try to manage conflicts when they arise rather than avoiding them.

Finally, we may have to coordinate our motivations to manage the conflict. We may be ready to manage the conflict today, but the other person is not. Tomorrow the other person may be ready and we are not. We can, however, consciously change our own motivation if we choose. *Reaching an agreement* occurs when we have a joint solution. Our agreement should specify how each person will act differently in the future, including both new things that the person will do in the future and things that will be avoided (e.g., criticism).

❏ Developing Relationships

In this section, I examine how we develop relationships with strangers. To put this discussion in context, however, it is necessary to begin with a discussion of how communication in interpersonal relationships is similar and different across cultures and ethnic groups.

SIMILARITIES AND DIFFERENCES ACROSS GROUPS

Before we can understand how we form relationships with members of different cultures or ethnic groups, we need to recognize how communication in relationships are similar and different across cultures. In this section I focus on similarities and differences in perceptions of the intimacy of our relationships, self-disclosure, how uncertainty is conceived and reduced, and how communication rules in relationships are similar and different.

Intimacy of Relationships. There are differences and similarities in how people communicate in interpersonal relationships across cultures. Japanese perceive ingroup relationships (i.e., co-worker and university classmate) to be more intimate than North Americans do (Gudykunst & Nishida, 1986b). The differences in perceived intimacy of relationships affect the way people communicate.[4] To illustrate, Japanese communicate more personally with members of their ingroups than with members of outgroups. In the United States, in contrast, there is not a large difference in how we communicate with members of our ingroups and outgroups, except when outgroup membership is determined by cultural background or ethnicity (Gudykunst & Hammer, 1988b; Gudykunst et al., 1992).

Generally, members of different cultures prefer to talk about their tastes and opinions and prefer to avoid discussing their physical attributes and personalities (Barnlund, 1975). There are, however, important cultural differences in self-disclosure. Overall, members of individualistic cultures are expected to self-disclose personal information about themselves more than members of collectivistic cultures (Gudykunst & Nishida, 1986a). One of the main ways we get to know others in individualistic cultures like the United States is by gathering personal information about them. This type of information is not critical in the early stages of relationship development in collectivistic cultures. In collectivistic cultures, individuals need to know information about others' ingroup memberships and status in order to predict their behavior. In best-friendships members of collectivistic cultures will self-disclose personal information at rates similar to those in individualistic cultures.

In addition to the cultural differences in perceived intimacy and self-disclosure, there are many similarities across cultures. People in Japan and the United States, for example, rate relationships with people they have never met as less intimate than relationships with acquaintances, relationships with acquaintances as less intimate than relationships with friends, and relationships with friends as less intimate than relationships with close friends (Gudykunst & Nishida, 1986b). The similarities in the perceived intimacy of relationships are manifested in our communication. Communication in both cultures becomes more personal as the perceived intimacy of the relationship increases (Gudykunst & Nishida, 1986a, 1986b). To illustrate, we talk about more intimate things about ourselves with friends than with acquaintances.

Uncertainty. The type of information that people seek for the purpose of reducing uncertainty varies across cultures (Gudykunst & Nishida, 1986a). In individualistic cultures like the United States, the focus tends to be on gathering personal information about the other person. Knowing another person's attitudes, beliefs, and values, for example, can be used to predict her or his behavior. In collectivistic cultures, in contrast, personal information is not necessarily useful in predicting others' behavior. Rather, group-based information is needed. Members of collectivistic cultures need to know whether another person is a member of one of their own ingroups. Information about another person's status (e.g., is he or she higher status than I am?), age, and so forth allows that person to be placed in the web of group affiliations. Person-based information does not lead to uncertainty reduction in collectivistic cultures as much as it does in individualistic cultures.

To illustrate the differences, consider a story that Chie Nakane (1974), a Japanese sociologist who taught at the University of Tokyo, tells. Professor Nakane was invited to give a talk at another university in Japan. She did not know the professor who invited her. Prior to her arrival she was apprehensive about interacting with the person meeting her. When she arrived at the lecture hall a man approached her and bowed. Before he said anything else, the man said "I am from the University of Tokyo," indicating to Professor Nakane that he had attended her university and thus shared an ingroup membership with her. The man then went on to give his name and present his business card. Nakane points out that once she knew that she shared an ingroup membership (the University of Tokyo) with the other professor, she relaxed because she knew she could predict his behavior.

Communication Rules. There also are similarities and differences in the rules used to guide communication across cultures and ethnic groups. Jennifer Noesjirwan (1978), for example, argues that there are different rules for dealing with other people in waiting rooms and at bus stops. The rule in both situations in Indonesia (collectivistic) requires one to talk to any other person present. The rule for Australians (individualistic), in contrast, requires one to ignore any other person present.

Michael Argyle and Monica Henderson (1984) suggest that there are six universal rules in personal relationships: (a) we should respect others' privacy; (b) we should look the other person in the eye during conversations; (c) we should or should not discuss that which is said in confidence with the other person; (d) we should or should not indulge in sexual activity with the other person; (e) we should not criticize the other person in public; and (f) we should repay debts, favors, or compliments no matter how small. The privacy rule receives the strongest endorsement across cultures (Argyle, Henderson, Bond, Iizuka, & Contarelo, 1986). The confidence rule receives strong support in Great Britain, Italy, and Hong Kong, but not in Japan. The public criticism rule is endorsed more strongly in Japan and Hong Kong than in Italy and Great Britain. These findings are to be expected given that Japan and Hong Kong are collectivistic cultures and Italy and Great

Britain are individualistic cultures. Harmony is maintained in collectivistic cultures by avoiding criticism of ingroup members.

In addition to differences in communication rules across cultures, there are differences among ethnic groups within cultures. Mary Jane Collier, Sydney Ribeau, and Michael Hecht (1986), for example, isolate rules for conversing with acquaintances in three subcultures in the United States. The rules for Mexican Americans are: "Be polite and show verbal and nonverbal concern for the other, acknowledge your cultural identity, conform to your sexual and professional role, be friendly, support your point of view, offer relevant comments and constructive criticism, be open-minded and direct" (p. 452). The rules for African Americans are: "Conform to societal and individual norms by acting verbally and nonverbally polite, support your position and stay on the topic, follow professional role prescriptions, but modify these to individual needs, be assertive yet open-minded, and be friendly" (p. 453). The corresponding rules for European American conversations are: "Be socially polite and show concern for the individual, especially through verbal behavior; follow professional, sexual, and personal role prescriptions; use relevant arguments and support them; be open-minded and friendly" (p. 453). Collier (1986) argues that behaviors that conform to mutually shared rules are more rewarding and self-concept affirming.

INTERGROUP RELATIONSHIPS

Most of our close interpersonal relationships are with people who are relatively similar to us. We tend to develop close relationships with members of our own culture and members of our ethnic group (Pogrebin, 1987). Constantia Safilios-Rothchild (1982) also points out that "there is considerable evidence that very often people do not want to enter unpredictable, and therefore, stressful interactions with visibly disabled people, and they avoid doing so by extending only 'fictional acceptance' which does not go beyond a polite, inhibited, and overcontrolled interaction" (p. 44). Paul Fussell (1983) claims that class differences similarly hinder members of different social classes from developing close relationships. With respect to intergenerational interactions, Lois

Tamir (1984) reports that age segregation in society "has hampered the opportunity for young and old to come to know one another. Hence, when they do come into contact, well-worn and often detrimental stereotypes may persist, and participants must make an active effort to dispel these preconceptions for a healthy dialogue to take place" (p. 39).

One reason why we do not have close relationships with members of other groups is that we do not have a lot of contact with strangers. Another reason is that our initial interactions and superficial contacts with strangers often result in ineffective communication. When our communication with strangers is not as effective and satisfying as we would like, we do not *try* to develop intimate relationships with strangers. If we understand the process of relationship development, however, we can make an informed conscious decision as to whether or not we want to have intimate relationships with strangers. In making such a decision, it is important to keep in mind that the more we know about strangers, the more accurately we can predict their behavior (Honeycutt, Knapp, & Powers, 1983).

Communication Satisfaction. One aspect of developing relationships with strangers is the degree to which we are satisfied with strangers' communication with us and strangers are satisfied with our communication with them. Satisfaction is an affective (i.e., emotional) reaction to communication that meets or fails to meet our expectations (Hecht, 1978). The more communication in a relationship is personalized and synchronized and the less difficulty people experience in communicating with their partner, the more satisfied they are with the communication in their relationship (Gudykunst, Nishida, & Chua, 1986). Also, the more partners self-disclose to each other, the more they are attracted to each other, the more similarities they perceive, and the more uncertainty they reduce about each other, the more satisfied they are (Gudykunst et al., 1986). Further, the more effective the partners judge each other's communication to be, the more satisfied they are.

Michael Hecht, Sydney Ribeau, and Jess Alberts (1989) isolate seven factors that contribute to African Americans' satisfaction with their conversations with European Americans. The first factor necessary for satisfaction is acceptance. To be satisfied, African Americans need to feel that they are respected, confirmed, and accepted by the European Americans with whom they communicate. Satisfying conversations with European Americans also included emotional expression and the European Americans being authentic (i.e., European Americans in satisfying conversations were perceived as genuine, whereas European Americans in dissatisfying conversations were perceived as evasive). African Americans also perceived that there was understanding (i.e., shared meanings) and goal attainment in satisfying conversations. They perceived negative stereotyping and felt powerless (e.g., manipulated or controlled) in dissatisfying conversations.

Michael Hecht, Sydney Ribeau, and Michael Sedano (1990) isolate factors Mexican Americans associate with satisfying and dissatisfying conversations with European Americans. Similar to African Americans, Mexican Americans see acceptance as an important aspect of satisfying conversations. Satisfying conversations with European Americans also included the expression of feelings and behaving rationally. The presence of self-expression and relational solidarity also contributed to satisfaction in conversations. Negative stereotyping and failure to discover a shared worldview (i.e., absence of perceived similarities) emerged as important factors in dissatisfying conversations.

European Americans need to communicate acceptance, express emotions, and avoid negative stereotyping for non-European Americans to be satisfied with interethnic conversations. Communicating acceptance and avoiding negative stereotyping are important in developing relationships across class, age, and disability lines as well (Pogrebin, 1987).

The questionnaire in Table 7.2 is designed to help you assess your satisfaction with your communication with strangers. Take a couple of minutes to complete the questionnaire now.

Scores on the questionnaire range from 10 to 50. The higher your score, the greater your satisfaction with communicating with strangers. Even though your perceptions of how you communicate with strangers are different than the strangers' perceptions, you can "reverse" the statements in Table 7.2 to assess your perceptions of your communication with strangers. Remember, however,

Table 7.2 Assessing Your Communication Satisfaction With Strangers

The purpose of this questionnaire is to help you assess your satisfaction with your communication with strangers. Respond to each statement by indicating the degree to which it is true of your communication with strangers: "Always False" (answer 1), "Usually False" (answer 2), "Sometimes True and Sometimes False" (answer 3), "Usually True" (answer 4), or "Always True" (answer 5).

_____ 1. I am satisfied with my communication with strangers.
_____ 2. Strangers are evasive when we communicate.
_____ 3. I enjoy communicating with strangers.
_____ 4. I do not feel confirmed when I communicate with strangers.
_____ 5. I feel accepted when I communicate with strangers.
_____ 6. I do not get to say what I want to say when I communicate with strangers.
_____ 7. I am able to present myself as I want to when I communicate with strangers.
_____ 8. Strangers do not understand me when we communicate.
_____ 9. Conversations flow smoothly when I communicate with strangers.
_____ 10. I do not accomplish my goals when I communicate with strangers.

To find your score, first reverse the responses for the even-numbered items (i.e., if you wrote 1, make it 5; if you wrote 2, make it 4; if you wrote 3, leave it as 3; if you wrote 4, make it 2; if you wrote 5, make it 1). Next, add the numbers next to each statement. Scores range from 10 to 50. The higher your score, the greater your satisfaction in communicating with this person.

SOURCE: Adapted from Hecht (1978).

that how you think you are coming across to strangers may not be the same as how they perceive your communication with them.

Perceived Similarity. The extent to which we perceive similarity of self-concepts with others influences our attraction to them. Ruth Wylie (1979), for example, points out that actual similarities in our self-concepts and others is _not_ related to our attraction to them. Rather, we are attracted to others we think see themselves similar to the way we see ourselves.

In addition to perceived similarity in self-conceptions, we are also attracted to others if we perceive similarities in attitudes, values, and communication styles. If we perceive that our attitudes are similar to others we will be attracted to them because the similarity in attitudes validates our view of the world (Byrne,

1971). We filter potential relational partners by the extent to which we perceive that they are similar to us (Duck, 1977). In the initial stages of getting to know others, we probably focus on general attitudes and opinions that we hold and search for similarities in central aspects of our worldviews (e.g., our core values).

Probably one of the most important similarities we search for in potential relational partners is similarity in our orientations toward interpersonal interactions (Sunnafrank, 1991). That is, if we perceive similarities in our orientations toward communication, we are likely to form close relationships with others. Recent research suggests close friends have similar orientations toward five specific communication activities: conflict management, ways to comfort each other, ways to persuade each other, ways to support each other's self-conceptions, and ways to tell stories and jokes (Burleson, Samter, & Lucchetti, 1992).

When we meet people from different cultures and ethnic groups, one of the main factors inhibiting the development of close relationships are the differences in cultures and ethnic groups. Although it is important to recognize genuine differences, it also is important to go beyond looking at differences. To do so and develop close relationships with members of other cultures or ethnic groups, we must talk with them and discover that we are similar in other areas.[5] Perceived similarities in attitudes, lifestyles, and worldviews are necessary for close relationships to develop between members of different cultures (Sudweeks, Gudykunst, Nishida, & Ting-Toomey, 1990).

Table 7.3 contains an assessment designed to help you determine the degree of perceived similarity in different relationships. Take a few minutes to complete it now.

Scores on the two scales range from 10 to 50. The higher your score, the more similarities you perceive in the relationship. In general, you probably perceive more similarities with your acquaintance from your own group than with the acquaintance from another group.

Uncertainty. The cultural differences in the types of information needed to reduce uncertainty can lead to interesting exchanges when individualists and collectivists meet for the first time.

Table 7.3 Assessing Perceived Similarity When Communicating in
              Different Relationships

The purpose of this questionnaire is to help you assess the amount of similarity you perceive when you communicate in different relationships. Respond to each statement by indicating the frequency that the statement applies in the particular relationship. If you "Never" have the experience, answer 1 in the space provided; if you "Almost Never" have the experience, answer 2; if you "Sometimes" have the experience and sometimes do not, answer 3; if you "Almost Always" have the experience, answer 4; if you "Always" have the experience, answer 5. Answer all questions for the amount of similarity you perceive with an acquaintance from a different group. Then answer all of the questions again thinking of an acquaintance from your own group. Think of specific individuals when you answer the questions.

OTHER GROUP	OWN GROUP	
___	___	1. I perceive that _____ and I have similar opinions.
___	___	2. I do not think that _____ and I have similar values.
___	___	3. I think that _____ and I have similar attitudes.
___	___	4. I do not think that _____ and I have similar beliefs.
___	___	5. I perceive that _____ and I have similar lifestyles.
___	___	6. I do not think that _____ and I have similar ways of telling stories and jokes.
___	___	7. I think that _____ and I have similar ways of managing conflict.
___	___	8. I do not think that _____ and I have similar ways of comforting each other.
___	___	9. I perceive that _____ and I have similar ways of persuading each other.
___	___	10. I do not think that _____ and I have similar ways of supporting each other's self-conceptions.

To find your scores, first reverse the responses for the even-numbered items (i.e., if you wrote 1, make it 5; if you wrote 2, make it 4; if you wrote 3, leave it as 3; if you wrote 4, make it 2; if you wrote 5, make it 1). Next, add the numbers next to each of the items. Scores range from 10 to 50. The higher your scores, the more similarity you perceive when interacting in the different relationships.

Individualists inevitably tell others personal information about themselves and seek this type of information from others, whereas collectivists tell others information about their group memberships and seek the same type of information from others. If we ask individualists what they do for a living, they will probably tell us their occupation. If we ask collectivists the same question, they will probably tell us the company for which they work. Collectivists might ask individualists their age so that they can determine who is older. Many individualists will take offense in being asked their age by strangers. Individualists, in contrast, might ask collectivists about their feelings or attitudes when they first meet. The collectivists would probably answer questions about their feelings or attitudes indirectly and avoid directly answering the individualists' question because they see these questions as too personal. Both parties will be frustrated—the collectivists because the individualists asked personal questions, the individualists because the collectivists did not answer their questions (e.g., Gudykunst, 1983; Lee & Boster, 1991).

Table 7.4 contains a questionnaire designed to help you assess the degree to which you experience uncertainty in you initial interaction with members of other groups and with members of your own group. Take a few minutes to complete it now.

Scores on the questionnaire in Table 7.4 range from 10 to 50. Most people will experience more uncertainty in their initial interactions with members of other groups than with members of their own group.

Anxiety. As indicated in Chapter 1, we experience more anxiety in our initial interactions with members of other groups than with members of our own group. Managing anxiety is associated closely with developing trust. *Trust* is "confidence that one will find what is desired from another, rather than what is feared" (M. Deutsch, 1973, p. 149). When we trust others, we expect positive outcomes from our interactions with them; when we have anxiety about interacting with others we fear negative outcomes from our interactions with them. When we first meet someone, "trust is often little more than a naive expression of hope" (Holmes & Rempel, 1989, p. 192). For us to have hope about the relationship, our anxiety must be below our maximum threshold. For relationships to become close,

> most people need to act *as if* a sense of [trust] were justified, and set their doubts aside. To do so requires a "leap of faith" in the face of evidence that can never be conclusive. Thus trust becomes . . . an

Table 7.4 Assessing Your Uncertainty When Communicating in
Different Relationships

The purpose of this questionnaire is to help you assess the amount of uncertainty you experience when you communicate in different relationships. Respond to each statement by indicating the frequency with which the situation in the statements occurs when you communicate in different relationships. If you "Never" have the experience, answer 1 in the space provided; if you "Almost Never" have the experience, answer 2; if you "Sometimes" have the experience and sometimes do not, answer 3; if you "Almost Always" have the experience, answer 4; if you "Always" have the experience, answer 5. Answer all questions for strangers from other groups first. Next, answer the questions again for your initial interactions with members of your own group.

OTHER GROUP	OWN GROUP	
___	___	1. I am not confident when I communicate with _____.
___	___	2 I can interpret _____'s behavior when we communicate.
___	___	3. I am indecisive when I communicate with _____.
___	___	4. I can explain _____'s behavior when we communicate.
___	___	5. I am not able to understand _____ when we communicate.
___	___	6. I know what to do when I communicate with _____.
___	___	7. I am uncertain how to behave when I communicate with _____.
___	___	8. I can comprehend _____'s behavior when we communicate.
___	___	9. I am not able to predict _____'s behavior when we communicate.
___	___	10. I can describe _____'s behavior when we communicate.

To find your scores, first reverse the responses for the even-numbered items (i.e., if you wrote 1, make it 5; if you wrote 2, make it 4; if you wrote 3, leave it as 3; if you wrote 4, make it 2; if you wrote 5, make it 1). Next, add the numbers next to each of the items. Scores range from 10 to 50. The higher your scores, the more uncertainty you experience when interacting in the different relationships.

emotionally charged sense of closure. It permits an illusion of control . . . where one can plan ahead without anxiety. (Holmes & Rempel, 1989, p. 204)

Without some minimal degree of trust, relationships cannot become close.

Table 7.5 contains a questionnaire designed to help you assess the amount of anxiety you experience when communicating with members of other groups and with members of your own group. Take a few minutes to complete it now.

Scores on the questionnaire in Table 7.5 range from 10 to 50. The higher your score, the more anxiety you experience. Most people will experience more anxiety in interacting with members of others groups than in interacting with members of their own group.

Relationship Development. As relationships between people from different groups become more intimate (i.e., move from initial interactions to close friendship), communication becomes more personal; for example, there are increases in self-disclosure, interpersonal attraction, perceived similarities, and uncertainty reduction (Gudykunst et al., 1986, 1987). Group similarities appear to have a major influence on our communication in the early stages of relationship development (i.e., initial interactions and acquaintance relationships), but not in the final stages (e.g., close friendship; Gudykunst, Chua, & Gray, 1987).[6]

I do not want to imply here that group differences are not problems in close relationships. Group differences can be sources of misunderstandings in intimate relationships, particularly in marital relationships. How to raise children, for example, is a central issue in intercultural or interethnic marriages. Group differences can be major problems if the partners are not mindful of their communication around core issues like this.

Although there may be problems in close relationships due to group differences, group differences have less of an effect on communication in close friendships than in acquaintance relationships.[7] The nature of the relationship development process itself appears to offer a reasonable explanation as to why group dissimilarities do not influence communication in close friendships as much as in earlier stages of relationships.[8] In early stages of relationship development, we must rely on cultural and social information to predict another person's behavior because we do not have sufficient information to use personal information in

Table 7.5 Assessing Your Anxiety When Communicating in Different Relationships

---

The purpose of this questionnaire is to help you assess the amount of anxiety you experience when you communicate in different relationships. Respond to each statement by indicating the frequency with which the statement applies in the particular relationship. If you "Never" have the experience, answer 1 in the space provided; if you "Almost Never" have the experience, answer 2; if you "Sometimes" have the experience and sometimes do not, answer 3; if you "Almost Always" have the experience, answer 4; if you "Always" have the experience, answer 5. Answer all questions for the amount of anxiety you experience when communicating with strangers from other groups for the first time. Next, answer the questions again regarding the amount of anxiety you experience interacting with people from your own group for the first time.

OTHER GROUP	OWN GROUP	
___	___	1. I feel calm when I communicate with _____.
___	___	2. I get frustrated when I communicate with _____.
___	___	3. I do not get ruffled when I communicate with _____.
___	___	4. I am insecure when I communicate with _____.
___	___	5. I feel composed when I communicate with _____.
___	___	6. I feel anxious when I communicate with _____.
___	___	7. I do not get excited when I have to communicate with _____.
___	___	8. I feel stress when I communicate with _____.
___	___	9. I feel relaxed when I communicate with _____.
___	___	10. I am worried when I communicate with _____.

To find your scores, first reverse the responses for the odd-numbered items (i.e., if you wrote 1, make it 5; if you wrote 2, make it 4; if you wrote 3, leave it as 3; if you wrote 4, make it 2; if you wrote 5, make it 1). Next, add the numbers next to each of the items. Scores range from 10 to 50. The higher your scores, the more anxiety you experience when interacting in the different relationships.

SOURCE: Adapted from Stephan and Stephan (1985).

making predictions. As the relationship develops and we gather information about the other person, we begin to use personal information. When we use personal information, we are differentiating how the other person is similar to and different from other members of his or her groups. In other words, we no longer rely on our stereotypes to predict the other person's behavior.

What is it about our initial interactions and our communication with acquaintances who are from other groups that allows the relationship to develop into a "friendship"? As indicated earlier, we must communicate in a way that signals we accept the other person, we must express our feelings, and we must avoid negative stereotyping. All of these factors combined suggested that our communication with the other person helps him or her have positive personal and social identities. Stated differently, we must support the other person's self-conceptions.[9]

We must perceive some degree of similarity between ourselves and the other person if an intimate relationship is to develop (Gudykunst, Gao, Sudweeks, Ting-Toomey, & Nishida, 1991; Sudweeks et al., 1990).[10] The display of empathy and mutual accommodation regarding differences in communication styles (i.e., adapting each other's style to the other person) also appears to be critical.[11] It is also important that at least one person have some competency in the other's language or dialect and that both parties demonstrate some interest in the other's group memberships. Other factors that appear to be important are similar to those in developing relationships with people from our own groups. We must, for example, make time available to interact with the other person and consciously or unconsciously attempt to increase the intimacy of our communication (i.e., talk about things that are important to us).[12]

When we communicate on automatic pilot, we often filter out members of other groups as potential friends simply because they are different and our communication with them is not as effective as our communication with people from our own group. Whether or not we want to act differently depends on our motivation. Letty Cottin Pogrebin (1987) points out that pluralistic friendships celebrate

> *genuine* differences arising out of life experiences and culture but reject *socially constructed* differences resulting from stereotypes or discrimination. . . .
>   Ethnicity is friendship-enhancing when it does not make another group into an "Other" group.

Ethnicity is friendship-enhancing when we make it an "and" not a "but." The difference is palpable: "She's my friend *and* she's Jewish" allows me the pride of difference that a "but" would destroy.

Group pride spawns both pride *and* prejudice. What makes a group special also makes it different. For some people, "different" must mean "better" or it is experienced as "worse." But people who do not need ethnic supremacy to feel ethnic pride find comfort and attitudinal regeneration among their "own kind" and also are able to make friends across racial and ethnic boundaries. (pp. 187-188)

Pogrebin's comments on ethnicity apply to other group differences (e.g., disability, age, social class) that affect relationship development as well.

Do we want to approach people who are different or continue to avoid them? I believe that relationships with strangers provide a chance for us to grow as individuals. The choice about developing these relationships, however, is an individual one. I encourage you to make a conscious choice about whether or not you want communicate effectively and develop relationships with strangers rather than relying on unconscious, mindless decisions. If you choose to approach strangers and are mindful of your communication, you will recognize real differences and eventually discover similarities between yourselves and the strangers with whom you communicate. The similarities you discover provide the foundation for developing intimate relationships.

❑ Building Community

As indicated in Chapter 1, Mother Teresa sees spiritual deprivation (i.e., a feeling of emptiness associated with separation from our fellow humans) as the major problem facing the world today (Jampolsky, 1989). One way to deal with this spiritual deprivation is to build community in our lives.

The term community is derived from the Latin *communitas*, which has two related, but distinct interpretations: (a) the quality of "common interest and hence the quality of fellowship" and (b) "a body of people having in common an external bond" (Rosenthal, 1984,

p. 219). Daniel Yankelovich (1984) argues that community evokes the "feeling that 'Here is where I belong, these are my people, I care for them, they care for me, I am part of them' . . . its absence is experienced as an achy loss, a void . . . feelings of isolation, falseness, instability, and impoverishment of spirit" (p. 227).

THE NATURE OF COMMUNITY

Martin Buber (1958, 1965) sees community as a choice around a common center; the voluntary coming together of people in a direct relationship that involves a concern for self, other, and group. He believes that community must begin in small groups and that it cannot be forced on organizations or nations. At the same time, Buber contends that some form of community is necessary to make life worth living.

> *Some form of community is necessary to make life worth living.*

In Buber's view, a community is *not* a group of like-minded people; rather, it is a group of individuals with complementary natures who have differing minds. Extending Buber's analysis, Maurice Friedman (1983) draws a distinction between a community of otherness and a community of affinity. A *community of affinity* is a group of like-minded people who have come together for security. Friedman argues that they feel safe because they use a similar language and the same slogans, but they do not have close relations with one another. A *community of otherness*, on the other hand, begins from the assumption that each member has a different point of view that contributes to the group. Members are not alike, but they share common concerns.

Buber sees openness, *not* intimacy, as the key to developing community. "A real community need not consist of people who are perpetually together; but it must consist of people who, precisely because they are comrades, have mutual access to one another and are ready for one another" (quoted in Friedman, 1986, p. xiii). The importance of openness becomes clear when we look at the distinctions Buber draws among three forms of communication: monologue, technical dialogue, and dialogue. *Monologues* are self-centered conversations in which the other person is treated as an object. *Technical dialogues* are information-centered conversations. Monologues and technical dialogues are necessary and appropriate at times, but problems emerge when they are used too frequently: when there is a lack of connection between the participants, community cannot develop. For community to develop, dialogue is necessary. *Dialogue* involves communication between individuals. In a dialogue, each participant's feeling of control and ownership is minimized; each participant confirms the other, even when conflict occurs.

Developing community requires a commitment to values higher than our own (Arnett, 1986). Glenn Tinder (1980) suggests that the values of civility, and tolerance of pluralism and diversity are necessary for community. It is important to recognize that holding these values requires that we accept that our own needs are not always met (Arnett, 1986).

The key to building community in Buber's view is for individuals to walk a narrow ridge. The concept of *narrow ridge* involves taking both our own and others' viewpoints into consideration in our dealings with others. Robert Arnett (1986) uses the metaphor of a tightrope walker to illustrate the narrow ridge. If a tightrope walker leans too much in one direction he or she will begin to loose his or her balance. To regain her or his balance, the tightrope walker must compensate by leaning in the other direction. The same is true of walking the narrow ridge in our dealings with others. If we give our own opinions too much weight in a conversation, we must compensate by considering the others' opinions of equal weight.

In walking the narrow ridge, we must try to understand others' points of view. Buber does not advocate that we take a nonjudgmental or relativistic attitude toward others. Rather, he argues that we openly listen to others, but if we are not persuaded by their arguments, we should maintain our original position; if we are persuaded, we should modify our opinions. There is a subtle difference between listening openly but not changing our minds and being close-minded. The difference depends on our intentions. If our intentions are seriously to consider others' opinions, we are walking the narrow ridge; if our intentions are not to consider others' opinions, then we are close-minded. It is the dual concern for self and other in walking the narrow ridge that stops polarized communication and allows community to develop (Arnett, 1986).

Buber (1958) argues that we should avoid giving in and accepting others' opinions just for the sake of peace. Rather, he suggests that we should accept others' opinions or compromise if it is the way to the best solution. Our commitment must be to principles, not false peace. It is also important to note that Buber does not suggest that we accept everything others say unquestioningly. Suspicion is sometimes warranted, but problems occur when suspicion becomes a norm of communication. When suspicion is always present, existential mistrust exists.

One factor that contributes to mistrust in low-context, individualistic cultures like the United States that value direct communication is looking for hidden meanings. Suspicion and looking for hidden meanings are only two of the factors that lead to mistrust. No matter how mistrust comes about, it always polarizes communication. Understanding strangers requires "a willing suspension of disbelief" (Trilling, 1968, p. 106). Developing superordinate goals and developing community require trust (Staub, 1989).

PRINCIPLES OF COMMUNITY BUILDING

To summarize, a community consists of diverse individuals who are honest and open with each other, trust each other, engage in ethical behavior, and are committed to living together. Members of a community are civil to each other and they value diversity even as they search for the commonalities humans share. Community is desirable because, as Buber points out, it is community that makes life worth living. Further, it is the existence of community that will make peace and intergroup harmony possible. Although community occurs in groups, individuals must take the responsibility for building community in their marriages, workplaces, schools, cities, nations, and the world.

To conclude, I want to synthesize the information presented into a set of principles for community building. These principles are based on seven assumptions:

1. Community is necessary to make life worth living and increase the potential for peace in the world. Peace is not possible without community. "Our experience of connection and community shape who we are, how we experience other people, and how we bear the stresses of both ordinary and extraordinary events" (Staub, 1989, p. 269).

2. Developing community is the responsibility of the individual. Each of us must take the responsibility for building community in our own life. "People who fully develop and harmoniously integrate their capabilities, values, and goals will be connected to others. The full evolution of the self . . . requires relationships and the development of deep connections and community—as well as the capacity for separateness" (Staub, 1989, p. 269).

3. Cultural and ethnic diversity (and all other forms of diversity, as well) are necessary resources for building community. A true community cannot exist without diversity.

4. Communities can be any size (e.g., a marriage, social organization, university, town, country, or even the world), but we must start building community in the smaller groups of which we are members (e.g., families) and work toward developing community in the larger groups (e.g., universities).

5. We are what we think. Gerald Jampolsky (1989), among others, points out that "everything in life depends on the thoughts we choose to hold in our minds and our willingness to change our belief systems" (p. 31). Similarly, in *The Dhammapada*, Buddha said that "our life is shaped by our minds; we become what we think."

6. Community cannot exist without conflict. Stuart Hampshire (1989) argues that we should expect "ineliminable and acceptable conflicts, and . . . rationally controlled hostilities, as the normal condition" (p. 189). Peck (1987) makes the point that we tend to assume that "if we can resolve our conflicts, then someday we will be able to live together in community" (p. 72). He argues that this assumption is mistaken. Actually, "if we can live together in

community, then someday we shall be able to resolve our conflicts" (p. 72). To develop community, therefore, we must engage in graceful fighting; try to persuade each other, but not coerce each other.

7. As Fisher and Brown (1988) suggest, one person can change a relationship and/or start the development of community. If one person follows the principles suggested below, people with whom this person comes in contact will change the way they interact.

Given these assumptions and the material summarized throughout the book, seven community-building principles can be isolated:

1. *Be committed.* We must be committed to the principle of building community in our lives, as well as to the individuals with whom we are trying to develop a community (Peck, 1987). Commitment to others is prerequisite for community to exist. If we are not committed, others will sense this and it will affect the quality of our relationships with them. Without commitment to our relationships with others, we cannot manage our conflicts with them. It is the commitment present in a community that allows the differences inherent in its diversity to be absorbed (Peck, 1987). We need to be committed to our collective (social) identities associated with our communities and to a participatory mode of politics within the community (Taylor, 1991). We must be committed to cooperating with others on our shared goals. We also need to be committed to principles, not being right (Buber, 1958).

2. *Be mindful.* We must think about what we do and say. If we communicate on automatic pilot, we will interpret others' behavior using our own frame of reference and evaluate them rather than try to understand them. If we are not mindful of our communication, we will interpret others' behavior from our own frame of reference and be more concerned for ourselves than others. This makes it impossible to develop community. When we are mindful, we need to focus on the process of our communication, not the outcome (Langer, 1989). Our emphasis should be on adapting

our messages so that others can understand them and interpreting others' messages using their frame of reference. We also need to be contemplative in examining our own behavior and that of the communities of which we are members (Peck, 1987).

3. *Be unconditionally accepting.* For community to develop, we must accept others as they are, and not try to change or control them (Fisher & Brown, 1988). If we try to change others, they will become defensive and building community will not be possible. We must accept others' diversity and not judge them based only on their group memberships. We need to recognize and support the personal and social identities others claim for themselves. If we do not support others' self-conceptions, we cannot develop satisfying relationships with them. We need to minimize our expectations, prejudices, suspicion, and mistrust (Peck, 1987). This can only be accomplished when we are mindful.

4. *Be concerned for both ourselves and others.* Communities are inclusive; they are *not* just groups of like-minded people. We must walk a narrow ridge in our interactions with others whenever practical (Buber, 1958). This means that we avoid polarizing our communication (Arnett, 1986), actively listen to others when they speak, and engage in dialogue whenever possible (Buber, 1958, 1965). Our survival depends on the survival of the communities of which we are members (Loewy, 1993). Being authentic (e.g., self-fulfilled, empowered) and identifying with others and our communities are *not* incompatible (Taylor, 1991). We need to be concerned with our own and others' personal and social identities. We must consult others on issues that affect them and be open to their ideas (Fisher & Brown, 1988). We must take others into consideration when there is a conflict, and fight gracefully (Peck, 1987).

5. *Be understanding.* We need to strive to understand others as completely as possible. As Martin Luther King, Jr. (1963) said, "shallow understanding from people of good will is more frustrating than absolute misunderstanding from people of ill will" (p. 88). To accomplish this, we must determine how others' interpretations of events or behaviors are different from and similar to our own. We also must recognize how culture, ethnicity,

and other forms of diversity affect the way we think and behave. We must understand real differences between our group and others' groups, not base our interpretations of differences on our stereotypes and prejudices. Building community requires "the appreciation of differences. In community, instead of being ignored, denied, hidden, or changed, human differences are celebrated as gifts" (Peck, 1987, p. 62). We also need to search for commonalities on which community can be built (Bellah et al., 1985). In our communication, we must balance emotion, anxiety, and fear with reason (Fisher & Brown, 1988).

6. *Be ethical.* We must engage in behavior that is not a means to an end, but morally right in and of itself (Bellah et al., 1985). We have to be reliable in what we say and do (Fisher & Brown, 1988). We must be morally inclusive (Optow, 1990) and engage in service to others (Lynberg, 1989). As Ervin Staub (1989) points out, "starting with common everyday acts and moving on to acts requiring greater sacrifice . . . can lead to genuine concern and a feeling of responsibility for people" (p. 276). This is not to say that we should not make moral judgments. We cannot avoid making ethical judgments, but we need to understand others' behavior in their frame of reference before we make judgments. A community is based on its moral principles (Etzioni, 1993).

7. *Be peaceful.* We must *not* be violent or deceitful, breach valid promises, or be secretive (Bok, 1989). Even if others engage in these behaviors toward us we are not justified in engaging in these behaviors toward them (Fisher & Brown, 1988). As Socrates pointed out, retaliation is never justified (Vlastos, 1991). We must strive for internal harmony (Prather, 1986) and harmony in our relations with others. "Practicing mindfulness in each moment of our daily lives, we can cultivate our own peace. With clarity, determination, and patience . . . we can sustain a life of action and be real instruments of peace" (Hanh, 1991, p. 99). If we are peaceful, everyone with whom we come into contact will benefit from our peace.

These seven principles are ideals for which we can strive. The more we are able to put them into practice individually, the greater the chance for community and peace in the world. We must not, however, punish ourselves when we fail to achieve the ideal. Achieving these ideals is a lifetime's work and requires extensive practice. If we are to tolerate others, we must begin by accepting our own mistakes. As Hugh Prather (1986) points out, when we find that we are not engaging in behaviors we want to practice (e.g., building community), we must forgive ourselves and start anew at practicing the behaviors. For most of us, this will occur numerous times a day initially. The behaviors suggested in the ideals are different from those we have learned from birth. To engage in these behaviors consistently, we must unlearn many of our normal behaviors (e.g., behaviors that occur at low levels of awareness such as reacting defensively and looking out only for ourselves). The critical thing is *not* the outcome, but the process. If we behave in a way consistent with these ideals (the process), community (the desirable outcome) will occur.

❏ Notes

1. I have cited only representative studies here. For a more detailed discussion, see Gudykunst and Ting-Toomey (1988).

2. My focus below is on European American-African American differences. Japanese American, Chinese American, and Mexican American patterns are similar to the cultural differences cited above. For other examples, see Boucher, Landis, and Clark (1987); and Strobe, Kruglanski, Bar-Tal, and Hewstone (1988).

3. Kochman's European American respondents may have been middle class and his African American respondents lower class. Social class, therefore, must be taken into consideration when interpreting the findings reported.

4. This research was an extension of Knapp, Ellis, and Williams's (1980) research in the United States.

5. Sunnafrank and Miller's (1981) research clearly indicates that communication can lead to perceptions of similarity where we initially thought there was only dissimilarity.

6. There are differences in the relationship labels used in the various studies. I have used the labels isolated above for illustrative purposes.

7. There obviously will be exceptions here. A man may want an "Oriental" wife, for example, because he thinks she will be passive and serve him.

8. Much of the argument I make in this section is drawn from Gudykunst (1989).

9. Self-concept support has been found to be critical in relationship development. See Cushman and Cahn (1985) for a summary of this research. These factors

also are related to Bell and Daly's (1984) "concern and caring" affinity-seeking strategy.

10. See Gudykunst (1989) for a summary of this research. Similarity is part of Bell and Daly's (1984) "commonalities" affinity-seeking strategy.

11. This is related to Bell and Daly's (1984) "politeness" affinity-seeking strategy.

12. These issues are related to Bell and Daly's (1984) "other involvement" affinity-seeking strategy.

References

Abelson, R. (1976). Script processing in attitude formation and decision making. In J. Carroll & J. Payne (Eds.), *Cognition and social behavior*. Hillsdale, NJ: Lawrence Erlbaum.

Alba, R. (1990). *Ethnic identity: The transformation of white America*. New Haven, CT: Yale University Press.

Alberti, R., & Emmons, M. (1986). *Your perfect right* (5th ed.). San Luis Obispo, CA: Impact.

Allport, G. (1954). *The nature of prejudice*. New York: Macmillan.

Almaney, A., & Alwan, A. (1982). *Communicating with the Arabs*. Prospect Heights, IL: Waveland.

Argyle, M., & Henderson, M. (1984). The rules of relationships. In S. Duck & D. Perlman (Eds.), *Understanding personal relationships*. Beverly Hills, CA: Sage.

Argyle, M., Henderson, M., Bond, M., Iizuka, Y., & Contarelo, A. (1986). Cross-cultural variations in relationship rules. *International Journal of Psychology, 21*, 287-315.

Arnett, R. C. (1986). *Communication and community*. Carbondale: Southern Illinois University Press.

Arnoff, C. (1974). Old age in prime time. *Journal of Communication, 24*, 86-87.

Ashford, S., & Cummings, L. (1983). Feedback as an individual resource. *Organizational Behavior and Human Performance, 32,* 370-398.

Ball-Rokeach, S. (1973). From pervasive ambiguity to definition of the situation. *Sociometry, 36,* 378-389.

Banks, S., Gao, G., & Baker, J. (1991). Intercultural encounters and miscommunication. In N. Coupland, H. Giles, & J. Wiemann (Eds.), *"Miscommunication" and problematic talk.* Newbury Park, CA: Sage.

Barbato, C., & Feezel, J. (1987). The language of aging in different age-groups. *Gerontological Society of America, 27,* 527-531.

Barnlund, D. (1962). Toward a meaning centered philosophy of communication. *Journal of Communication, 2,* 197-211.

Barnlund, D. (1975). *Public and private self in Japan and the United States.* Tokyo: Simul.

Barnsley, J. (1972). *The social reality of ethics.* London: Routledge & Kegan Paul.

Barringer, F. (1993, May 16). Pride in a soundless world. *New York Times,* pp. 1, 14.

Barth, F. (1969). *Ethnic groups and boundaries.* London: Allen & Unwin.

Bateson, G. (1979). *Mind and nature.* New York: Dutton.

Beck, A. (1988). *Love is never enough.* New York: Harper & Row.

Bell, R. (1987). Social involvement. In J. McCroskey & J. Daly (Eds.), *Personality and interpersonal communication.* Newbury Park, CA: Sage.

Bell, R., & Daly, J. (1984). The affinity-seeking function of communication. *Communication Monographs, 51,* 91-115.

Bellah, R. N., Madsen, R., Sullivan, W. M., Swidler, A., & Tipton, S. M. (1985). *Habits of the heart: Individualism and commitment in American life.* Berkeley: University of California Press.

Bennett, M. (1979). Overcoming the Golden Rule: Sympathy and empathy. In D. Nimmo (Ed.), *Communication yearbook 3.* New Brunswick, NJ: Transaction.

Benson, P., & Vincent, S. (1980). Development and validation of the sexist attitude toward women scale. *Psychology of Women Quarterly, 5,* 276-291.

Berger, C. R. (1979). Beyond initial interactions. In H. Giles & R. St. Clair (Eds.), *Language and social psychology.* Oxford, UK: Blackwell.

Berger, C. R., & Bradac, J. (1982). *Language and social knowledge.* London: Edward Arnold.

Berger, C. R., & Calabrese, R. (1975). Some explorations in initial interactions and beyond: Toward a developmental theory of interpersonal communication. *Human Communication Research, 1,* 99-112.

Berger, C. R., & Douglas, W. (1982). Thought and talk. In F. Dance (Ed.), *Human communication theory.* New York: Harper & Row.

Berlo, D. (1960). *The process of communication.* New York: Holt.

Bernstein, B. (1973). *Class, codes, and control* (Vol. 1). London: Routledge & Kegan Paul.

Bidney, D. (1968). Cultural relativism. In D. Sills (Ed.), *International encyclopedia of the social sciences* (Vol. 3). New York: Free Press.

Blanchard, F., Lilly, T., & Vaughn, L. (1991). Reducing the expression of racial prejudice. *Psychological Science, 2,* 101-105.

Bloom, L., Coburn, K., & Pearlman, J. (1975). *The new assertive woman.* New York: Dell.

Bodenhausen, G., Gaelick, L., & Wyer, R. (1987). Affective and cognitive factors in intragroup and intergroup communication. In C. Hendrick (Ed.), *Group processes and intergroup relations.* Newbury Park, CA: Sage.

Bok, S. (1989). *A strategy for peace: Human values and the threat of war.* New York: Pantheon.

Bolton, R. (1990). Listening is more than merely hearing. In J. Stewart (Ed.), *Bridges not walls.* New York: McGraw-Hill.

Bond, M. H., Wan, K., Leung, K., & Giacalone, R. (1985). How are the responses to verbal insults related to cultural collectivism and power distance? *Journal of Cross-Cultural Psychology, 16,* 111-127.

Boucher, K., Landis, D., & Clark, K. (Eds.). (1987). *Ethnic conflict.* Newbury Park, CA: Sage.

Boulding, E. (1988). *Building a global civic culture.* Syracuse, NY: Syracuse University Press.

Bourhis, R. (1985). The sequential nature of language choices in cross-cultural communication. In R. Street & J. Cappella (Eds.), *Sequence and pattern in communicative behavior.* London: Edward Arnold.

Boyer, E. (1990, June 20). Letter to the editor. *Chronicle of Higher Education,* p. B4.

Bradac, J. (1990). Language attitudes and impression formation. In H. Giles & P. Robinson (Eds.), *Handbook of language and social psychology.* London: John Wiley.

Breakwell, G. (1979). Women: Group and identity. *Women's Studies International Quarterly, 2,* 9-17.

Brewer, M. B. (1981). Ethnocentrism and its role in interpersonal trust. In M. Brewer & B. Collins (Eds.), *Scientific inquiry and the social sciences.* San Francisco: Jossey-Bass.

Brewer, M. B., & Miller, N. (1988). Contact and cooperation: When do they work? In P. Katz & D. Taylor (Eds.), *Eliminating racism.* New York: Plenum.

Brislin, R. W., Cushner, K., Cherrie, C., & Yong, M. (1986). *Intercultural interactions: A practical guide.* Beverly Hills, CA: Sage

Brodie, H. K. (1989, September 9). No we're not taught to hate, but we can overcome instinct to fear "the other." *Los Angeles Times,* Part II, p. 16.

Bruner, J. (1958). Social psychology and perception. In E. Maccoby, T. Newcomb, & E. Hartley (Eds.), *Readings in social psychology* (3rd. ed.). New York: Holt, Rinehart & Winston.

Buber, M. (1958). *I and thou.* New York: Scribner.

Buber, M. (1965). *Between man and man.* New York: Macmillan.

Burgoon, J., & Hale, J. (1988). Nonverbal expectancy violations. *Communication Monographs, 55,* 58-79.

Burleson, B., Samter, W., & Lucchetti, A. (1992). Similarity in communication values as predictors of friendship choices. *Southern Communication Journal, 57,* 260-276.

Burns, D. (1989). *The feeling good handbook.* New York: William Morrow.

Butler, R. (1969). Age-ism: Another form of bigotry. *Gerontologist, 9,* 243-246.

Byrne, D. (1971). *The attraction paradigm.* New York: Academic Press.

Cantor, N., Mischel, W., & Schwartz, J. (1982). Social knowledge. In A. Isen & A. Hastorf (Eds.), *Cognitive social psychology.* New York: Elsevier.

Carroll, R. (1988). *Cultural misunderstandings: The French-American experience.* Chicago: University of Chicago Press.

Chaika, E. (1982). *Language: The social mirror.* Rowley, MA: Newbury House.

Chinese Culture Connection. (1987). Chinese values and the search for culture-free dimensions of culture. *Journal of Cross-Cultural Psychology, 18,* 143-164.

Cissna, K., & Sieburg, E. (1981). Patterns of interactional confirmation and disconfirmation. In C. Wilder-Mott & J. Weaklund (Eds.), *Rigor and imagination.* New York: Praeger.

Clark, H., & Marshall, C. (1981). Definite reference and mutual knowledge. In A. Joshi, B. Webber, & I. Sag (Eds.), *Elements of discourse understanding.* New York: Cambridge University Press.

Cohen, R. (1987). Problems in intercultural communication in Egyptian-American diplomatic relations. *International Journal of Intercultural Relations, 11,* 29-47.

Coleman, L., & De Paulo, B. (1991). Uncovering the human spirit: Moving beyond disability and "missed" communication. In N. Coupland, H. Giles, & J. Wiemann (Eds.), *"Miscommunication" and problematic talk.* Newbury Park, CA: Sage.

Collier, M. (1986). Culture and gender. In M. McLaughlin (Ed.), *Communication yearbook 9.* Beverly Hills, CA: Sage.

Collier, M., Ribeau, S., & Hecht, M. (1986). Intracultural communication rules and outcomes within three domestic cultures. *International Journal of Intercultural Relations, 10,* 439-458.

Condon, J. (1984). *With respect to the Japanese.* Yarmouth, ME: Intercultural Press.

Condor, S. (1986). Sex role beliefs and "traditional" women. In S. Wilkenson (Ed.), *Feminist social psychology.* Milton Keynes: Open University Press.

Coupland, J., Nussbaum, J., & Coupland, N. (1991). The reproduction of aging and ageism in intergenerational talk. In N. Coupland, H. Giles, & J. Wisemann (Eds.), *"Miscommunication" and problematic talk.* Newbury Park, CA: Sage.

Coupland, N., Coupland, J., Giles, H., & Henwood, K. (1988). Accommodating the elderly. *Language in Society, 17,* 1-42.

Covey, H. (1988). Historical terminology used to represent older people. *Gerontologist, 28,* 291-297.

Crocker, J., & Luhtanen, R. (1990). Collective self-esteem and ingroup bias. *Journal of Personality and Social Psychology, 58,* 60-67.

Crockett, W., & Friedman, P. (1980). Theoretical explorations in the process of initial interactions. *Western Journal of Speech Communication, 44,* 86-92.

Csikszentmihalyi, M. (1990). *Flow: The psychology of optimal experience.* New York: Harper & Row.

Cushman, D. P., & Cahn, D. (1985). *Interpersonal communication.* Albany: State University of New York Press.

Cushman, D. P., Valentinsen, B., & Dietrich, D. (1982). A rules theory of interpersonal relationships. In F. Dance (Ed.), *Human communication theory.* New York: Harper & Row.

Dahnke, G. (1983). Communication between handicapped and nonhandicapped. In M. McLaughlin (Ed.), *Communication yearbook 6.* Beverly Hills, CA: Sage.

Davidson, A., & Thompson, E. (1980). Cross-cultural studies of attitudes and beliefs. In H. Triandis & R. Brislin (Eds.), *Handbook of cross-cultural psychology* (Vol. 5). Boston: Allyn & Bacon.

Davis, F. (1977). Deviance disavowal. In J. Stubbins (Ed.), *Social and psychological aspects of disability.* Baltimore, MD: University Park Press.

Deaux, K. (1993). Reconstructing social identity. *Personality and Social Psychology Bulletin, 19,* 4-12.

Detweiler, R. (1975). On inferring the intentions of a person from another culture. *Journal of Personality, 43,* 591-611.

Detweiler, R. (1978). Culture, category width, and attributions. *Journal of Cross-Cultural Psychology, 11,* 101-124.

Deutsch, K. (1968). Toward a cybernetic model of man and society. In W. Buckley (Ed.), *Modern systems theory for the behavioral scientist.* Chicago: Aldine.

Deutsch, M. (1973). *The resolution of conflict.* New Haven, CT: Yale University Press.

Devine, P. (1989). Stereotypes and prejudice. *Journal of Personality and Social Psychology, 56,* 5-18.

DeVos, G. (1975). Ethnic pluralism. In G. DeVos & L. Romanucci-Ross (Eds.), *Ethnic identity.* Palo Alto, CA: Mayfield.

Douglas, M. (1986). *How institutions think.* Syracuse, NY: Syracuse University Press.

Downs, J. (1971). *Cultures in crisis.* Chicago: Glencoe.

Duck, S. (1977). *The study of acquaintance.* Farnborough, UK: Saxon House.

Duran, R. L. (1983). Communicative adaptability. *Communication Quarterly, 31,* 320-326.

Edwards, J. (1985). *Language, society, and identity.* Oxford, UK: Blackwell.

Ehrenhaus, P. (1983). Culture and the attribution process. In W. Gudykunst (Ed.), *Intercultural communication theory.* Beverly Hills, CA: Sage.

Erickson, F. (1981). *Anecdote, rhapsody, and rhetoric.* Paper presented at the Georgetown University Roundtable on Language and Linguistics, Washington, DC.

Essed, P. (1991). *Understanding everyday racism.* Newbury Park, CA: Sage.

Etzioni, A. (1993). *The spirit of community.* New York: Crown.

Faulkender, P. (1985). Relationships between Bem sex-role inventory and attitudes of sexism. *Psychological Reports, 57,* 227-235.

Fisher, B. A. (1978). *Perspectives on human communication.* New York: Macmillan.

Fisher, R., & Brown, S. (1988). *Getting together: Building relationships as we negotiate.* New York: Houghton Mifflin.

Fitzgerald, T. (1993). *Metaphors of identity.* Albany: State University of New York Press.

Friedman, M. (1983). *The confirmation of otherness: In family, community and society.* New York: Pilgrim Press.

Friedman, M. (1986). Forward. In R. Arnett, *Communication and community.* Carbondale: Southern Illinois University Press.

Fuentes, C. (1992). *The buried mirror.* Boston: Houghton Mifflin.

Fussell, P. (1983). *Class.* New York: Summit.

Gaertner, S., & Bickman, L. (1971). Effects of race on the elicitation of helping behavior. *Journal of Personality and Social Psychology, 20,* 218-222.

Galston, W. (1991). Rights do not equal rightness. *Responsive Community, 1,* 7-8.

Gans, H. (1979). Symbolic ethnicity. *Ethnic and Racial Studies, 2,* 1-20.

Gao, G., & Gudykunst, W. B. (1990). Uncertainty, anxiety, and adaptation. *International Journal of Intercultural Relations, 14,* 301-317.

Gardner, R. (1985). *Social psychology and second language learning.* London: Edward Arnold.

Garreau, J. (1981). *The nine nations of North America.* New York: Houghton Mifflin.

Garrett, P., Giles, H., & Coupland, N. (1989). The contexts of language learning. In S. Ting-Toomey & F. Korzenny (Eds.), *Language, communication, and culture.* Newbury Park, CA: Sage.

Gass, S., & Varonis, E. (1984). The effect of familiarity on the comprehensibility of nonnative speech. *Language Learning, 34,* 65-89.

Gass, S., & Varonis, E. (1985). Variations in native speaker speech modification on nonnative speakers. *Studies in Second Language Acquisition, 7* 37-58.

Gass, S., & Varonis, E. (1991). Miscommunication in nonnative speaker discourse. In N. Coupland, H. Giles, & J. Wiemann (Eds.), *"Miscommunication" and problematic talk.* Newbury Park, CA: Sage.

Geertz, C. (1973). *The interpretation of cultures.* New York: Basic books.

Genesse, F., & Bourhis, R. (1982). The social psychological significance of code switching in cross-cultural communication. *Journal of Language and Social Psychology, 1,* 1-28.

Gerbner, G. (1978). The dynamics of cultural resistance. In G. Tuchman et al. (Eds.), *Health and home.* New York: Oxford University Press.

Gerbner, G., Gross, L., Morgan, M., & Signorielli, N. (1980). The "mainstreaming" of America. *Journal of Communication, 30,* 10-29.

Gibb, J. (1961). Defensive communication. *Journal of Communication, 11,* 141-148.

Giles, H. (1973). Accent mobility. *Anthropological Linguistics, 15,* 87-105.

Giles, H., Bourhis, R., & Taylor, D. (1977). Towards a theory of language in ethnic group relations. In H. Giles (Ed.), *Language, ethnicity, and intergroup relations.* London: Academic Press.

Giles, H., & Byrne, J. (1982). The intergroup theory of second language acquisition. *Journal of Multilingual and Multicultural Development, 3,* 17-40.

Giles, H., Coupland, N., & Wiemann, J. (1992). "Talk is cheap . . ." but "my word is my bond." In R. Bolton & H. Kwok (Eds.), *Sociolinguistics today.* London: Routledge.

Giles, H., & Johnson, P. (1981). The role of language in ethnic group relations. In J. Turner & H. Giles (Eds.), *Intergroup behavior.* Chicago: University of Chicago Press.

Giles, H., & Johnson, P. (1987). Ethnolinguistic identity theory. *International Journal of the Sociology of Language, 68,* 69-90.

Giles, H., Mulac, A., Bradac, J., & Johnson, P. (1987). Speech accommodation theory. In M. McLaughlin (Ed.), *Communication yearbook 10.* Newbury Park, CA: Sage.

Giles, H., & Smith, P. (1979). Accommodation theory. In H. Giles & R. St Clair (Eds.), *Language and social psychology.* Oxford: Blackwell.

Gilligan, C. (1982). *In a different voice.* Cambridge: Harvard University Press.

Glazer, N., & Moynihan, D. (1975). *Ethnicity.* Cambridge: Harvard University Press.

Goffman, E. (1963). *Stigma.* Englewood Cliffs, NJ: Prentice Hall.

Gonzalez, D. (1992, November 15). What's the problem with Hispanic? Just ask a Latino. *Los Angeles Times,* p. E6.

Gordon, M. (1964). *Assimilation in American life.* Oxford, UK: Oxford University Press.

Gotanda, P. K. (1991). Interview with Philip Kan Gotanda. *Los Angeles Performing Arts, 25(1),* 9-11.

Gouldner, A. (1960). The norm of reciprocity. *American Sociological Review, 25,* 161-179.

Greeley, A. (1989). Protestant and catholic: Is the analogical imagination extinct? *American Sociological Review, 54,* 485-502.

Grove, T., & Werkman, D. (1991). Communication with able-bodied and visually disabled strangers. *Human Communication Research, 17*, 507-534.

Gudykunst, W. B. (1983). Similarities and differences in perceptions of initial intracultural and intercultural encounters. *Southern Speech Communication Journal, 49*, 49-65.

Gudykunst, W. B. (1987). Cross-cultural comparisons. In C. Berger & S. Chaffee (Eds.), *Handbook of communication science*. Newbury Park, CA: Sage.

Gudykunst, W. B. (1988). Uncertainty and anxiety. In Y. Kim & W. Gudykunst (Eds.), *Theories in intercultural communication*. Newbury Park, CA: Sage.

Gudykunst, W. B. (1989). Culture and communication in interpersonal relationships. In J. Anderson (Ed.), *Communication yearbook 12*. Newbury Park, CA: Sage.

Gudykunst, W. B. (1993). Toward a theory of interpersonal and intergroup communication: An anxiety/uncertainty management (AUM) perspective. In R. Wiseman & J. Koester (Eds.), *Intercultural communication competence*. Newbury Park, CA: Sage.

Gudykunst, W. B. (in press). Anxiety/uncertainty management theory. In R. Wiseman (Ed.), *Intercultural communication theory* (tentative). Thousand Oaks, CA: Sage.

Gudykunst, W. B., Chua, E., & Gray, A. (1987). Cultural dissimilarities and uncertainty reduction processes. In M. McLaughlin (Ed.), *Communication yearbook 10*. Newbury Park, CA: Sage.

Gudykunst, W. B., Gao, G., Schmidt, K., Nishida, T., Bond, M. H., Leung, K., Wang, G., & Barraclough, R. A. (1992). The influence of individualism-collectivism on communication in ingroup and outgroup relationships. *Journal of Cross-Cultural Psychology, 23*, 196-213.

Gudykunst, W. B., Gao, G., Sudweeks, S., Ting-Toomey, S., & Nishida, T. (1991). Themes in opposite-sex Japanese-North American relationships. In S. Ting-Toomey & F. Korzenny (Eds.), *Cross-cultural interpersonal communication*. Newbury Park, CA: Sage.

Gudykunst, W. B., & Hammer, M. R. (1988a). Strangers and hosts. In Y. Kim & W. Gudykunst (Eds.), *Cross-cultural adaptation*. Newbury Park, CA: Sage.

Gudykunst, W. B., & Hammer, M. R. (1988b). The influence of social identity and intimacy of interethnic relationships on uncertainty reduction processes. *Human Communication Research, 14*, 569-601.

Gudykunst, W. B., & Kim, Y. Y. (1984). *Communicating with strangers: An approach to intercultural communication*. New York: McGraw-Hill.

Gudykunst, W. B., & Kim, Y. Y. (1992). *Communicating with strangers: An approach to intercultural communication* (2nd ed.). New York: McGraw-Hill.

Gudykunst, W. B., & Lim, T. S. (1985). Ethnicity, sex, and self-perceptions of communicator style. *Communication Research Reports, 2* (1), 68-75.

Gudykunst, W. B., & Nishida, T. (1986a). Attributional confidence in low- and high-context cultures. *Human Communication Research, 12*, 525-549.

Gudykunst, W. B., & Nishida, T. (1986b). The influence of cultural variability on perceptions of communication behavior associated with relationship terms. *Human Communication Research, 13*, 147-166.

Gudykunst, W. B., & Nishida, T. (1994). *Bridging Japanese/North American differences*. Thousand Oaks, CA: Sage.

Gudykunst, W. B., Nishida, T., & Chua, E. (1986). Uncertainty reduction processes in Japanese-North American relationships. *Communication Research Reports, 3,* 39-46.

Gudykunst, W. B., Nishida, T., & Chua, E. (1987). Perceptions of social penetration in Japanese-North American relationships. *International Journal of Intercultural Relations, 11,* 171-190.

Gudykunst, W. B., & Ting-Toomey, S., with Chua, E. (1988). *Culture and interpersonal communication.* Newbury Park, CA: Sage.

Gudykunst, W. B., Ting-Toomey, S., Hall, B. J., & Schmidt, K. L. (1989). Language and intergroup communication. In M. K. Asante & W. B. Gudykunst (Eds.), *Handbook of international and intercultural communication.* Newbury Park, CA: Sage.

Gumperz, J. (1982). *Discourse strategies.* Cambridge, UK: Cambridge University Press.

Gumperz, J., & Hernandez-Chavez, E. (1972). Bilingualism, bidialectism and classroom interaction. In C. Cazden, V. John, & D. Hymes (Eds.), *Functions of language in the classroom.* New York: Teacher's College Press.

Gurin, P., & Townsend, A. (1986). Properties of gender identity and their implications for gender consciousness. *British Journal of Social Psychology, 25,* 139-148.

Gutmann, A. (1992). Introduction. In A. Gutmann (Ed.), *Multiculturalism and the politics of recognition.* Princeton, NJ: Princeton University Press.

Hall, E. T. (1959). *The silent language.* New York: Doubleday.

Hall, E. T. (1976). *Beyond culture.* New York: Doubleday.

Hamilton, D., Sherman, S., & Ruvolo, C. (1992). Stereotyped based expectancies. In W. B. Gudykunst & Y. Y. Kim (Eds.), *Readings on communicating with strangers.* New York: McGraw-Hill. (Originally published in *Journal of Social Issues,* 1990, *46*[2], 35-60)

Hampshire, S. (1989). *Innocence and experience.* Cambridge, MA: Harvard University Press.

Hanh, T. N. (1991). *Peace in every step.* New York: Bantam.

Haslett, B. (1990). Social class, social status and communicative behavior. In H. Giles & W. Robinson (Eds.), *Handbook of language and social psychology.* Chichester, UK: John Wiley.

Haslett, B., & Ogilvie, J. (1988). Feedback processes in small groups. In R. Cathcart & L. Samovar (Eds.), *Small group communication: A reader* (5th ed.). Dubuque, IA: William C. Brown.

Hass, R., Katz, I., Rizzo, N., Bailey, J., & Moore, L. (1992). When racial ambivalence evokes negative affect. *Personality and Social Psychology Bulletin, 18,* 786-797.

Hayashi, R. (1990). Rhythmicity, sequence and synchrony of English and Japanese face-to-face conversations. *Language Sciences, 12,* 155-195.

Hecht. M. (1978). The conceptualization and measurement of communication satisfaction. *Human Communication Research, 4,* 253-264.

Hecht, M., & Ribeau, S. (1991). Sociocultural roots of ethnic identity. *Journal of Black Studies, 21,* 501-513.

Hecht, M., Ribeau, S., & Alberts, J. (1989). An Afro-American perspective on interethnic communication. *Communication Monographs, 56,* 385-410.

Hecht, M., Ribeau, S., & Sedano, M. (1990). A Mexican-American perspective on interethnic communication. *International Journal of Intercultural Relations, 14,* 31-55.

Heider, F. (1958). *The psychology of interpersonal relations*. New York: John Wiley.

Henley, N., Hamilton, M., & Thorne, B. (1985). Womanspeak and manspeak. In A. Sargent (Ed.), *Beyond sex roles*. New York: West.

Henry, W. (1990, April 9). Beyond the melting pot. *Time*, pp. 28-31.

Herman, S., & Schield, E. (1961). The stranger group in a cross-cultural situation. *Sociometry, 24*, 165-176.

Herskovits, M. (1950). *Man and his works*. New York: Knopf.

Herskovits, M. (1955). *Cultural anthropology*. New York: Knopf.

Hewstone, M., & Brown, R. (1986). Contact is not enough. In M. Hewstone & R. Brown (Eds.), *Contact and conflict in intergroup encounters*. Oxford, UK: Blackwell.

Hewstone, M., & Giles, H. (1986). Stereotypes and intergroup communication. In W. Gudykunst (Ed.), *Intergroup communication*. London: Edward Arnold.

Hewstone, M., & Jaspars, J. (1984). Social dimensions of attributions. In H. Tajfel (Ed.), *The social dimension* (Vol. 2). Cambridge, UK: Cambridge University Press.

Hirokawa, R., & Miyahara, A. (1986). A comparison of influence strategies utilized by managers in American and Japanese organizations. *Communication Quarterly, 34*, 250-265.

Hodges, H. (1964). *Social stratification*. Cambridge, MA: Schenkman.

Hofman, T. (1985). Arabs and Jews, Blacks and Whites: Identity and group relations. *Journal of Multilingual and Multicultural Development, 6*, 217-237.

Hofstede, G. (1979). Value systems in forty countries. In L. Eckensberger, W. Lonner, & Y. Poortinga (Eds.), *Cross-cultural contributions to psychology*. Lisse, Netherlands: Swets & Zeitlinger.

Hofstede, G. (1980). *Culture's consequences*. Beverly Hills, CA: Sage.

Hofstede, G. (1991). *Cultures and organizations*. London: McGraw-Hill.

Hofstede, G., & Bond, M. (1984). Hofstede's culture dimensions. *Journal of Cross-Cultural Psychology, 15*, 417-433.

Holmes, J., & Rempel, J. (1989). Trust in close relationships. In C. Hendrick (Ed.), *Close relationships*. Newbury Park, CA: Sage.

Honeycutt, J. M., Knapp, M. L., & Powers, W. G. (1983). On knowing others and predicting what they say. *Western Journal of Speech Communication, 47*, 157-174.

Howell, W. S. (1982). *The empathic communicator*. Belmont, CA: Wadsworth.

Hoyle, R., Pinkley, R., & Insko, C. (1989). Perceptions of social behavior: Evidence of differing expectations for interpersonal and intergroup behavior. *Personality and Social Psychology Bulletin, 15*, 365-376.

Hraba, J., & Hoiberg, E. (1983). Origins of modern theories of ethnicity. *Sociological Quarterly, 24*, 381-391.

Hwang, J., Chase, L., & Kelly, C. (1980). An intercultural examination of communication competence. *Communication, 9*, 70-79.

Infante, D. (1987). Aggressiveness. In J. McCroskey & J. Daly (Eds.), *Personality and interpersonal communication*. Newbury Park, CA: Sage.

Infante, D. (1988). *Arguing constructively*. Prospect Heights, IL: Waveland.

Inkeles, A. (1974). *Becoming modern*. Cambridge, MA: Harvard University Press.

Ittelson, W., & Cantril, H. (1954). *Perception, a transactional approach*. Garden City, NY: Doubleday.

Jackman, M., & Jackman, R. (1983). *Class awareness in the United States*. Berkeley: University of California Press.

Jackson, J. (1964). The normative regulation of authoritative behavior. In W. Grove & J. Dyson (Eds.), *The making of decisions*. New York: Free Press.

Jampolsky, G. (1989). *Out of darkness into the light*. New York: Bantam.

Janis, I., & Mann, L. (1977). *Decision making*. New York: Free Press.

Johnson, D. (1986). *Reaching out* (3rd ed.). Englewood Cliffs, NJ: Prentice Hall.

Johnstone, L., & Hewstone, M. (1991). Intergroup contact. In D. Abrams & M. Hogg (Eds.), *Social identity theory*. New York: Springer-Verlag.

Jussim, L., Coleman, L., & Lerch, L. (1987). The nature of stereotypes. *Journal of Personality and Social Psychology, 52,* 536-546.

Kanouse, D., & Hanson, L. (1972). Negativity in evaluations. In E. Jones, D. Kanouse, H. H. Kelley, R. Nisbett, S. Valins, & L. Petrullo (Eds.), *Attribution: Perceiving the causes of behavior*. Morristown, NJ: General Learning Press.

Karniol, R. (1990). Reading people's minds. In M. Zanna (Ed.), *Advances in experimental social psychology* (Vol. 23). New York: Academic Press.

Katz, D., & Braly, K. (1933). Racial stereotypes of 100 college students. *Journal of Abnormal and Social Psychology, 28,* 280-290.

Keesing, R. (1974). Theories of culture. *Annual Review of Anthropology, 3,* 73-97.

Kellermann, K. (1986). Anticipation of future interaction and information exchange in initial interactions. *Human Communication Research, 13,* 41-65.

Kellermann, K. (1993). Extrapolating beyond: Processes of uncertainty reduction. In S. Deetz (Ed.), *Communication yearbook 16*. Newbury Park, CA: Sage.

Kellermann, K., & Reynolds, R. (1990). When ignorance is bliss: The role of motivation to reduce uncertainty in uncertainty reduction theory. *Human Communication Research, 17,* 5-75.

Kelley, H. H. (1967). Attribution theory in social psychology. *Nebraska Symposium on Motivation, 15,* 192-238.

Kelley, H. H. (1972). Causal schemata and the attribution process. In E. Jones, D. Kanouse, H. H. Kelley, R. Nisbett, S. Valins, & B. Weiner (Eds.), *Attribution: Perceiving the causes of behavior*. Morristown, NJ: General Learning Press.

Kennerley, H. (1990). *Managing anxiety*. New York: Oxford University Press.

King, M. L., Jr. (1963). Letter from Birmingham jail. In *Why we can't wait*. New York: Harper & Row.

Kitayama, S., & Burnstein, E. (1988). Automaticity in conversations. *Journal of Personality and Social Psychology, 54,* 219-224.

Kluckhohn, F., & Strodtbeck, F. (1961). *Variations in value orientations*. New York: Row, Peterson.

Knapp, M., Ellis, D., & Williams, B. (1980). Perceptions of communication behavior associated with relationship terms. *Communication Monographs, 47,* 262-278.

Kochman, T. (1981). *Black and white: Styles in conflict*. Chicago: University of Chicago Press.

Krauss, R., & Fussell, S. (1991). Constructing shared communicative environments. In L. Resnick, J. Levine, & S. Behrend (Eds.), *Perspectives on socially shared cognition*. Washington, DC: American Psychological Association.

Kraut, R., & Higgins, E. (1984). Communication and social cognition. In R. Wyer & T. Srull (Eds.), *Handbook of social cognition* (Vol. 3). Hillsdale, NJ: Lawrence Erlbaum.

Laing, D. (1961). *The self and others*. New York: Pantheon.

Lakoff, R. (1990). *Talking power*. New York: Basic Books.

Langer, E. (1978). Rethinking the role of thought in social interaction. In J. Harvey, W. Ickes., & R. Kidd (Eds.), *New directions in attribution research* (Vol. 2). Hillsdale, NJ: Lawrence Erlbaum.

Langer, E. (1989). *Mindfulness*. Reading, MA: Addison-Wesley.

Larkey, L., Hecht, M., & Martin, J. (1993). What's in a name? African-American ethnic labels and self-distinctions. *Journal of Language and Social Psychology, 12*, 302-317.

Lazarus, R. (1991). *Emotion and adaptation*. New York: Oxford University Press.

Lebra, T. S. (1987). The cultural significance of silence in Japanese communication. *Multilingua, 6*, 343-357.

Lee, H., & Boster, F. (1991). Social information for uncertainty reduction during initial interactions. In S. Ting-Toomey & F. Korzenny (Eds.), *Cross-cultural interpersonal communication*. Newbury Park, CA: Sage.

Lee, S. (1990, July 12). Interview on "48 Hours." CBS Television.

Lennox, R., & Wolfe, R. (1984). Revision of the self-monitoring scale. *Journal of Personality and Social Psychology, 46*, 1349-1364.

Levin, J., & Levin, W. (1980). *Ageism: Prejudice and discrimination*. Belmont, CA: Wadsworth.

Levine, D. (1979). Simmel at a distance. In W. Shack & E. Skinner (Eds.), *Strangers in African societies*. Berkeley: University of California Press.

Levine, D. (1985). *The flight from ambiguity*. Chicago: University of Chicago Press.

LeVine, R. A., & Campbell, D. T. (1972). *Ethnocentrism: Theories of conflict, ethnic attitudes, and group behavior*. New York: John Wiley.

Lieberson, S. (1985). Unhyphenated whites in the United States. *Ethnic and Racial Studies, 8*, 158-180.

Linville, P., Fisher, G., & Salovey, P. (1989). Perceived distributions of the characteristics of in-group and out-group members. *Journal of Personality and Social Psychology, 57*, 165-188.

LoCastro, V. (1987). *Aizuchi*: A Japanese conversational routine. In L. Smith (Ed.), *Discourse across cultures*. Englewood Cliffs, NJ: Prentice Hall.

Loewy, E. (1993). *Freedom and community*. Albany: State University of New York Press.

Longmore, P. (1987). Screening stereotypes. In A. Gartner & T. Jol (Eds.), *Images of the disabled, disabling images*. New York: Praeger.

Loveday, L. (1982). Communicative interference. *International Review of Applied Linguistics in Language Teaching, 20*, 1-16.

Lukens, J. (1978). Ethnocentric speech. *Ethnic Groups, 2*, 35-53.

Lynberg, M. (1989). *The path with heart*. New York: Fawcett.

Maltz, D., & Borker, R. (1982). A cultural approach to male-female miscommunication. In J. Gumperz (Ed.), *Language and social identity*. New York: Cambridge University Press.

Markus, H., & Kitayama, S. (1991). Culture and the self: Implications for cognition, emotion, and motivation. *Psychological Review, 98*, 224-253.

May, R. (1977). *The meaning of anxiety*. New York: Washington Square Press.

McArthur, L. (1982). Judging a book by its cover. In A. Hastorf & A. Isen (Eds.), *Cognitive social psychology*. New York: Elsevier.

McConahay, J. B. (1986). Modern racism, ambivalence, and the modern racism scale. In J. Dovidio & S. Gaertner (Eds.), *Prejudice, discrimination, and racism*. New York: Academic Press.

McConnell-Ginet, S. (1978). Address forms in sexual politics. In D. Butturff & E. Epstein (Eds.), *Women's language and styles*. Akron, OH: L&S Books.

McFall, L. (1987). Integrity. *Ethics, 98*, 5-20.

McFall, R. (1982). A review and reformulation of the concept of social skills. *Behavioral Assessment, 4,* 1-33.

McGinn, N., Harburg, E., & Ginsburg, G. (1973). Responses to interpersonal conflict by middle class males in Guadalajara and Michigan. In F. Jandt (Ed.), *Conflict resolution through communication.* New York: Harper & Row.

McLeod, J., & Chaffee, S. (1973). Interpersonal approach to communication research. *American Behavioral Scientist, 16,* 469-499.

McPherson, K. (1983). Opinion-related information seeking. *Personality and Social Psychology Bulletin, 9,* 116-124.

Messick, D., & Mackie, D. (1989). Intergroup relations. *Annual Review of Psychology, 40,* 45-81.

Miller, G., & Steinberg, M. (1975). *Between people.* Chicago: Science Research Associates.

Miller, G., & Sunnafrank, M. (1982). All is for one but one is not for all. In F. Dance (Ed.), *Human communication theory.* New York: Harper & Row.

Morris, M. L. (1981). *Saying and meaning in Puerto Rico.* Elmsford, NY: Pergamon.

Morrison, T. (1992). *Playing in the dark: Whiteness in the literary imagination.* Cambridge: Harvard University Press.

Mullen, B. (1991). Group composition, salience, and cognitive representations. *Journal of Experimental Social Psychology, 27,* 297-323.

Mullen, B., & Johnson, C. (1993). Cognitive representations in ethnophaulisms as a function of group size. *Personality and Social Psychology Bulletin, 19,* 296-304.

Nakane, C. (1970). *Japanese society.* Berkeley: University of California Press.

Nakane, C. (1974). The social system reflected in interpersonal communication. In J. Condon & M. Saito (Eds.), *Intercultural encounters with Japan.* Tokyo: Simul Press.

Neuberg, S. (1989). The goal of forming accurate impressions during initial interactions. *Journal of Personality and Social Psychology, 56,* 374-386.

Nilsen, A. (1977). Sexism as shown through the English vocabulary. In A. Nilsen, H. Bosmajian, H. Gershuny, & J. Stanley (Eds.), *Sexism and language.* Urbana, IL: National Council of Teachers of English.

Nilsen, A., Bosmajian, H., Gershuny, H., & Stanley, J. (Eds.). (1977). *Sexism and language.* Urbana, IL: National Council of Teachers of English.

Noesjirwan, J. (1978). A rule-based analysis of cultural differences in social behavior. *International Journal of Psychology, 13,* 305-316.

Noller, P. (1980). Misunderstandings in marital communication. *Journal of Personality and Social Psychology, 39,* 1135-1148.

Nozick, R. (1974). *Anarchy, state, and utopia.* New York: Basic Books.

Nozick, R. (1989). *The examined life.* New York: Simon & Schuster.

Nuessel, F. (1984). Ageist language. *Maledicta, 8,* 17-28.

Ogden, C., & Richards, I. (1923). *The meaning of meaning.* New York: Harcourt, Brace.

Okabe, R. (1983). Cultural assumptions of east and west: Japan and the United States. In W. B. Gudykunst (Ed.), *Intercultural communication theory.* Beverly Hills, CA: Sage.

Olsen, M. (1978). *The process of social organization* (2nd ed.). New York: Holt, Rinehart & Winston.

Omi, M., & Winant, H. (1986). *Racial group formation in the United States.* New York: Routledge.

Optow, S. (1990). Moral exclusion and injustice: An introduction. *Journal of Social Issues, 46* (1), 1-20.

Palmore, E. (1982). Attitudes toward the aged. *Research on Aging, 4,* 333-348.

Park, R. E. (1950). Our racial frontier in the Pacific. In R. Park (Ed.), *Race and culture.* New York: Free Press.

Peck, M. S. (1978). *The road less traveled.* New York: Simon & Schuster.

Peck, M. S. (1987). *The different drum: Community making and peace.* New York: Simon & Schuster.

Peng, F. (1974). Communicative distances. *Language Sciences, 31,* 32-38.

Pettigrew, T. F. (1978). Three issues in ethnicity. In Y. Yinger & S. Cutler (Eds.), *Major social issues.* New York: Free Press.

Pettigrew, T. F. (1979). The ultimate attribution error. *Personality and Social Psychology Bulletin, 5,* 461-476.

Pettigrew, T. F. (1982). Cognitive styles and social behavior. In L. Wheeler (Ed.), *Review of personality and social psychology* (Vol. 3). Beverly Hills, CA: Sage.

Planalp, S., Rutherford, D., & Honeycutt, J. (1988). Events that increase uncertainty in interpersonal relationships II. *Human Communication Research, 14,* 516-547.

Pogrebin, L. C. (1987). *Among friends.* New York: McGraw-Hill.

Powers, W., & Lowry, D. (1984). Basic communication fidelity. In R. Bostrom (Ed.), *Competence in communication.* Beverly Hills, CA: Sage.

Prather, H. (1986). *Notes on how to live in the world and still be happy.* New York: Doubleday.

Pritchard, M. (1991). *On becoming responsible.* Lawrence: University of Kansas Press.

Pyszczynski, T., & Greenberg, J. (1981). Role of disconfirmed expectancies in the instigation of attributional processing. *Journal of Personality and Social Psychology, 40,* 31-38.

Regan, T. (1983). *The case for animal rights.* Berkeley: University of California Press.

Renteln, A. (1988). Relativism and the search for human rights. *American Anthropologist, 90,* 56-72.

Roach, C., & Wyatt, N. (1988). *Successful listening.* New York: Harper & Row.

Rodriguez, R. (1982). *Hunger of memory.* New York: Bantam.

Rokeach, M. (1951). A method for studying individual differences in "narrow-mindedness." *Journal of Personality, 20,* 219-233.

Rokeach, M. (1960). *The open and closed mind.* New York: Basic Books.

Rokeach, M. (1972). *Beliefs, attitudes, and values.* San Francisco: Jossey-Bass.

Rogers, C. (1980). *A way of being.* Boston: Houghton-Mifflin.

Rogers, E., & Kincaid, D. L. (1981). *Communication networks.* New York: Free Press.

Roosens, E. (1989). *Creating ethnicity.* Newbury Park, CA: Sage.

Rose, A. (1965). The subculture of aging. In A. Rose & W. Peterson (Eds.), *Older people and their social world.* Philadelphia: F. A. Davis.

Rose, T. (1981). Cognitive and dyadic processes in intergroup contact. In D. Hamilton (Ed.), *Cognitive processes in stereotyping and intergroup behavior.* Hillsdale, NJ: Lawrence Erlbaum.

Rosenthal, P. (1984). *Words and values.* Cambridge, UK: Cambridge University Press.

Ross, L. (1977). The intuitive psychologist and his shortcomings. *Advances in Experimental and Social Psychology, 10,* 174-220.

Ruben, B. (1976). Assessing communication competency for intercultural adaptation. *Group and Organizational Studies, 1,* 334-354.

Ruben, B., & Kealey, D. (1979). Behavioral assessment of communication competency and the prediction of cross-cultural adaptation. *International Journal of Intercultural Relations, 3,* 15-48.

Rubin, T. I. (1990). *Anti-Semitism: A disease of the mind.* New York: Continuum.

Ryan, E., Hewstone, M., & Giles, H. (1984). Language and intergroup attitudes. In J. Eiser (Ed.), *Attitudinal judgment.* New York: Springer-Verlag.

Sachdev, I, & Bourhis, R. (1990). Bilinguality and multilinguality. In H. Giles & W. Robinson (Eds.), *Handbook of language and social psychology.* Chichester, UK: John Wiley.

Safilios-Rothchild, C. (1982). Social and psychological parameters of friendship and intimacy for disabled people. In M. Eisenberg, C. Giggins, & R. Duval (Eds.), *Disabled people as second class citizens.* New York: Springer.

Saleh, S., & Gufwoli, P. (1982). The transfer of management techniques and practices: The Kenya case. In R. Rath et al. (Eds.), *Diversity and unity in cross-cultural psychology.* Lisse, The Netherlands: Swets & Zeitlinger.

Schlenker, B. R. (1986). Self-identification. In R. F. Baumeister (Ed.), *Public self and private self.* New York: Springer-Verlag.

Schmidt, K. L. (1991). *Exit, voice, loyalty, and neglect: Responses to sexist communication in dating relationships.* Unpublished doctoral dissertation, Arizona State University.

Schneider, J., & Hacker, S. (1973). Sex role imagery and the use of the generic "man" in introductory texts. *American Sociologist, 8,* 12-18.

Schwartz, S. (1990). Individualism-collectivism: Critique and proposed refinements. *Journal of Cross-Cultural Psychology, 21,* 139-157.

Scotton, C. (1993). *Social motivations for code-switching.* New York: Oxford University Press.

Shearer, A. (1984). *Disability: Whose handicap?* Oxford, UK: Blackwell.

Sieburg, E. (1975). *Interpersonal confirmation* (ERIC document No. ED 098 634).

Simmel, G. (1950). The stranger. In K. Wolff (Ed. & Trans.), *The sociology of Georg Simmel.* New York: Free Press. (Originally published 1908)

Skevington, S. (1989). A place for emotion in social identity theory. In S. Skevington & D. Baker (Eds.), *The social identity of women.* London: Sage.

Snyder, M. (1974). Self-monitoring of expressive behavior. *Journal of Personality and Social Psychology, 30,* 526-537.

Sorrentino, R. M., & Short, J. A. (1986). Uncertainty orientation, motivation, and cognition. In R. M. Sorrentino & E. T. Higgins (Eds.), *Handbook of motivation and cognition.* New York: Guilford.

Spitzberg, B., & Cupach, W. (1984). *Interpersonal communication competence.* Beverly Hills, CA: Sage.

Stanley, J. (1977). Paradigmatic women. In D. Shores & C. Hines (Eds.), *Papers in language variation.* Tuscaloosa: University of Alabama Press.

Staub, E. (1989). *The roots of evil.* New York: Cambridge University Press.

Stephan, W. G. (1985). Intergroup relations. In G. Lindzey & E. Aronson (Eds.), *Handbook of social psychology* (3rd ed., Vol. 2). New York: Random House.

Stephan, W. G., & Rosenfield, D. (1982). Racial and ethnic stereotyping. In A. Millar (Ed.), *In the eye of the beholder.* New York: Praeger.

Stephan, W. G., & Stephan, C. W. (1985). Intergroup anxiety. *Journal of Social Issues, 41*, 157-166.

Stephan, W. G., & Stephan, C. W. (1989). Antecedents of intergroup anxiety in Asian-Americans and Hispanic-Americans. *International Journal of Intercultural Relations, 13*, 203-219.

Stewart, J. (1990). Interpersonal communication. In J. Stewart (Ed.), *Bridges not walls* (5th ed.). New York: McGraw-Hill.

Stewart, J., & Thomas, M. (1990). Dialogic listening. In J. Stewart (Ed.), *Bridges not walls* (5th ed.). New York: McGraw-Hill.

Stewart, L. P., Stewart, A., Friedley, S., & Cooper, P. (1990). *Communication between the sexes* (2nd ed.). Scottsdale, AZ: Gorsuch Scarsbrick.

Stone, C. (1974). *Should trees have standing?* Los Altos, CA: Kaufmann.

Strobe, W., Kruglanski, A., Bar-Tal, D., & Hewstone, M. (Eds.). (1988). *The social psychology of intergroup conflict.* New York: Springer-Verlag.

Sudweeks, S., Gudykunst, W. B., Nishida, T., & Ting-Toomey, S. (1990). Relational themes in Japanese-North American relationships. *International Journal of Intercultural Relations, 14*, 207-233.

Sumner, W. G. (1940). *Folkways.* Boston: Ginn.

Sunnafrank, M. (1991). Interpersonal attraction and attitude similarity. In J. Anderson (Ed.), *Communication yearbook 14.* Newbury Park, CA: Sage.

Sunnafrank, M., & Miller, G. (1981). The role of initial conversation in determining attraction to similar and dissimilar strangers. *Human Communication Research, 8*, 16-25.

Tajfel, H. (1978). Social categorization, social identity, and social comparisons. In H. Tajfel (Ed.), *Differentiation between social groups.* London: Academic Press.

Tajfel, H. (1981). Social stereotypes and social groups. In J. Turner & H. Giles (Eds.), *Intergroup behavior.* Chicago: University of Chicago Press.

Tajfel, H., & Turner, J. (1979). An integrative theory of intergroup conflict. In W. Austin & S. Worchel (Eds.), *The social psychology of intergroup relations.* Monterey, CA: Brooks/Cole.

Tamir, L. (1984). The older person's communicative needs. In R. Dunkle, M. Haig, & M. Rosenberg (Eds.), *Communications technology and the elderly.* New York: Springer.

Tannen, D. (1975). Communication mix and mixup or how linguistics can ruin a marriage. *San Jose State Occasional Papers on Linguistics*, 205-211.

Tannen, D. (1979). Ethnicity as conversational style. In *Working papers in sociolinguistics* (Number 55). Austin, TX: Southwest Educational Development Laboratory.

Tannen, D. (1993, June 9). Commencement address at State University of New York at Binghamton. *Chronicle of Higher Education*, p. B5.

Taylor, C. (1991). *The ethics of authenticity.* Cambridge, MA: Harvard University Press.

Taylor, C. (1992). Multiculturalism and the politics of recognition. In A. Gutmann (Ed.), *Multiculturalism and the politics of recognition.* Princeton, NJ: Princeton University Press.

Taylor, S., & Fiske, S. (1978). Salience, attention, and attribution. In L. Berkowitz (Ed.), *Advances in experimental social psychology* (Vol. 11). New York: Academic Press.

Tempest, R. (1990, June 12). Hate survives a holocaust: Anti-Semitism resurfaces. *Los Angeles Times*, pp. H1, H7.

Thomas, K. (1983). Conflict and its management. In M. Dunnette (Ed.), *Handbook of industrial and organizational psychology*. New York: John Wiley.

Tinder, G. (1980). *Community: Reflections on a tragic ideal*. Baton Rouge: Louisiana State University Press.

Ting-Toomey, S. (1985). Toward a theory of conflict and culture. In W. Gudykunst, L. Stewart, & S. Ting-Toomey (Eds.), *Communication, culture, and organizational processes*. Beverly Hills, CA: Sage.

Ting-Toomey, S. (1986). Conflict styles in black and white subjective cultures. In Y. Kim (Ed.), *Current research in interpersonal communication*. Beverly Hills, CA: Sage.

Ting-Toomey, S. (1988). A face negotiation theory. In Y. Kim & W. Gudykunst (Ed.), *Theories in intercultural communication*. Newbury Park, CA: Sage.

Ting-Toomey, S. (1989). Identity and interpersonal bonding. In M. Asante & W. Gudykunst (Eds.), *Handbook of international and intercultural communication*. Newbury Park, CA: Sage.

Ting-Toomey, S. (1994). Managing intercultural conflicts effectively. In L. Samovar & R. Porter (Eds.), *Intercultural communication: A reader* (7th ed.). Belmont, CA: Wadsworth.

Trafimow, D., Triandis, H. C., & Goto, S. (1991). Some tests of the distinction between the private self and the collective self. *Journal of Personality and Social Psychology, 60*, 649-655.

Triandis, H. C. (1975). Culture training, cognitive complexity, and interpersonal attitudes. In R. Brislin, S. Bochner, & W. Lonner (Eds.), *Cross-cultural perspectives on learning*. Beverly Hills, CA: Sage.

Triandis, H. C. (1977). *Interpersonal behavior*. Monterey, CA: Brooks/Cole.

Triandis, H. C. (1980). Values, attitudes, and interpersonal behavior. In M. Page (Ed.), *Nebraska symposium on motivation* (Vol. 27). Lincoln: University of Nebraska Press.

Triandis, H. C. (1983). Essentials of studying culture. In D. Landis & R. Brislin (Eds.), *Handbook of intercultural training* (Vol. 1). Elmsford, NY: Pergamon.

Triandis, H. C. (1984). A theoretical framework for the more efficient construction of cultural assimilators. *International Journal of Cultural Relations, 8*, 301-330.

Triandis, H. C. (1988). Collectivism vs. individualism. In G. Verma & C. Bagley (Eds.), *Cross-cultural studies of personality, attitudes, and cognition*. London: Macmillan.

Triandis, H. C., Brislin, R., & Hui, C. H. (1988). Cross-cultural training across the individualism-collectivism divide. *International Journal of Intercultural Relations, 12*, 269-289.

Triandis, H. C., Leung, K., Villareal, M., & Clack, F. (1985). Allocentric vs. idiocentric tendencies. *Journal of Research in Personality, 19*, 395-415.

Trilling, L. (1968). *Beyond culture*. New York: Viking Press.

Turner, J. C. (1982). Towards a cognitive redefinition of the social group. In H. Tajfel (Ed.), *Social identity and intergroup relations*. Cambridge, UK: Cambridge University Press.

Turner, J. C. (1987). *Rediscovering the social group*. Oxford, UK: Blackwell.

Turner, J. H. (1988). *A theory of social interaction*. Stanford, CA: Stanford University Press.

van Dijk, T. (1984). *Prejudice in discourse.* Amsterdam: Benjamins.

Varonis, E., & Gass, S. (1985). Nonnative/native conversations: A model for negotiation of meaning. *Applied Linguistics, 6,* 71-90.

Vassiliou, V., Triandis, H. C., Vassiliou, G., & McGuire, H. (1972). Interpersonal contact and stereotyping. In H. Triandis, *Analysis of subjective culture.* New York: John Wiley.

Vlastos, G. (1991). *Socrates, ironist and moral philosopher.* Ithaca, NY: Cornell University Press.

Wallace, A. (1952). Individual differences and cultural uniformities. *American Sociological Review, 17,* 747-750.

Waterman, A. (1984). *The psychology of individualism.* New York: Praeger.

Waters, M. (1990). *Ethnic options.* Berkeley: University of California Press.

Watts, A. (1966). *The book: On the taboo against knowing who you are.* New York: Pantheon.

Watzlawick, P., Beavin, J., & Jackson, D. (1967). *The pragmatics of human communication.* New York: Norton.

Weiner-Davis, M. (1992). *Divorce busting.* New York: Summit.

White, S. (1989). Back channels across cultures: A study of Americans and Japanese. *Language in Society, 18,* 59-76.

Wiemann, J. M., & Backlund, P. (1980). Current theory and research in communication competence. *Review of Educational Research, 50,* 185-199.

Wiemann, J. M., & Bradac, J. (1989). Metatheoretical issues in the study of communicative competence. In B. Dervin (Ed.), *Progress in communication sciences* (Vol. 9). Norwood, NJ: Ablex.

Wiemann, J. M., Chen, V., & Giles, H. (1986). *Beliefs about talk and silence in cultural context.* Paper presented at the Speech Communication Association convention, Chicago.

Wiemann, J. M., & Kelly, C. (1981). Pragmatics of interpersonal competence. In C. Wilder-Mott & J. Weaklund (Eds.), *Rigor and imagination.* New York: Praeger.

Wilder, D. A., & Shapiro, P. (1989). Effects of anxiety on impression formation in a group context. *Journal of Experimental Social Psychology, 25,* 481-499.

Williams, J. (1984). Gender and intergroup behavior. *British Journal of Social Psychology, 23,* 311-316.

Worchel, S., & Norwell, N. (1980). Effect of perceived environmental conditions during co-operation on intergroup attraction. *Journal of Personality and Social Psychology, 38,* 764-772.

Wylie, R. (1979). *The self-concept.* Lincoln: University of Nebraska Press.

Yamada, H. (1990). Topic management and turn distributions in business meetings: American versus Japanese strategies. *Text, 10,* 271-295.

Yankelovich, D. (1984). *New rules: Searching for self-fulfillment in a world turned upside down.* New York: Random House.

Zajonc, R. (1980). Feeling and thinking. *American Psychologist, 35,* 151-175.

Zerubavel, E. (1991). *The fine line.* New York: Free Press.

Zoglin, R. (1993, June 21). All you need is hate. *Time,* p. 63.

Name Index

Subject Index

251

About the Author

William B. Gudykunst is Professor of Speech Communication at California State University, Fullerton. The focus of his work is on developing a theory to explain effective interpersonal and intergroup communication, and applying this theory to help people improve their communication with members of other groups. He has written several books on the topic, including *Communicating With Strangers* (with Young Yun Kim, McGraw-Hill), *Culture and Interpersonal Communication* (with Stella Ting-Toomey, Sage), and *Bridging Japanese/North American Differences* (with Tsukasa Nishida, Sage). He also has edited several books, including *Communication in Japan and the United States* (State University of New York Press), *Intergroup Communication* (Edward Arnold), *Handbook of International and Intercultural Communication* (with Molefi K. Asante, Sage), *Language and Ethnic Identity* (Multilingual Matters), and three volumes of the *International and Intercultural Communication Annual* (all published by Sage). The first edition of *Bridging Differences* was translated into Japanese. He was elected a Fellow of the International Communication Association in 1992.

ACR 8608